KU-766-985

[Odin Teatret 2000]

Edited by John Andreasen
and Annelis Kuhlmann

Acta Jutlandica LXXVI:1

Aarhus University Press

Copyrights: The individual contributors
and Aarhus University Press, 2000
Cover: Alexander Thieme
Graphic design: Jørgen Sparre
Printed in Denmark at the Narayana Press, Gylling
Drawings: Ulla Madsen
Photos: Bo Amstrup, Jan Rüsz, Tony D'Urso
and Poul Østergaard

ISBN 87 7288 872 5
ISSN 0065 1354 (Acta Jutlandica)
ISSN 0106 0556 (Humanities Series)

AARHUS UNIVERSITY PRESS
Langelandsgade 177
DK - 8200 Århus N
www.unipress.dk

Published with final support from
Aarhus University Research Foundation

**Books are to be returned on or before
the last date below.**

2 0 JAN 2006

LIBREX —

LIVERPOOL JOHN MOORES UNIVERSITY
Aldham Robarts L.R.C.
TEL. 0151 231 3701/3634

LIVERPOOL JMU LIBRARY

3 1111 00933 3038

[Contents]

5

[Act II] *Text & Performance*

[Act III] *Social Function, Philosophy & Theatre*

[Contents]

[Act IV] *Behind the Curtain*

Editors' Prologue to

[Odin Teatret 2000]

I am searching for the country where one does not die ... I have found it! This is a theatre, and in theatre time can be manipulated at pleasure, like an accordion. Years can be minutes and seconds can be hours, nothing is easier but to let time go in different directions all together.

But who is it that gives life to a theatre performance? Is it an actor? A dancer? Someone who interprets texts? Someone who moves well? Someone who identifies with the character? Someone who uses the *verfremdung* distancing effect? Someone who is carried away by emotions? Someone who coldly leans on technique?

Julia Varley, Aarhus, 22 March, 2000

Odin Teatret 2000 is a performance in four acts. Act I, on *Theatre & Traditions*, opens with Peter Laugesen's new, 'wild' poem *Roman Meditations*, which gives a Dionysian atmosphere to the history of Odin Teatret. Eugenio Barba follows with *Tacit Knowledge: Heritage and Waste*, where he draws a historiographical sketch of movements in the theatre. The challenge of heritage seems to have been on Barba's mind ever since he founded Odin Teatret in 1964. Janne Risum in her article, *The Impulse and the Image. The Theatre Laboratory Tradition and Odin Teatret*, follows the line of theatre laboratories in the 20th century, beginning with Stanislavsky and presenting Odin Teatret in the opposite end of the tradition of traditions. Erik Exe Christoffersen's article, *Odin Teatret: Between Dance and Theatre*, traces a historical portrait of the characteristics of some of the performances of Odin Teatret. Roberta Carreri presents for the very first time the text, that corresponds to her working demonstration *Traces in the Snow*. By inspiration follows Annelis Kuhlmann's *Foot and fantasy. Act in shoes*, where she provides a survey of the importance of shoes in the history of drama and theatre. Finally, Frans Winther gives in *Odin Teatret and the Music* a score of different voices and instruments in the important role that the music plays in Odin Teatret.

Act II takes in discussions about *Text & Performance*. Elin Andersen discusses in *A Doll's House: Odin meets Ibsen* choices of working approaches when a so-called naturalistic play is transformed by two actors from a non-naturalistic tradition. Klaus Hoffmeyer tells in *Directing Shakespeare* about his personal working experiences with a couple of plays by Shakespeare's hand — inspired by Artaud. Morten Kyndrup's interpretation in *Mythos — Text and Performance* reveals the creative lines of both the poet and the director of *Mythos*. This reading is followed by Julia Varley's text, *Dramaturgy according to Daedalus*, in which she tells about the genesis of her character in *Mythos*. In *Fragments of an Actor's Diary* Iben Nagel Rasmussen also tells a story of creativity, namely the story of how she began to rewrite a part of her personal biography into an artistic text for *Itsi Bitsi*, in which she as an actress has played the major part since 1990. Act II reaches its end with Sven Erik Larsen's article, *As Time Goes By ... Theatre and Memory*, where he reflects the issue of handling memories on stage.

Act III deals with *Social Function, Philosophy & Theatre*. John Andreasen's contribution, *The Social Space of Theatre — including Odin Teatret*, tries to encircle central elements creating both a concrete and a mental 'social space' in theatre in general as well as in Odin Teatret in particular. Niels Lehmann and Steen Sidenius look on Odin Teatret in a philosophical perspective with their article, *Post-romantic Romanticism. A Note on the Poetics of the Third Theatre*. Torunn Kjølner ends act III with her article, *Searching for Differences*, in which she frames some characteristics of the organic theatre, according to Barba's definitions concentrating on a comparison between 'First' and 'Third' theatre.

The IVth and final act of *Odin Teatret 2000* takes the reader to other stages seen from *Behind the Curtain*. In April 2000 Eugenio Barba was awarded the Sonning Prize. Rector of the University of Copenhagen, Kjeld Møllgård, motivates the choice, followed by Kirsten Hastrup's principal speech, *For Odin*, given at the official ceremony. On behalf of Odin Teatret Eugenio Barba in his *Sonning Prize Acceptance Speech* tells the story of the importance of the artist's isolation and of the necessity of performances becoming burning books. Chr. Ludvigsen's very personal statement, *Open Letter 36 years later — a Framework of Moles*, throws light on the early days of Odin Teatret. In *Pictures of Odin* Tony D'Urso comments a few of his favourite photographs of Odin Teatret from more than 25 years. Janne Risum follows with a survey of the coherence in the history of the International School of Theatre Anthropology in *ISTA — What's in a Name?* As a former actor in Odin Teatret, now being part of the administrative staff, Ulrik Skeel writes *Dancing without light. A Note from the Administration*. From an organisational point of view Jørn Bjerre writes on management systems seen from *Odin Teatret and the Art of Perpetuating Creativity through Difference*. John Andreasen's *Ode to Odin 2000* was recited in Danish as a farewell poem just before the end of the seminar with Odin Teatret in Aarhus, April 2000. Alexander Thieme has created the cover as a montage of theatre masks and of Odin's eye. As a short epilogue of each contributor to *Odin Teatret 2000* is given a small 'portrait' in order to identify who is who.

9

Half of the contributions are created especially for *Odin Teatret 2000*, and the other half are either dense or dilated versions of speeches held at the conferences during the seminar with Odin Teatret at Department of Dramaturgy, Aarhus University in Denmark, March 19 - April 11 2000. On the initiative of Erik Exe Christoffersen and in collaboration with different Arts and Language Studies and Kulturhus Aarhus a special Odin Teatret Festival took place containing eight performances, a six days workshop, four 'barters', eight one day conferences and a symposium including actors, dancers, writers, directors, choreographers, speech trainers, students and university scholars.

The performances were: *In the Skeleton of the Whale, Mythos, The Castle in Holstebro II, Judith, Ode to Progress, Doña Musica's Butterflies, White as Jasmin* and *Itsi Bitsi*. The symposium including Granhoj Dance was held under the headline Dance and Theatre. The conferences had various themes like: Theatre and philosophy, Theatre and text (modern and classic), Interpreting text, Acting traditions, The voice and the music, Theatre and the social space, and Spaces of memory. And during this period Eugenio Barba was visiting professor at Aarhus University.

As editors, we are grateful to all the contributors for a variety of personal viewpoints on Odin Teatret 2000. We send warm thanks to Stacey Marie Cozart and Patricia Lunddahl for their help in correcting our foreign languages.

> You want me to speak about dance and theatre, theatre in dance and dance in theatre.
>
> You want me to reveal my technical skills and secrets, or maybe do you expect me to tear out the heart of the scenic figures I've represented over the years and then serve them for you pumping like a dance macabre.
>
> Maybe you think you've understood, but I tell you from where you sit — from where you watch and with all the notebooks in the world you'll never be able to capture the secret behind the mask — on the other side within the dance itself lies the vast country of wisdom — dance, dance, dance and you will understand — but then — oh — paradox of paradoxes — your words will be like my words, your speaking like my speaking, just a shadow — just a shadow of the real.
>
> *Iben Nagel Rasmussen, Aarhus, 22 March 2000*

Peter Laugesen

[**Roman Meditations**]

*We roared through the old gates. Iron doors hanging
all grey, with bricks mossed over and gone into chips
dogs walked through.*
LeRoi Jones

Two theatre-groups that we all followed back then: From
the United States of America, ladies and gentlemen, let's have
a round of applause for the LIVING THEATRE! And from Holstebro,
Denmark, and don't you dare applaud: the ODIN TEATRET!
Violent, outgoing, rooted in beatnik land and Piscator's
teachings on worker's theatre in New York City. Didn't they
shoot real heroin up on stage during Jack Gelber's THE CONNECTION?

TWO   And silent, enclosed safeguarded until ready to pop out
TRIBES   like spoiled children from another age, like beginning anew,
             oriental influence and more like hippies, younger. COME AND
             THE DAY WILL BE OURS!

Yet, maybe paradoxically, also an ACADEMIC theatre. Basing
itself on post-68 drama-students as well as on bartering with
real life people in out-of-the-way places. Both however real
theatres of potlatch, latter day indians from Etrurias yet to
emerge from the darkness released by hydrogen bombs in the
desert, fallout citizens of castaway empires. Towering
presences awakened from the dead and stalking the streets of
Rome like dancing sculpture. Voices from the dark slimy tombs
emptied long ago by wayward robbers, crazy clowns of eternity.

DISTURBANCE!

Shaking the walls, stilting the streets. Patrolling the borders,
unarmed. Ambassadors everywhere of poetic reality. Both of these
tribes came out like exploding carnivals of repressed desires,
unfolding fragmented flags of forgotten beauty in patterns
of possible new cities, risking absurdity and death. Chained and
gagged, mummified only to unroll the bandages of authority
and cast them to the winds of constant change, for everyone to
see the terribly tender truth inside.

ETRURIAN ODIN

Bird's body with a dog's head wanders up the empty street
sweeping dust of withered houses.
Dying modernity flowers into chaotic prologue.
Time jumps from every hole in the gone walls like supernova
polar bears in disco quickstep while the night goes lollipop.
Textures of mornings to come on the grey skeletons of industrialism.
Bags of virus waiting on flakes of tropical ice for the cocktail rain of empty bottles.
Neon lungs drip blood on every flag.
Rafaello workers say good-bye and tears are rolling.

Teatro India, Rome-Brabrand, June 2000

Eugenio Barba

[Tacit Knowledge]

Heritage and Waste

[What the feet know]

Theatre people often say that an actor must know how to think with the whole body, that not just the head, but also the feet must be able to reflect, and that this reflection is *knowledge-in-action*.

This is not strange. Every type of physical training tends to strengthen certain patterns or plans of action which enable us to act without having to think about *how* to put them into practice. It is as if the body itself, a hand, a foot, the spine were doing the thinking, without involving the head. In the same way, for example, we learn to drive a car after a period in which every movement must be understood, learned and memorised. In the end we are able to drive without having to call to mind every single procedure, reacting appropriately and immediately if something unexpected happens, while at the same time we may be listening to music, speaking with a passenger or following a train of thought.

The ability to react appropriately and immediately does not mean automatically following a memorised pattern of action. It consists in knowing how to imagine a new and unforeseen pattern and executing it even before you are aware of where it is leading, according to a behaviour whose precise rules have been incorporated.

To learn the actor's craft means to incorporate certain competences, skills, ways of thinking and behaving that, on stage, become 'second nature', to use the words of Stanislavski. For the trained actor, scenic behaviour becomes just as 'spontaneous' as daily behaviour. It is the result of a re-elaborated spontaneity. The aim of this 're-elaboration of spontaneity' is a capacity to perform actions decisively so that they become organic and effective to the senses of the spectator.

Re-elaborated spontaneity is not simply an unconstrained, free and easy manner that *simulates* spontaneous behaviour. It is the result of a process which rebuilds a dynamic equivalent to that which governs our daily behaviour within the extra-ordinary realm of art: the balance between that which we are aware that we know and that which we know without knowing it: our tacit knowledge.

[Inculturation and acculturation]

Actors have followed two separate paths to 're-elaborate spontaneity': as a point of departure they have adopted a process of *acculturation* which imposes new models of behaviour; or else they have started out from the behaviour that each individual unwittingly learns within the culture in which s/he has grown up, according to those processes we call inculturation.

These two divergent paths govern in different though equivalent ways the relationship between the actor's explicit knowledge, communicated and communicable through words, and his or her profound, implicit and organic knowledge. Or, to use Michael Polanyi's terminology, the distance between 'focal knowledge' and 'tacit knowledge'. Artistic effectiveness and the possibility to transform inherited knowledge without it becoming wasted or fossilised in a rigid system capable only of repetition depend on the coexistence of and the relationship between these two dimensions of knowledge.

The decisive factors in both paths are the way in which the transmission of experience takes place, the characteristics of the environment and the interpersonal relationships during the period of apprenticeship.

a) *Acculturation as a point of departure* — The first path towards the 're-elaboration of spontaneity' goes from simplification towards the creation of a diverse and artificial complexity. It is the path of the 'codified' artistic traditions: the classical theatres of Asia, ballet, pantomime, mime and, for the voice, the tradition of 'bel canto'. Among humankind's endless possibilities, certain aspects of 'natural' daily behaviour are isolated, re-elaborated, redesigned and enhanced until they often become unrecognisable (to such an extent that we often speak of 'non-realism' or 'anti-realism').

The procedure consists in selecting a limited number of basic movements and positions and combining these in progressively more complex and varied units until the equivalent of the unforeseeable variety of individual reactions is reached. Thus a sort of 'alternative nature' is elaborated. The apprenticeship concerns above all the physical aspects of behaviour, starting with the most elementary situations: how to stand, walk, sit, look, use the hands and compose the face into a range of expressions representing as many basic emotions.

The multiple combination and linking of these few codified forms becomes a continuous flow inside which the actor-dancer can be free, creative and can *improvise*. But the first long phases of apprenticeship are characterised by the necessity to imitate and to execute with precision the pattern of movements with which the student must comply. It is a question of a process of acculturation similar to that by means of which we learn a language other than our own mother tongue.

I am giving this example in order to avoid certain negative associations attached to the term 'acculturation' which can be the result of violence and not of free choice, as in the case of cultural colonialism or forced homogenisation. The decisive factor is the initial choice, whether free or not. From the moment that someone *chooses* to train within one of the performative genres, whether ballet or classical Chinese theatre, the process is not unlike that of forced acculturation. The patterns imposed from the outside do not originate from the autonomous decisions of the pupil but are supplied ready made and simply have to be complied with. They collide with the normal behaviour of the pupil's culture, biography, family circle and experiences, deforming everything that s/he has learned 'naturally' through the painless process of inculturation.

One of the consequences of this method is that it becomes very difficult to distinguish between 'theatre' and 'dance' according to the paradigms of western culture. Another even more important consequence concerns the deep personal roots which grow from the established forms when the actor-dancers *have made them their own*.

The process of *acculturation* which transforms (de-forms) physical behaviour has an effect on two different levels: one is external, defining a belonging to the collective identity of a tradition or style; the other is intimate and profoundly personal. The pupils have incorporated forms which do not belong to them but which, nevertheless, coincide with the collective style of a performative genre. They have introduced these forms to the secret universe of their associations and their personal rituals, nourishing the silent and subterranean dialogue that each of us has with our own 'body', i.e. with ourselves. The forms imposed become a part of the experience of our own *being*, through that sixth sense known as kinaesthesia in which the so-called 'physical' and 'mental' (or 'spiritual') cross over the confines of the other.

The tensions between these two poles — one collective and the other intimate — are one of the sources of the artists' strength enabling them to detach themselves from the learned models, at the very moment when they embody and execute them. It is here too that the masters derive their strength when they are able to transform the incorporated knowledge into practical reflection and therefore to transmit to the pupils not only patterns of action but also personal attitudes.

b) *Inculturation as a point of departure* — The other path towards the 're-elaboration of spontaneity' is not selective but uses as its basis the entire range of 'natural' daily behaviour. This procedure consists in creating specific conditions that modify the inculturated reactions, transforming them into scenic behaviour, i.e. into actions which are organic and effective to the senses of the spectator. The assumptions may be generic and vague. For example: to be an actor it is enough to know how to make your reactions visible from a distance and to make yourself heard, to be able to imitate daily behaviour, to interest the spectators, to catch and guide their attention.

This initial vagueness may grow into a wealth of details when confronted by the events and characters in the stories presented on stage. The *characters* trigger the detailed process of acculturation which was not present at the level of basic physical behaviour. The characters are *potential presences* transmitted through the texts, dialogues or monologues, through their actions which have been established once and for all, and through the thoughts, opinions and feelings as these may be deduced or imagined from what is said and done.

Without a confrontation and a clash with the characters, or rather without that forced process called *interpretation*, the vagueness of a non-codified scenic behaviour can be very useful material in the hands of a director and also of interest to the spectators, but it does not provide the actor with an independent territory in which to grow.

When, along this path, the actors take upon themselves the task of *giving life* to the many different characters from the stories to be staged, they need to know the 'secrets of the craft' or else to invent them for themselves. They have to find the equivalent of the clear-cut, formalised and shared codification that is the starting point of the other path. Here it is hidden, personal and informal. But without this informal, personal and therefore hidden knowledge which steers the use of their own scenic presence, the actors would not be able to render visible and credible their interpretation, their creative intentions and personal visions concerning the characters they embody. It is important for the actor to play *many* and *diverse* characters. The actor's task is to mould them individually and in detail in order to differentiate the characters from one another. This develops the variety and the complexity of an actor's personal technique.

This second path is especially characteristic of so-called 'dramatic' theatre of European origin, as opposed to theatre of dance, mime or song. In China, for example, performances following the European and North American tradition are known as 'spoken' theatre to distinguish them from the traditional forms. This is not because it is based solely on words but because only the text is transmitted in a fixed and precise form while the rest — which is codified in the classical forms — is left entirely to the actors, i.e. to their ability to create a personal physical language.

Between these two poles whose characteristics I have summarised here, there is a vast range of nuances, a tangle of different tracks and roads along which we come up against situations and experiences which are difficult to classify. Where would we place Meyerhold, for instance, and what about Kazuo Ohno?

But the simplification inherent in classification allows us to uncover a burning problem. It does not concern the differences between the ways in which the actor's pro-fessional identity is forged, but rather the *heart* that must beat in each of these ways: a heart whose diastole is constituted by the transmission of knowledge that is both for-malised and can be formulated, and whose systole is the occurrence of a silent subter-ranean process which cannot be programmed. It is a profoundly personal process, not because it is subjective but because it helps to shape the personalities of those who want to immerse themselves in the craft, guiding them towards individuality (*in-dividuus*: undivided, whole).

The schools' didactic programmes are insufficient because they can only refer to knowledge which is communicable and formalised, thus reducing teaching to one dimension only. In this sense those who affirm that the art of the actor *cannot be taught* are right. The point is whether it can be learnt. And on what conditions.

[The many faces of the guru, and the collective guru]

Traditional apprenticeship in theatre has always been based on the one hand on the professional authoritativeness of the master, the *guru*, the *sensei* or certain models, and, on the other, on the tradition (or the breaking of tradition) that they represent.

Today *guru* is a common word, even outside the Indian context. Its use is often the fatuous sign of a fashion, but it also points to an unsatisfied need: an apprenticeship which establishes a pedagogical relationship that is difficult, full of risks, rigorous, demanding; that is, more profound and personal than a scholastic one.

For centuries, in theatre practice, continuity and also the seeds of change have been rooted in a situation in which apprenticeship took place in a real work situation, not separated from that of the public exercise of the profession. The process of learning was pragmatic and was integrated into the daily routine of repetition, variation and competition within a family or a company.

In Asian traditions the relationship between master and pupil was (and often still is) modelled on the relationship between parents and children, in a culture in which the authority of the parents is absolute and, equally, their commands represent a moral imperative. In many cases it is actually a question of biological parents and children. In others the master 'adopts' the chosen pupil, giving the child the family name and thus creating a veritable dynasty, as with *kabuki*, *noh* and certain families of actors and dancers in Bali and India. Like kings and popes, great *kabuki* actors succeed one an-other in a long line in which the different individuals are distinguished by a number indicating the continuity of a single lineage running through the changing generations: Ichikawa Danjûrô I, Ichikawa Danjûrô II, Ichikawa Danjûrô III up until Ichikawa Danjûrô XII, spanning the period from 1660 to the present day.

Apprenticeship consists of much practical routine work, of imitation and identification with the professional norms embodied by the master. In addition to the pupil's professional duties, there are sometimes filial ones such as taking care of the day-to-day needs of the master-parent. In return, the parent-master feels responsible for the development of the pupil-son and not merely for his ability within the profession.

The process of selection is a personal one: the apprentice chooses the master and the master the apprentices. The long trial period before making a final choice allows possible merits and weaknesses to come to light on both sides. This is the very opposite of what happens in modern theatre schools (in Asia, Europe or any other continent) where the entrance exam lasts an hour at the most and attempts to take into account the aspiring pupil's talent, maturity, age, previous studies and predisposition towards the art.

In the traditional relationship between master and pupil, *learning by doing* is not limited to three or four years, but takes place in a slow succession of phases allowing the pupil to absorb and take possession of the craft. This craft does not consist merely of skills but also of certain intuitive knowledge for which no rules exist. There is no didactic system or formalised method of teaching when it comes to matters such as how long to insist on certain details, how to confront an impasse during the rehearsals, or how to deal with the conflicts that arise in the working relationships.

If it is true that the art of the actor cannot be taught, and yet that certain people can learn it, this means that *the characteristics of the relationships within the working environment* make more or less possible the assimilation of scenic knowledge.

In many traditions, in Asia as in classical ballet, emphasis is placed on the mute aspect of apprenticeship in which words are considered to be superfluous. The skills and values that the pupil gradually incorporates are not necessarily translatable into precise formulas. When an apprenticeship is successful, the pupils know far more than they think they know. Only *a posteriori*, when they themselves are ready to become masters, do they begin to question themselves about the principles that are implicit in what they have incorporated.

The master, the *guru*, has many faces. S/he is a keeper of technical knowledge as well as a spiritual guide. S/he is a professional and a moral authority. S/he is master and parent and, at the same time, head of the working ensemble or family. S/he is the indisputable judge of the quality of the work, thus allowing the pupil not to be kept on a tight rein by the fickle and imprecise tastes of the 'public'.

It cannot be emphasised enough how important it is for actors, for their independence and above all for their courage, to be able to address themselves to *one* spectator whom they trust completely and whose judgement is worth more than that of all the other spectators or all successes and failures.

In the environment in which transmission occurs within the relationship of master-parent and pupil-son (or -daughter), the guru retains this position with all its authority for as long as s/he lives, even when the pupil has become an expert artist, perhaps even more skilled and famous than the *guru*, and even when the pupil is transformed into a master.

This method of guaranteeing the handing down of experience appears today to be 'archaic' and contrasts with the criteria which rule modern society. It survives with difficulty and is an exception, an exoticism. Today those who train for the profession rarely manage to resist the need to do many things and all of them in a hurry, programming their time, the *curriculum* and the itinerary to be taken. A way of thinking prevails in which having your own personality means *doing without* outside influences instead of constantly *struggling* with them.

Very soon there will be no true *gurus* left, not so much because they themselves will disappear, but because the conditions which make their function possible will no longer exist. *Gurus* are being replaced by teachers.

'How can we call them back to life?' This is not an appropriate question. The right one would be: 'How do we avoid wasting the essence of the relationships they were able to establish?'

In the tradition of Western theatre (which has the path of inculturation as its point of departure) there has never been anything comparable to the apprenticeship guaranteed by the relationship with a *guru*. Something similar can be found in the ballet or in the 'bel canto' tradition, but this is a forced similarity.

It is true that often, in the history of Western theatre, experience seemed to pass from parents to children since many actors came from a family of artists. But even when actors received their training in their theatrical family, the learning process did not involve the intensity and the dangerous relationship characterising the bond between the *guru* and his pupil.

Nevertheless there was a *guru*: a collective one.

Let us see what happened when an actor was trained within a theatre company or by moving from one company to another. There was no separation between the moment of learning and that of exercising the profession. The environment with its hierarchies, habits and customs, with its tacit rules of behaviour, shaped the attitude of the apprentice towards the craft. It provided a vast range of artistic models, some based on routine, others on exceptional originality. They could be observed at close hand, evening after evening for months and years, opening possibilities for choices and comparisons. In the beginning the apprentice imitated. But s/he could decide on the direction to take, thereby discovering a didactic path in a context with many examples of high quality. By combining imitated elements, selecting them here and there and re-organising them, s/he was able to obtain original effects.

The apprentice played small roles (he was a kind of unskilled theatre worker and as such suffered financial exploitation) until faced by the challenge of a more demanding role that provided him with a foothold to advance in his career. He did not have a master who had the time and desire to dedicate himself to him. From time to time his companions — the more experienced and skilful actors — let fall a word of advice or a piece of practical information. It was a reticent form of teaching, one drop at a time, with many voices and often abounding in contradictions mingled with shows of indifference, disapproval or appreciation from the spectators.

The young actor was moulded by the presence of two different audiences: spectators and fellow actors. The first were quick to applaud and to disapprove, and ferocious in their indifference; the second were more sceptical and cautious, familiar with the tricks of the trade, difficult to surprise or convince, clever at noticing the details and symptoms of a so-far unexpressed potentiality, accustomed to fighting against the audience's tastes without giving in. The older actors' language, information and explanations contributed to developing the *reflection-in-action* of the younger inexperienced actor (a 'reflective practitioner' in today's terminology).

The rigour of the 'collective *guru*' was not revealed in the person of the master-parent, but through a wearisome routine with little time for indulgence and beautiful words, where nobody seemed anxious to teach, where the word 'steal' seemed more suitable than 'learn' when referring to the appropriation of a technique or of a 'secret' of the craft, where the numerous characters interpreted were at the same time the instruments and the proof of advancement in one's career, and where almost every evening one had to confront a frightening audience.

The situation that we have called the 'collective *guru*' seems wretched and chaotic when compared to the other, which is characterised by the presence of a master-parent. It is surprising to note, however, that in spite of appearances it was an appropriate response to a process of learning based on inculturation and in which the only fixed elements were the texts from the repertoire. Rigid relationships between master and pupil would have been counterproductive. Learning could only happen through trial and error, along the rough path of autodidactism.

Autodidactism can be defined as the capacity to have a dialogue with a master who is not there. It presupposes the ability to discern *what may be of use*, labouriously picking it out from among all the information, rules, encounters, misunderstandings, relationships and clashes within the context in which one lives. It demands, above all, an attitude of hanging on doggedly to something which at first one is unable to grasp.

It would be easy to accentuate the negative aspects of apprenticeship with a traditional *guru* or with a 'collective *guru*' or, on the contrary, to idealise the 'archaic' systems of theatre apprenticeship, contrasting them with modern deficiencies. But the systems of the past are neither good nor bad. They are *past*. Our task today is to create an equivalent of their positive characteristics.

Almost everything can be eliminated from the traditional theatre apprenticeship, except for the capacity to organise an environment in which learning is not the direct consequence of a teaching programme.

It was precisely *the quality of this environment* that this century's theatre reformers tried to achieve while struggling against the tendencies of our time; or rather against the ideology (or the illusion) of an industrialised society that makes people believe that an actor's learning process consists only in absorbing everything a group of teachers in a school is able to teach according to an efficient didactic method and programme.

[Many schools]

Parallel with these schools whose goal was the creation of a new theatre ethos, other more 'normal' institutions grew up that were less revolutionary and aimed at high professional quality. These schools too — from which the official theatre schools that exist in many countries today were derived — were born out of a need for order as well as a pedagogical and social equity: to introduce young people into the craft in a less fortuitous and limited way, freeing them from the distortions of the theatrical market.

Since the eighteenth century in Europe, enlightened intellectuals such as Voltaire, Diderot and particularly d'Alembert considered the establishment of theatre schools to be a means of surmounting the actor's ambiguous moral and social status. Their motivations were as follows: the actors' social marginalisation is not a consequence of their profession. Their profession is marginalised because it selects its members from among the marginalised. Actors as a whole can never become a respectable and respected class. The majority of actors will continue to be recruited from among the numbers of the rejected, maladjusted and asocial as long as — in order to become actors — they have to abandon their families, withdraw from the daily life of civil society and join a wandering theatre company.

The schools that the intellectuals of the Enlightenment dreamed about never saw the light of day.

The first theatre schools appeared in Europe in the eighteenth century (although the first school was founded in Russia as early as 1673). In the nineteenth century their numbers increased. Sometimes they were conceived as being preliminary to the engagement of actors in great theatres like the Conservatoire in Paris, which was linked to the Comédie Française, or like the school attached to the Alexandrinski Theatre in Moscow. Sometimes they were small academies in which experienced actors taught acting to amateurs, in the same way that professional musicians, singers and ballet dancers gave lessons to children from wealthy families. There were also classes at the music conservatories and art academies based on the assumption that opera singers also had to know how to act, and that painters and sculptors could better depict the passions and actions of historical, mythological and religious heroes if they had some notion of the actor's *savoir faire*.

Alongside these schools, classes and courses, there also flourished a whole literary branch consisting of treatises on acting, recitation, declamation and gesticulation presented sometimes as a theory or — as they said at the time — a 'philosophy' of scenic art. They were works by scholars, philosophers and physiognomists (like the treatises by Sainte-Albine, Diderot's *The Actor's Paradox*, and *Letters on Mimicry* by Engel), or by actors (such as Luigi and Francesco Riccoboni, Garrick, as well as innumerable other great performers of the nineteenth century). These schools and books constitute a pedagogical nebula that is of interest to theatre historians. On the whole, however, they had little influence on the actors' practical life, where the principal way of apprenticeship was via the criteria set forth by what we have called the *collective guru*.

This 'pedagogical nebula', on the other hand, became influential in the twentieth century, with new tones, ambitions and prospects. It was in the twentieth century that the idea of training actors far from the routine of the craft prevailed, beyond the influence of an environment that was characterised by clichés, routine and the necessity to 'tread the boards' prematurely. It offered the possibility of initiating and completing a fruitful process of apprenticeship, developing personal creative capacities without being exploited financially by the directors of companies.

The term 'school' defines profoundly different and often incomparable realities: from the institutions organised by the State with a general programme preparing for work; to prolonged courses offered by professional actors or directors; and to 'schools' that teach the *method* of a master, or the style of one of the great Asian theatre traditions.

The economic law of supply and demand — on the one hand those who wish to be introduced to theatre practice, and on the other those who consider they have the competence to transmit it — has made such proliferation possible. In the twentieth century a 'market of methods' has also sprung up in which different masters or traditions are treated like any other 'subject'. A host of schools or workshops claim in their programmes to be able to introduce the pupil to the 'method' of Stanislavski, Meyerhold, Michael Chekhov, Piscator, Brecht, Decroux, the Actor's Studio, The Living Theater, Grotowski, *kathakali, noh* or the Peking Opera.

A 'method' is not in itself an effective formula that works for all those who wish to achieve a particular result. Method means literally path: an indication of a process which needs a certain context, particular times, places, relationships and stable presences in order to exist.

I have hinted several times at the drawbacks arising from a scholastic education which dull the tension between formalised knowledge and tacit knowledge. I will add one last example: even the theatre traditions which are based on a precise 'codification' of behaviour undergo a deterioration when they are handed down according to the scholastic model. In school one can learn perfectly well how to perform the score of an Indian or Balinese dance-drama or that of the characters in the Peking Opera or *kabuki*. In these cases there is something concrete to teach. But at the cost of sterilising it, reducing it to an unalterable form whose only changes, in time, stem from a progressive lack of precision and from the attempts to simplify or emphasise the points of departure. In this way one of the most powerful preconceptions is reinforced: that in changing, traditions deteriorate. Change is the lifeblood of tradition, based on the dialectic between preservation and innovation. This dialectic can only come about when there are artists capable of reformulating, sometimes even to the point of unrecognizability, the forms that are rooted in their tacit knowledge. The submerged part of the iceberg of one's knowledge prevents one from veering off course, even when redrawing the map of the journey. This capacity to redesign previously defined forms is what makes a 'codified style' into a true *art*.

Not all the 'schools' are scholastic. Some of them were able to realise, for reasonably long periods and in different ways, the equivalent of the elements that are essential to the traditional process of learning. The schools created alongside the theatres of the twentieth century reformers are examples of this. Limiting ourselves to the first half of the century, suffice it to think of Stanislavski, Meyerhold, Copeau, or the projects of Craig, Appia, Fuchs and of the Bauhaus, or the intransigent extremism of Decroux.

Taking these examples into account, a synthetic discourse is possible since, in spite of differences in choices and methods, we find a recurring criteria: to reconstruct the equivalent of the complexity and the wholeness of an environment and a tradition.

These environments may be small, consisting of only a few dozen people. But around this nucleus, the diverse components of a theatrical culture congregate in concentric circles: actors, dancers, directors, musicians, playwrights, experts in figurative and architectural art, craftsmen, scholars and intellectuals interested in historical and theoretical research into the performance arts, as well as passionate and knowledgeable spectators.

Such environments constitute 'small traditions' which do not sink their roots into an age-old history — or one that is assumed to be so — but compensate for their youth with research into a transcultural dimension, or better still trans-stylistic. They do not try to pass on a style that corresponds to the tastes of the founders, or a new and original codification, but the roots of the craft, those principles of scenic behaviour that permit choices in the most diverse artistic directions. Often the actors' sources of knowledge are investigated at the elementary levels of human behaviour, the physical principles that characterise their movements, their 'bio-mechanics', their 'scenic *bios*', the mental processes that govern their actions and the pragmatic laws of perception.

It is not necessary to establish if and to what extent the initial hypotheses are truly scientific and well-grounded. It is important to note how this attitude implies, not a vision of knowledge as a whole, but a continuous process of knowing. Learning, in theatre, is not thought of as the appropriation of established competences, but as continual experimental research within the domain of the stage. The pedagogical paradigm is replaced by that of the scientific laboratory, and it is no longer possible to differentiate between 'school' and 'ensemble'.

Well before Grotowski compared his small ensemble to a laboratory for scientific research, this tendency had already developed in the work of the reformers at the beginning of the century. Here too Grotowski showed how that which is expressed effectively in a programme or a slogan ('poor theatre') is determined by whatever has been absorbed as tacit knowledge through a long historical and biographical process. What seems to be a programme awaiting realisation is in fact the ascertainment, *a posteriori*, of something that has been experienced.

In the changing conditions of theatre and of the socio-cultural system which surrounds it, the 'non-scholastic schools' adequately resolve the fundamental problem of learning. This cannot be based solely on articulated knowledge, formulated and organised in teaching programmes, but must also shape and nourish the submerged knowledge which is metabolised by each individual — everything s/he *knows, without knowing that s/he knows it.*

We may call them 'schools', 'workshops' or 'laboratories'. In fact they function like true theatrical microcosms in which professional competence is only a part of a cultural identity, an ethos.

We could say that they are places for work involving the individual as a human being and not merely as a professional. But we could assert that this ambition — or illusion — to change the 'human being' or to 'work on oneself' is one of the ways in which we formulate our awareness of the efficacity of the submerged and tacit parts of professional knowledge.

[Behind the recipes]

I aroused a reaction of surprise and reproach from the theatre historians with whom I share the experience of ISTA (yet again the word 'school': International School of Theatre Anthropology) when I proposed putting together a small book of recipes for young people who are entering the profession. I wanted to condense into a few sentences the practical know-how implied in the words of masters such as Decroux, Stanislavski or Grotowski, Piscator or Copeau, Craig or Mejerhold, Brecht, Michael Chekhov or Artaud.

It would be a way to freeze history into a catalogue of advice according to the do-it-yourself concept that is so popular with our consumer society. I admit, however, that speaking of the importance of tacit knowledge that cannot be put into words, while at the same time offering recipes, seems rather an exaggerated way of exercising the art of contradiction.

It is also interesting to observe how few operative principles are contained in the teachings of even the most eloquent masters of the twentieth century, starting with Stanislavski: no more than one, two, or at the most three recipes for each of them.

While the 'great traditions' reveal to us a myriad details and precepts, the masters of the twentieth-century theatre reform concentrate on one point alone, one single principle, like scientists who search for the answer to one single obsessing question. They examine it from every side, through a thousand examples which constitute the many lines of the same perspective.

Restricting the field is the condition for reaching depth.

Behind their 'recipes' there is no *knowledge* which is acquired and confirmed by belonging to a style, but rather the personal involvement in a *process of knowing*. It is this process that allows the acquired knowledge to be incorporated, to become 'tacit', i.e. second nature. It is a metabolism that presupposes a favourable environment.

Environments exist that are formed through an organic process, while others are formed mechanically. An environment is formed mechanically when a company signs up its actors for one production at a time, complying with the rules of casting, according to the procedures in the system of today's theatre production. Many permanent companies have an environment which has been formed mechanically. Here the different components (actors, technicians, directors, dramaturge) remain together for long periods, but as a corporate organisation based on the rigid division of work and functions.

To define an environment as formed mechanically is not a negative definition. It simply means that it is organised with a view to a result, and that its profile and internal dynamic must depend on the objectives it hopes to achieve. It may nurture profound personal motivations and human relationships, but this is a wish, not an automatic consequence. When the aim is the standard of quality of the product, it is essential to recruit a good team of experts, provide them with good tools and well thought out work plans, and then to proceed in such a way that their relationships may function more or less harmoniously. In such cases the professional experience of the individual people in the team is a necessary condition. The training cannot be the objective.

Other examples of environments which are formed mechanically are those schools that follow the paradigms, the formal structures and the way of thinking of scholastic regulations (specialised teachers for the different subjects, pre-established courses, exams, diplomas). Such organisation is a necessary condition in order to guarantee the same opportunities to every single pupil. Any school that offers *equal education for all* must be *impersonal*. It may involve commitment in relationships but must exclude personal ties between teachers and pupils.

The learning process in schools is often conceived as a continuous progression from incompetence to competence. In fact, learning implies two stages connected by a period of transition. The first stage involves the acquisition of common basic knowledge. The pupil can take over a patrimony of impersonal knowledge, in so much as it is considered useful to everybody. The second stage is a non-scholastic one in which the totality of the acquired knowledge is adapted and absorbed in depth. Technique, as a conscious factor or a problem, disappears when the young artist masters it to such an extent that s/he can concentrate on the essential question: what to do with this technique and to what end, and what meaning to give it. This second stage, however, is preceded by a period of transition that is fundamental to the development of the individual.

In certain cases this transitional phase is clearly identified and organised. Before starting out along their own road, the young artisans of past centuries left their master and set out on a long educative journey, going from one country and language to another, visiting different workplaces and new masters. The same thing applies today in many professions, from doctors to pilots, with a period of 'trial' or 'practical experience' between the scholastic 'curriculum' and the exercise of a profession. But on the whole, the students who have finished theatre school are left to their own devices and must manage alone during the decisive period in which their experience is consolidated. This is the transitional phase in which discursive knowledge must become active knowledge, capable of changing, adapting itself and interacting with the context.

The theatre school is only concerned with the first stage of the apprenticeship. Sometimes there is no connection between what is taught there and what is practised in the real world of the craft. Thus the transition, which guarantees the *continuity* between what is considered to be the foundation common to all and the personalised practice of the profession, is lacking.

Theatre today has many ways of being and has many different practices that are not even comparable amongst themselves. How can we establish a valid common basis for all of them, or for the theatre in which the schools must train their pupils? Whereas the performance market is ruled by the technical and financial demands of cinema and television, the theatre's margins of freedom are broader and more elastic. But it is difficult to define which skills and techniques are necessary for the would-be actor. Thus the continuity between basic learning and its personalisation runs the risk of being lost.

Against the theatre schools I have set the 'non-scholastic' schools that consider the craft as an unknown quantity whose foundations are to be investigated. They fuse, in a new synthesis, the actual working conditions of the 'company' with those of a 'school'. These are rare situations that are difficult to promote and keep alive, although very much present in the history of twentieth century theatre. They are made up of *small groups* in which the distinctions between the period of apprenticeship and the practice of the craft, between school and artistic production, between master and pupil, have disappeared.

The environments of small theatre groups are often formed through an organic process. The force of this process does not derive from a clear idea about the objectives to be reached, but from the urgency of different motivations which assemble and guide individuals who cannot or will not pass through a theatre school. In this case, the personal motivations and the quality of the relationships are the premises that determine the character and the results of the work.

The prospect is overturned: it is not the group, the team or the company that is formed with the aim of attaining certain results; but it is the results, the artistic products, which take form according to whatever is feasible and imaginable within the group.

According to the orthodox way of thinking, organising and practising theatre, this seems to be a paradox. But this 'paradoxical theatre' includes a vast region which is not always — as in Europe — submerged. It is enough to know what happens in Latin America to realise how inappropriate it is to consider as a theatrical exception something that is the rule there.

It is, in fact, just *another rule* of the entire twentieth-century theatre. This *other rule* is represented by theatres formed through an organic process. These are neither a continuation of the traditional company, which has characterised theatre history from the sixteenth to the twentieth centuries, nor do they correspond to today's companies. They are the unrecognisable and often involuntary development of 'workshops', 'studios' or 'laboratories' that, during the first decades of the twentieth century, set about trying to create a solid foundation for the knowledge of the actor by combining 'school' and 'company'.

It was this type of environment that, at the beginning of the twentieth century, formed the Russian and French theatre generations with their strong fighting spirit: the 'studios' and 'workshops' connected with Stanislavski and his Art Theatre, with the activities of Vakhtangov, with the theatres of Meyerhold and Tairov, Copeau and Dullin. It was in Joan Littlewood's Theatre Workshop that some of the protagonists of the second half of twentieth-century British theatre were trained. Similar environments had been created in the United States by the exiles Richard Boleslavski, Erwin Piscator, Michail Chekhov and later by Harold Clurman, Lee Strasberg and Stella Adler.

Apparently the 'studios', 'ateliers' and Art Theatre schools at the start of the twentieth century have nothing in common with theatre groups. The former were the theatre aristocracy of their time, an aristocracy that was rebellious, industrious and adventurous as well as being heir to the most refined knowledge and the most subtle aesthetic taste. Small theatre groups apply, whether by choice or by necessity, an auto-didactism that, as far as ideas are concerned, obliges them to invent a tradition with which they can identify and which, on a practical level, forces them to learn by continually moving from one course to another. The former rejected the legacy of the theatre of the past. The latter experienced the condition of the disinherited. But in both cases we find an environment that is not only able to guarantee creative continuity, but also the handing down of the craft.

In order not to remain superficial knowledge, these heterogeneous techniques which have been learnt on the outside, must be metabolised and put down roots. The process that leads to the incorporation is made possible, not only by the effectiveness of the teaching methods, but above all by the existence of an independent territory, by a network of relationships and commitments and by certain conditions capable of filtering and personalising everything learnt on the outside. It is for this reason that, in spite of their enormous differences, the small, apparently marginal, theatre groups that grew up spontaneously can be compared to the outposts of the theatre aristocracy of the beginning of the twentieth century. In both cases a particular environment, and not a single individual, whether director or outstanding actor, is the premise for creativity. In both cases the theatrical environment fulfills the function of 'school' and 'workplace for the apprenticeship'. It safeguards the transition and continuity between the phase in which basic techniques are learned and the phase in which these are *forgotten*, become incorporated, tacit, and are translated into personalised actions.

Preparation for a creative profession is an education to excellency, comparable to the training of an athlete. Excellency should not be understood as the exceptional feat of an opportune moment, as success, grace, talent or fortune, but as a *habit* as well as a *habitat*, characterised by the discovery of one's own limits and by the need to go beyond them. Learning a technique is the first step towards liberating oneself from it, rejecting it, contradicting it. Training achieves its aim only if it creates something similar to an iceberg where the emerged part is *discursive knowledge* and the submerged part is *active knowledge* that is explicit in action and only subsequently able to be put into words.

This is why the quality of the apprenticeship coincides with the quality of the environment. It is a question of *ethos*, a combination of know-how and values, an ethological behaviour but also an ethic.

Twentieth-century theatre has been traversed by two visible and conscious forces: the rejection of the customs and conventions which have governed scenic practice for several centuries and the need to draw from the sources of the diverse traditions. A third force, on the other hand, has acted unwittingly, constituting a true waste or cultural entropy. Ironically, this waste is the consequence of the need to transform theatre in order to adapt it to the changing times or to new artistic and social visions. While trying to 'clean up' the remains of the past, the stereotypes, conditions and circumstances which hampered the creativity of the actor, certain practices which apparently did not correspond to the times and the new needs were obliterated. However, they had a vital function and we realise this as we become aware of their loss.

The force of waste can be seen at work in the case of theatre apprenticeship where the conditions that shape one's tacit knowledge are squandered: programmes instead of environments. The force of waste is particularly evident in the indifference and misunderstandings that encompass the theatre groups which live out their own autonomy and autodidactism in a context in which 'normality' is defined by institutions. Autonomy, anomaly, autodidactism and research are not the same as avant-garde, originality or novelty. They are the conditions for the development of environments in which it is possible to shape and pass on the process of knowing and the values that make theatre a precious asset. The actor's tacit knowledge is no longer a normal and obvious fact. It is a cultural asset under threat. Dealing with this threat is problematic because it compels us to recognise that conditions suitable for learning exist, even in contexts which apparently have nothing whatever to do with what we associate with a pedagogical process, a school or a teaching method.

Moreover, it forces us to concentrate on those very levels of experience whose fertility depends on their not being exposed. Once again, these are the zones in which technical competence is interwoven with professional identity, with the unformulated system of values underlying the *ethos* of theatre people, allowing each of them to build up a personal method of orientation — an ethic.

Behind those feet which — in the words of theatre people — *know how to reflect*, there is the awareness of an incorporated knowledge that coincides with the road, the time, the encounters, the environments through which we have passed, without the illusion of an ultimative goal. It is a knowledge that does not separate thought and action, means and objectives, which can be learned and passed on little by little, directly and indirectly. And it cannot be schematised or reproduced.

This article was written for the international symposium 'Tacit Knowledge — Heritage and Waste' which was held in Holstebro from 22 to 26 September 1999 on the occasion of Odin Teatret's thirty-fifth anniversary.

Translation by Judy Barba

Janne Risum

[The Impulse and the Image]

The Theatre Laboratory Tradition

and Odin Teatret

The Italian Renaissance academies, a handful of actors' academies in the 18th century, Goethe's experimental court theatre in Weimar, Antoine's Théâtre Libre in Paris, Lugnë-Poe's Théâtre l'Œuvre, the Moscow Art Theatre — this is the frail and labyrinthic line of descent to the first modern theatre laboratory, Meyerhold's in 1905.

> What name other than 'love' can we give to the passion which has bound certain theatre artists one to another, transforming into viable possibilities those ideas which dispassionate people considered at the time to be the obsessions of solitary maniacs? [...] the Master [...] reveals himself, only to disappear. (Barba 1999, 12)

It was the child of a close and complex relationship between a talented master of acting and directing, Konstantin Stanislavsky, and a gifted and rebellious apprentice, Vsevolod Meyerhold. At stake were the questions of life and meaning central to modern art, and so the relation between the impulse and the image.

[The impulse. The real action]

When Stanislavsky directed Meyerhold in the role of Tusenbach in *Three Sisters* (1901), he gave him a hard lesson for life in real stage actions. After what seemed like endless repetitions of his first entry heading for the piano stool, Meyerhold still struck a pose to recite his lines. Finally taking pity on him, Stanislavsky gave him a simple physical action and rhythm to perform: picking up a piece of paper.

> Stanislavsky climbed up on the stage, threw a piece of paper on the floor and asked me to break up my text in the following way: after having said three lines, I would see the

paper, pick it up, continue to speak, then unfold it and speak further. [...] The oratory disappeared as if by magic. (Gladkov 1997, 149)

Stanislavsky prescribed another physical action, opening a bottle of wine, as a simple remedy to release inner tension. As Meyerhold explains,

> I was as cold as a dog's nose. Then he gave me a sealed bottle of wine, telling me to open it with the corkscrew and at the same time say my lines. The physical difficulty of opening the bottle and the energy needed for doing it immediately awoke me. (Gladkov 1997, 150)

Reminiscing about this with his actors in 1936, Meyerhold points out that such 'a living gesture' invariably releases 'a living intonation' (Schmidt 1980, 130-31).

Yet, after the closure of his theatre in 1938, Meyerhold returned from Stanislavsky, having planned with him their future artistic cooperation all day, exclaiming:

> At the end of life our roads met, Meyerhold strongly agitated said, taking off his fur coat. He was silent for a second, and then he added: Anyhow, it was I who said first that you have to begin with the action. (Vendrovskaja 1967, 568)

Entangling themselves in such tragicomic contradictions was essential to their creative dynamic.

[The theatre laboratory]

Many ears earlier Stanislavsky had spent the winter of 1877 wearing a kimono and holding a fan, learning Japanese body language and dance. Meyerhold especially admired his gestures. Stanislavsky had exercises for the hands that used them as objects. He used a special rubber device for finger and carpus exercises, and also explored ways of handling all sorts of objects.

> how to pick up a glass, a jug. (Mejerchol'd 1968: 2, 92-93)

Stanislavsky performed Løvborg in Ibsen's *Hedda Gabler* (1899) with a theatricality which Meyerhold identifies as an assimilated Asian inspiration.

> just like a Japanese or Chinese actor. Especially his acting in the scene with the loss of the manuscript [...] the Japanese acting devices Konstantin Sergeevič actually effectuated, but dropped again for certain reasons. (Mejerchol'd 1968: 2, 90)

Meyerhold did not. The result was his theatre laboratory in 1905. As Stanislavsky defined,

> Our plans required preparatory laboratory work. [...] We needed a special institution which Vsevolod Èmil'evič aptly named 'a theatre studio'. This is not a finished theatre and not a school for beginners, but a laboratory for the experiments of more or less experienced actors. (Stanislavskij 1988-: 1, 358)

A century before, E.T.A. Hoffmann had founded his proposal for a basic theatre reform on music, pointing out the counterpoint as being its most efficient device (Hoffmann 1990, 51). Hoffmann explains that a theatre reform means educating a group of inexperienced young actors from scratch.

> Meinem Grundsatz gemäss werbe ich nur Künstler an, die noch nie ein Theater betreten haben. (Hoffmann 1924, 265)

Meyerhold linked Hoffmann's principles with the devices of a series of old strong theatre conventions on an East-West axis, including Noh and Kabuki. His more immediate model was the symbolist theatre inspired by Noh.

However, his radical recombination of their acting devices significantly coincides with Picasso painting his first major cubist work in Paris, *Les Demoiselles d'Avignon* (1906).

In 1906-07 Meyerhold summarizes the set of basic rules that a theatre laboratory must follow. I find the following rules: 1) It must have an artistic director. 2) It must join the forces of aesthetics and scholarship. 3) It must be a permanent group, 4) It must remain independent of the normal production economy of theatre. 5) It must be founded on free interaction between the actor and the spectator. 6) It must remain independent of existing performance conventions. 7) It must a priori define acting and theatre in the broadest possible sense, and thus not accept any historical separations such as those between acting, dancing, and singing, or between the arts. 8) It must study the basics of acting and theatre in the strongest theatre conventions in European and Asian theatre history. 9) Its acting devices must be founded on music. 10) It must use the method of collective creation. 11) It must use improvisation. 12) It must explore all means of human expression separately, investigating their possible range of devices when isolated or combined, and thus, contrary to the tradition of rhetoric, allow for the fact that in human behaviour plasticity and words may not correspond and may have different rhythms. 13) To be able to do so as theatre, it must develop études (fixed scores of action). 14) For the same reason, it must also mount productions. 15) It must establish a theatrical convention. 16) The studio must dissolve, when it stops being inventive (Meyerhold 1991, 23-64). 17) since the actor *is* the theatre, he or she may perform anywhere (Meyerhold adds in 1914).

> For the actor, the theatre is any stage, which he can construct for himself — without the assistance of a builder, wherever and however necessary, and as quickly as his skill will allow (read about the Chinese travelling companies). (Meyerhold 1991, 147)

By sticking to these basics, the group dynamics will eventually generate new experience, and consequently an autonomous mode of artistic expression for as long as its creative spirit is alive.

[The image. The opposite action]

Meyerhold's key device is the opposite image. You should do the opposite of what you would really or habitually do. The prerequisite for this is minimalism.

> To say a lot with a little — that's the secret. The task of the artist is to use the greatest riches with the most prudent economy. The Japanese have only to draw one blossoming twig to evoke an entire spring. (Meyerhold 1991, 97)

He treats everything, including language, as possible artistic material, breaking it up into fragments, if necessary unrecognizable ones, and recomposing it in unexpected ways.

> the more obvious the artifice, the more powerful the sensation of life (Meyerhold 1991, 63)

Pasternak defines this method as pursuing 'the rare and fulgurant summit of art where one can speak of the absolute indistinguishability of the material' (Schmidt 1996, 145), and Eisenstein labels Meyerhold, his own teacher, 'this most eminent master of surprising and opposite interpretation' (Ėjzenštejn 1964-1971: 4, 96).

[The grotesque]

'The soul of the grotesque and the soul of the theatre will be one', Meyerhold's credo says (Meyerhold 1991, 142). Only an unexpected maximum of theatrical contrast, which may be simultaneously tragic and comic, realistic and fantastic, sensuous and cognitive, familiar and strange, will provoke such a maximum of synesthetic sensation and ambivalence in each spectator that it will make them lose their habitual orientations and perceive anew, each new counterpoint only intensifying the process by establishing yet another coincidence of oppositions.

> Is it not the task of the grotesque in the theatre to preserve this ambivalent attitude in the spectator by switching the course of the action with strokes of contrast? The basis of the grotesque is the artist's constant desire to switch the spectator from the plane he has just reached to another which is totally unforeseen. (Meyerhold 1991, 139)

Meyerhold's grotesque is hyperprecision. As if studying reality under a magnifying glass, it expands realism to the maximum through a combination of poetic and musical devices, based on the laws of paradox and counterpoint. As in Japanese haiku poems, the artistic collision of images may have been found by chance.

> Given men's powers of memory, the existence of two facts in juxtaposition prompts their correlation; no sooner do we begin to recognize this correlation than a composition is born and its laws begin to assert themselves. (Meyerhold 1991, 322)

His actor-poet creates a montage of physical and vocal images in which every little change involves the change of the whole body.

> Every movement is a hieroglyph with its own peculiar meaning. (Meyerhold 1991, 200)

Executing this montage in a personal rhythm, always in deliberate counterpoint to the general tempo-rhythm of the performance and its music, the actors' concentration and excitation will spread among the spectators, 'what we used to call 'gripping' the spectator':

> It is this excitation which is the very essence of the actor's art. (Meyerhold 1991, 199)

Considering all sound to be music, and carefully orchestrating the sound patterns which his actors perform, Meyerhold labels his grotesque 'musical realism' (Mejerchol'd 1968:2, 140). At times the sound may be almost mute,

> a sort of secret jazz-band where the sound comes from God knows where, like the rumbling of a stomach. (Meyerhold; Picon-Vallin 1990, 307)

As a theorist Meyerhold always remains a practitian. It was Eisenstein who established a consistent theory on the montage as attractions (Eisenstein 1998, 29-34), and as a collision of images.

> The shot is a montage cell.
> [...] montage is conflict. (Eisenstein 1998, 87-88)

You have 'the optical counterpoint', 'the conflict between the acoustic and the optical', and 'the conflict between the frame of the shot and the object' (Eisenstein 1998, 89), and in musical terms you have four levels of montage: metric, rhythmic, tonal, and overtonal (Eisenstein 1998, 111-23). The human behaviour that we call art rearranges 'the identity of the part and the whole' as it appears to the senses (Eisenstein 1949, 131-33).

> there takes place in it a dual process: an impetuous progressive rise along the lines of the highest explicit steps of consciousness and a simultaneous penetration by means of the structure of the form into the layers of profoundest sensual thinking. (Eisenstein 1949, 144-45)

The grotesque reveals this process.

[The impulse and the image]

Stanislavsky's 'I am' and Meyerhold's 'I represent' are interdependent choices of priorities relating to an even larger sum of existing acting devices. Stanislavsky sums up in 1926:

> Meyerhold's theatre? Whatever is the same, I sign too, I want just the same. With the only difference that they present the very result of life, but not the life process of the human spirit. That is, only the spectator's impressions. However in itself, the result which is represented on the stage, as life, will be a supreme achievement. (Vendrovskaja 1967, 593)

However, as Eisenstein emphasizes, 'the master — regardless of school — accomplishes the full process including both phases' (Ėjzenštejn 1964-1971: 4, 434).
They agree in basing the work of the actor on real actions. However their terminologies focus on complementary aspects.

Stanislavsky gives priority to the perspective of the actor. He focuses on the actor's psycho-physical process, on his or her line of actions and its motivation, thus centring his terminology in everyday language, and the task of the actor in the impulse, grammatically expressed by the active verb.

Meyerhold gives priority to the perspective of the spectator. He focuses on the spectator's perceptive process, on the flow of theatrical situations and images that he or she experiences, thus centring his terminology in the field of music, and the task of the actor in the image grammatically expressed by the concrete noun.

It is significant that over time they both start investigating the complementarity of acting all over again, and end up doing so together. Meyerhold wonders:

> What he calls 'the task' I call 'the motif'. But we are speaking of one and the same thing. (Gladkov 1997, 168)

In 1937-38 they return to the laboratory in private. 'It was a persistent work atmosphere, two artists exchanging their experiences.' (Mejerchol'd 1968: 2, 475). Allowing for their artistic differences they present each other with the essence of their knowledge.

> I shall present to Constantin Sergeevič on this small saucer the good which I have. Here is my small part, like these ashes, the rest is trash. The trash you may throw out. [...] And I [...] I shall take something for myself. (Mejerchol'd 1968: 2, 475)

They agree that

> We represent two complementary systems. [...] we have no great divergences as to principles, the two systems will find their unity, when people who know the subject will carry out scientific research on those systems. (Mejerchol'd 1968: 2, 579)

Keeping up the full tension between their complementary points of view, they keep exploring the basic challenge in acting, that of preserving the element of improvisation. As they hope,

> inevitably, somewhere in the middle we must meet. (Gladkov 1997, 167)

[Don Giovanni's impulses]

They kept their nerve. When Stalin closed Meyerhold's theatre in 1938, Stanislavsky immediately let him into his own last refuge and laboratory, his Opera-Dramatic Studio. Of all times, the two of them considered this critical moment to be just the right opportunity for Meyerhold to stage Mozart's signally ambiguous portrait of the archetypal seducer, his opera *Don Giovanni*, at the Stanislavsky Opera. That summer day, sitting in private on Stanislavsky's small balcony in the shade of the apple tree, their joint invention of the production plan for the opera at once turns into a happy dance of reciprocal impulses. Their ideas prompt each other so rapidly that the assistant, the only eye witness, to his despair soon has to give up writing down the succession of images. Their conversation culminates in a warm and humorous handshake between two Don Juans. In defiance of Stanislavsky's serious physical condition, as well as of the spooky Moscow setting which surrounds their deceivingly sunny idyll, their hands meet to surpass the fatal handshake of the opera.

> The summer was bright and rather hot. Each day around noon I phoned Konstantin Sergeevič, asked him how he felt, and whether he might receive Meyerhold. The answer was almost always in the affirmative. Then I went to pick up Vsevolod Èmil'evič in Brjusov Lane, and we reached Stanislavsky together. Usually he was already sitting and waiting for us on the small balcony in the shade of his beloved apple tree. [...] One conversation is especially unforgettable. Stanislavsky opened it. He started talking about that it would be very good to mount Mozart's *Don Giovanni*. In a few minutes the conversation became so animated, that the eyes of both interlocutors began to sparkle as in their youth. Without restraint they spoke all at once, complementing each other, fantasized, made the most intriguing plans, took each other's hints. When Meyerhold stated that in his opinion the opera should have not less than fifteen-eighteen scenes, Stanislavsky interrupted him: 'Not enough! Twenty, twenty-five'. Meyerhold consented at once and added: 'But they must succeed each other with lightning speed!' 'But without that the performance is ruined', Stanislavsky straightaway put in. Their conversation was a brilliant display of fireworks — of plans, fantasies, inspiration. I listened as if bewitched, and not only did I not manage to take notes, but I was also unable to remember the priceless ideas which the interlocutors lavished in such plenty. The day was bright, but a bit chilly. Stanislavsky was sitting in his warm pyjamas with a plaid thrown over his legs. Suddenly he interrupted the discussion and asked Meyerhold: 'But you are not cold?' 'What are you driving at? Not in the least', Vsevolod Èmil'evič replied. 'Now come on, shake my hand!' — Stanislavsky took Meyerhold's hand, felt it, and only when having satisfied himself that it was not cold, he continued the discussion ...
>
> That day we remained sitting for a long time. We were electrified. (Bachrušin; Vendrovskaja 1967, 587)

Those impulses dancing between them under the apple were to remain the sole performance of their production plan for *Don Giovanni*.

[Grotowski]

Meyerhold pertinaciously defends the books of his deceased friend against reductionism and sanctification. He reminds us that Stanislavsky used experiences he had by his colleagues and pupils, for instance by himself and Vakhtangov (Mejerchol'd 1968: 2, 469).

Seventeen years later, at the Russian State Theatre Institute GITIS in 1955-56, Vakhtangov's principal actor, Yuri Zavadsky, initiated the young Pole Jerzy Grotowski into the basics of the Russian theatre laboratory tradition. In May 1996, two years before his death, Grotowski participated in his own pupil Eugenio Barba's 10. ISTA session in Copenhagen. During a conversation I asked him whom he considered to be the principal reformer of Stanislavsky's early method of re-experiencing, Meyerhold or Vakhtangov. He took out his pipe and gave me a firm look: 'Vakhtangov'. I reminded him of Vakhtangov's dilemma, that towards the end of his life he had asked himself how to choose between the approaches of Stanislavsky and Meyerhold. He looked at me even more firmly: 'It was Vakhtangov'. I replied that I would think it over.

No reductionism will account for so many artistic counterpoints of such precision.

Showing Grotowski all his privileges, Zavadsky had warned him, only once, against repeating his own mistake. He had been bought.

> they have broken me. Remember, Jerzy, *nie warto*, it is not worth it. This is the harvest of compromise.
>
> Forty years on, in Holstebro, Grotowski talked to me of this moment as of a turning point in his life. Every time he thought about it he saw it as the opposite of the scene in which Satan tempted Christ. He asked himself if, without this situation and without these words, he would have been able to stand firm in Poland. Zavadsky had been his great master. (Barba 1999, 24-25)

Always acknowledging that 'You are Someone's Son' (Grotowski 1987, 30-41), Grotowski did the opposite. He dressed in black and studied hinduism and shamanism. Founding his small theatre in the marginal Polish town of Opole in 1959, he established his own theatre laboratory. Working under grotesquely banal restrictive conditions, his introverted and religious pursuits symbolically rejected them by staging extreme coincidences of oppositions and finally abolishing the physical separation between the actors and the spectators altogether.

If I had to define our scenic research in a single term I would refer to the myth of the

Dance of Shiva. [...] It is an attempt to absorb reality in all its aspects, with its multiplicity of facets, yet at the same time remaining outside and distant. To express it in another way, it is the dance of form, the pulsation of form, the flowing and fissile multiplicity of theatre conventions, styles, acting traditions. But it is also the construction of contraries: the intellectual game in impetuosity, the seriousness in the grotesque, the mockery in pain. [...] The essence of the theatre for which we are searching is 'pulsation, movement and rhythm'. (Grotowski; Barba 1999, 54-55)

Grotowski developed his own training. For his own experimental purposes he stripped down all the acting techniques he knew, selecting as most important for his purposes Dullin's rhythm exercises, Delsarte's extroversion and introversion, Stanislavsky's physical actions, Meyerhold's biomechanics, Vakhtangov's synthesis, the Peking opera, Kathakali, and Noh.

I have studied all the major actor-training methods of Europe and beyond. (Grotowski 1968, 16)

Biomechanics gave him the key to understanding the actor's bios.

'behind each gesture of the actor, the whole of his body stands'. This formula was a major discovery. (Flaszen; Kumiega 1987, 121)

One morning in 1963 a visitor depicts a training session. The degree of transformation which the original exercises have already undergone, springs to the eye.

There is a long, low room, about 40 by 15 feet, bare, its walls painted black. Two big rostra, like trestle tables, run the length of the room... eight actors are lined up on the tables. Grotowski, still in black, sits silent in the corner. The actors are performing their exercises. Every morning at ten they come, and for three hours work on breathing, voice, balance and acrobatics... Voice work aims at discovering extra resonators, rarely used by the European theatre. Oriental techniques and Meyerhold's biomechanics help the actor to divide effort between parts of his body, and, like a conjuror, force the audience's attention on one part at the expense of the rest. 'The actor is a sorcerer, doing things beyond the spectator's means, affecting his subconscious. His face can express heroism, hands doubt, and his feet panic'. Grotowski is trying to build a resolutely *artificial theatre language*. Naturalism is left behind: vocal and physical 'compositions' (as in the Japanese theatre) are yoked to a developed sense of irony to create a style of playing which, not literally, but by association and allusion, calls up responses deep-rooted in the collective imagination. (Kustow; Kumiega 1987, 40)

No doubt in another corner of the room, the young Italian director-to-be, Eugenio Barba, is busy noting down the exercises (Barba; Grotowski 1968, 101-41). For two and a half intensive years, 1962-64, he assists Grotowski in everything, night after night indulging with him in 'an unceasing reformulation of a vision of theatre' (Barba 1999, 50) aiming at a transgression of taboos.

> sitting and watching the progress of rehearsals and training sessions and then, sitting alone with Grotowski, making comments, expressing doubts, asking for explanations, making suggestions, opening up for all my associations, impressions and questions. This I did for thirty months. (Barba 1999, 34)

Ever since they continued their 'A Thousand and one Nights' in Opole whenever they saw the chance.

> The two Sheherazades remain undaunted while outside the world changes. (Barba 1999, 113)

Devoting his last years exclusively to the performer's work on himself, beyond and beneath all distinctions between genres, Grotowski defines the execution of the impulse to act within a precise structure as the essence of performing: 'Knowledge is a matter of doing' (Grotowski 1988). He nevertheless keeps asking himself how the two registers of Art as presentation and Art as vehicle might be possible within the same performative structure (Grotowski; Richards 1995, 132).

 [Barba]

In 1964 Barba founded his theatre laboratory, Odin Teatret, in Oslo, moving it to Holstebro, Denmark, in 1966. Barba emphasizes that 'Theatre is work on oneself, on that part of us which lives in exile', and defines 'chance as the key to multidimensional experience'. With Grotowski he shares a fundamental rejection of dualism and consequently of the notion of avant garde, thus sharing his original determination to keep working within the basic dynamics of theatre as a social encounter. However, the unique feature of Barba's dramaturgy is his gradual inversion of Grotowski's more introverted method into a theatrical balance between introversion and extroversion. Without discarding the link to ritual or the Stanislavsky heritage, he has applied the training principles and experimental dramaturgy that Grotowski taught him to resume the radical modernism of Meyerhold and Eisenstein in its quality of anthropological investigation. 'A subtle insight', he calls the Meyerhold grotesque, the montage 'actually the construction of meaning' (Barba and Savarese 1991, 157-58). His method in turning this bricolage into viable stage montages is deceptively simple. It is the poetic device of arranging a maximum coincidence of oppositions on all levels imaginable.

Barba began to do so at a time when many Western theatre artists considered the rationalism of Brecht to be a more appropriate counterpoint to naturalism than quaint and bygone Russian theatricalities or the ritual pursuits of Grotowski. However, such reasoning is dualistic.

Stanislavsky's real actions, Meyerhold's grotesque, Vakhtangov's phantastic realism, Eisenstein's collision montage, Grotowski's poor theatre, Barba's poetic theatre anthropology, these are all valid dramaturgic strategies. They all conform to the fundamental law of theatre: to exclude no possibility. They exist between the impulse and the image.

The Eurasian foundation of modern theatre is basic to Odin Teatret (Barba; Pavis 1996, 217-22). As if arriving directly from Kabuki, the actors are normally seen walking on an eternal *hanamichi*. In the streets they enter a culturally created footbridge. And just like the Kabuki footbridge divides the auditorium in two, the amphitheatre in two parts which Odin Teatret uses for its group performances is placed so as to face the acting space from opposite directions. The spectators study each other as well. More like the No theatre, the Odin actors condense their solo performances around a minimal frontal scenography.

Regardless of any habitual context, they may use any physical or vocal action as their material. However, they base any action on a personal logic. They may establish their own material of physical or vocal scores during their training. To create a new score they may also improvise, then fix the score of the improvisation, simultaneously remembering their personal logic behind it. Combining their physical and vocal scores, they may combine any physical action with any vocal action or any text. Moving them to this new context, the montage, they freely decompose or recompose them to make them fit, if necessary also modifying their original personal logic. They may adapt their scores so many times that the original versions and their logic are no longer recognizable.

The Odin musicians — a violinist, a guitarist, and an accordionist, all of whom have been there for years — work along the same lines. They also act. All sounds produced by the actors and the musicians are carefully composed so as to form part of the total acoustic orchestration of the performance. Its counterpoints may originate from any source.

Already during their training a central device to the actors is to do the opposite. Their individual scores, their character work, and the visual and acoustic orchestration of the whole performance form a montage based on the principle of maximum coincidence of oppositions. On all levels of the performance opposite visual images and acoustic counterpoints abound. Each moment has at least one.

As though in homage of Stanislavsky, a real physical action — that of opening a bottle of wine — opens their latest performance, *Mythos* (1999). More obviously, the montages of Odin Teatret are saturated with the principles of Meyerhold's grotesque. Odin Teatret presents a polyphonic conception of life, meaning, and art. Executed by the actors as a maximum collision of sight and sound images, its performances transform any dualism into a simultaneous complementarity, thus also frequently juxtaposing elements from myths or rituals of historically conflicting cultural origin without judging them.

Barba insists how productive misunderstandings can be.

> You can totally misunderstand what I say and do, and nevertheless do something which is inspiring for you and others. (Baumrin 1999, 44)

What a waste? If you study the zigzag pattern of authentic artistic solutions that have grown out of the theatre laboratory tradition and its global meetings, you will notice that at each new bend soneone uses a counterbalance to start from zero.

References

Barba, Eugenio 1999. *Land of Ashes and Diamonds. My Apprenticeship in Poland.* Aberystwyth: Black Mountain.

Barba, Eugenio and Nicola Savarese (eds.) 1991. *The Secret Art of the Performer. A Dictionary of Theatre Anthropology.* London and New York: Routledge.

Baumrin, Seth 1999. My Grandfather Konstantin Sergeivich. Interview with Eugenio Barba. *Mime Journal 1998-1999.* Claremont, California: Pomona College, 29-51.

Eisenstein, Sergei 1949. *Film Form. Essays in Film Theory.* (ed.) Jay Leyda. New York: Harcourt, Brace & Co.

Ėjzenštejn, Sergej 1964-1971. *Izbrannye proizvedenija* 1-6. Moskva: Iskusstvo.

Eisenstein, Sergei 1998. *The Eisenstein Reader.* (ed.) Richard Taylor. London: BFI.

Gladkov, Aleksandr 1997. *Meyerhold Speaks. Meyerhold Rehearses.* (ed.) Alma Law. Amsterdam: Harwood.

Grotowski, Jerzy 1968. *Towards a Poor Theatre.* (ed.) Eugenio Barba. Holstebro: Odin Teatrets Forlag.

Grotowski, Jerzy 1987. Tu es le fils de quelqu'un/You are Someone's Son. *The Drama Review* 31: 3, 1987, 30-41.

Grotowski, Jerzy 1988. Performer. *Centro di lavoro di Jerzy Grotowski. Workcenter of Jerzy Grotowski.* Pontedera: Centro per la sperimentazione e la ricerca teatrale, 36-40.

Hoffmann, E.T.A. 1924. *Die vier grossen Gespräche und die kleinen Schriften über Literatur und Theater*. Weimar: Erich Lichtenstein.

Hoffmann, E.T.A. 1990. *Fantasiestücke in Callots Manier*. Frankfurt am Main: Insel.

Kumiega, Jennifer 1985. *The Theatre of Grotowski*. London and New York: Methuen.

Mejerchol'd, Vsevolod 1968. *Staty, Pis'ma, Reči, Besedy* 1-2. (eds.) Aleksandr V. Fevral'skij og Boleslav I. Rostockij. Moskva: Iskusstvo.

Meyerhold, Vsevolod 1991. *Meyerhold on Theatre*. (ed.) Edward Braun. London: Methuen.

Pavis, Patrice (ed.) 1996. *The Intercultural Performance Reader*. London and New York: Routledge.

Richards, Thomas 1995. *At Work With Grotowski On Physical Actions*. London and New York: Routledge.

Schmidt, Paul (ed.) 1980. *Meyerhold at Work*. Austin: University of Texas Press.

Stanislavskij, K. S. 1988. *Sobranie sočinenij* 1. *Moja žizn' v iskusstve*. Moskva: Iskusstvo.

Vendrovskaya, Lyubov and Galina Kaptereva (eds.) 1982. *Evgeny Vakhtangov*. Moscow: Progress.

Vendrovskaja, Ljubov' D. et al. (eds.) 1967. *Vstreči s Mejerchol'dom. Sbornik vospominanij*. Moskva: VTO.

Erik Exe Christoffersen

Odin Teatret

[Between Dance and Theatre]

For 35 years Odin Teatret has existed as a group theatre in a *borderland:* it resides in the town of Holstebro, far away from the capital and the centre for theatre, and tours far-away countries. What makes this theatre special compared to other theatres in Denmark is that it comprehends theatre as a specific social and spatial reality, often expressed through the metaphor of a monastery, ghetto or exile.

Odin Teatret was founded in 1964 in Norway by the Italian Eugenio Barba (1936) and a group of uneducated young actors who had been refused admission to the established drama schools. Since 1966 Holstebro has been the centre for Odin Teatret, or the theatre laboratory, which comprises many more activities than merely creating theatre performances. Over the years the theatre has arranged a number of seminars, conferences and meetings with theatre people from all over the world. Odin Teatret has published a series of books and magazines about theatre technique and theory and produced films and videos. The theatre has also organised a number of cultural manifestations such as for example the recurring festival week in Holstebro, which in various ways is related to the central themes taken up by Odin Teatret, namely, travelling. Amongst other things the theatre has survived because it has succeeded in creating a comprehensive international network, ISTA (International School of Theatre Anthropology), run by Eugenio Barba. ISTA has explored various transhistoric and transcultural forms of movement among dancers and actors from various cultures and styles.

The network consists of actors, dancers, directors, producers, theoreticians, and of course spectators who all participate in the development of its pedagogical and professional profile. The theatre has created a new type of actors, but it has also created a new type of audience. An audience that forms the network of this particular theatre.

The history of Odin Teatret is closely connected with the fundamental changes of the concept of theatre which took place during the 1960s. These changes do not relate to the mere art of theatre, they are changes in art itself. The birth of new art forms such as Event, Happening, Performance Art, Body Art, Minimalism and so forth demon-

44

strated that art can be anything at all, and that the limitations of art are a question of definition, choice or designation. Art does not hold any essence — for instance, a special beauty or professional quality — it becomes art where it is introduced as art.

In the 1960s Odin Teatret was hardly recognised as theatre, nor was perceived as such. Only after a slow process of self-definition did a *theatre* based on its own values and rules emerge. This applies both to the question of the definition of an actor and to the role and the function of the theatre as a cultural place. The changes in the concept of theatre were primarily a clash with the relation of representation: the fact that the performance represented a text and the actor represented a character. The traditional framing, the position of the audience, and the relation of fiction were dissolved so as to allow a formalised presence between audience and actors (performers). The form of the work itself tended to become an event, an action or a performance. This created a kind of interaction between the actor's body or presence and the audience.

This is apparent in the picture from the training session taken in the late 1960s. Where are the costumes, where is the stage, where is scenography? The picture merely shows us a real action in a room. No fiction, no spectators, only the possibility of presence in the form of jumping at precisely the same time.

The 1960s witnessed the development of various tendencies within theatre and visual art in the borderland. Theatre as a social action (Living Theatre), theatre as a personal meeting (Grotowski), a ritual act, political theatre, visual performance, popular theatre (Dario Fo), and a number of dance-like forms which were orientated towards different forms of movement. Odin Teatret possesses elements from most of these tendencies, perhaps with special emphasis on the relation between theatre and dance and theatre as a social relation.

In this heterogeneous field Odin Teatret has defined a way which Barba calls the Third Theatre. It is not traditional theatre representing texts, nor is it anti-representative avant-garde theatre. It is a third kind of theatre, primarily based on the concept of theatre as an ethical and social relation.

Whereas many theatre forms of the 1960s removed themselves entirely from theatre and approached visual art, making the actors part of mobile visiual and spatial structure, Odin Teatret turned to the tradition of theatre, with the ambition of redefining the organic artistic process and artistic scenic behaviour. Odin Teatret was not interested in the actor of representation, nor in the actor of anti-representation, but in the personal actor who creates his presence through self-definition. The theatre has developed various techniques of improvisation and training that permit a self-definition in which the actor represents himself, his profession and his function, and in which the role or the character is of secondary importance. It has been possible to use techniques from the psychological realism of the theatre that represented texts (Stanislavsky), from the avant-garde theatre's (Meyerhold, Eisenstein, Brecht) emphasis on the functional and sensory effects on the audience (the montage of attraction) or from popular theatre forms by Copeau, Decroux and Fo, who renewed the art of mime, and from elements of the Commedia dell' arte. Odin Teatret has transcended its historical background and has become a transhistoric 'floating island'.

What is special about Odin Teatret, however, is that it has taken several steps further and has examined so-called techniques of self-definition in a much broader perspective. Odin Teatret has tried to distill so-called *recurrent principles* which characterise the actor and the dancer of different cultures and styles. It can even be said that connecting with Tradition is part of the self-definition of Odin Teatret. And an essential part of the work of Odin Teatret consists in exploring and communicating this knowledge which is concealed in the tradition concretely related to principles of training. The definition of self being a central part of this tradition, like a kind of individuation, Odin Teatret is also a group of individuals, each going their own way, following their own principles, only tied together by a common history and organisation and common performances. The tendency of recent years has been clear: Odin Teatret is an individualistic project of continuous artistic education, as demonstrated by their solo performances and work demonstrations: for instance the autobiographical and monologic dance-music-theatre performance *Itsi Bitsi* and work demonstrations such as Roberta Carreri's *Spor i sneen* (Traces in the snow), which is the artist's artistic autobiography. Over different periods of time most of the actors work with activities of exploration and communication, of which ISTA is the most comprehensive one. Odin Teatret actors work with administration, producing films, editing and publishing magazines or pedagogy and teaching methods.

The issue here is a significant renewal of the actors' creative potentials. This is not merely based on expressivity on stage, it is also based on the creation of the context which the actor builds around artistic and pedagogical principles, theoretical reflections, and networks which create and continue knowledge and tradition.

In his first performances, Eugenio Barba worked with finished manuscripts, but later the theatre's performances were created from the actors' improvisations and from montages of various types of dramatic, literary and scientific texts. Therefore, the production and performance periods are long. Since 1964 Odin Teatret has only produced approximately twenty performances, all of which in various ways create a confrontation or dialogue between the theatre and the audience in different kinds of scenic arrangements. On the other hand, their work is coherent, based on a group culture consisting of the same people. The production time is rather long and the performances often run for two to three years. The touring done by the theatre means that the performances must be movable.

The concept of *travelling* plays a very important part in various myths and fairy tales. Characters like the wanderer, the fool, the trickster, the angel or the shaman are all in transition from one place to another. They are often characterised by a kind of madness, by magic or by supernatural skills which make them active and efficient in the transition process. They are in harmony with nature and can change from visible to invisible, from man to woman. They have power over darkness, life and death by virtue of technique or mental strength. In the figure of the trickster lie the first seeds of the actor embracing opposites.

Odin Teatret embodies this myth of cultural development. It is on a chronic journey or in a state of emergency (the 'exile'). It is a fairy tale about the outcast who endures hardships and sufferings (the actor's training), and who seeks his identity in confrontations with the unknown.

This personal basis or starting point, the 'longing' for finding or losing oneself, might be mistaken for a therapeutic process. It is, however, a *cultural* process which has created a 'society' (monastery, ghetto, exile) outside and independent of what Barba calls the spirit of the time (the *Zeitgeist*). Distance is the basis of the theatre's identity. The anonymity of the exile walks hand in hand with something personal. The 'loss' is a central impetus behind the development of Odin Teatret, both at the personal and the professional level, and it is the foundation of the special *Odin pathos*.

Odin Teatret's actors have developed a special technique. Like dance it differs from normal everyday life, but in it the voice plays an important part. It is a physical and intellectual behaviour that has obtained an organic and natural form. It is the easiness and naturalness of a ballerina walking on tiptoe, although compared to everyday life it is deeply unnatural. In their diversity the Odin actors unite elements from dancing, singing and musical traditions while creating theatrical figures like other actors, some meant for indoor, some for outdoor use. Some of the figures continue to exist through various performances and become a kind of archetype, like the ones we know from the Commedia dell'arte or Asian theatrical forms. It is 'the other' who is alive in the actor's body as a physical and vocal score, but who also becomes a living, independent figure who starts to articulate the actor. Odin Teatret's archetypal figures — the town crier dressed in white, carrying a drum and wearing a mask with a tear; the demon on stilts; the 'Androgyne' and Mr. Peanut, and 'death' on stilts — have been developed by individual actors over a number of years. By now they are, however, charac-ters that have been passed on to new actors, like a living 'text' with its own kind of biography, identity and narration. In this the theatre is approaching a personal ritual: a confrontation or 'conversation' with another reality. In its form the theatre is being transgressed and is becoming a kind of self-reflective action changing the life lived. Each actor defines an individual meaning of theatre through professional actions and relations. Odin Teatret is an *anthropological theatre* where the actor is confronted with his own identity. The theatre creates what Artaud called the actor's double, or what Barba calls the actor's exile-part. The training or continuous education of the actor is not an issue of learning how to act, reciting a certain text, or showing the actions of a certain character, as is the traditional way of seeing the job of the actor. Instead it is an issue of finding the principles which can develop, renew and vary the individual energy, because these principles are independent of a dramatic context. This means that the material of the actors is not fixed but can be moved from one connection to the other without losing its basic quality. Different improvisations create new material, or old material is varied, like the jazz musician who makes variations on a certain theme. The performance achieves depth and force through this long and patient work during which the actions of the actors are mounted, cut and brought into a dramatic connection that finally leads to a complex staging of the audience's attention.

In modern theatre, this phenomenological tradition can be localised to Artaud's manifests on the Theatre of Cruelty. Artaud's dream of a type of theatre as *poetry in space* is about a theatre that is directly perceptible and that opposes representation and the urge of Western culture to create a hierarchy between the language and the sense perception in the room. Artaud wanted to oppose theatre as representation in order to create theatre as life or presence. This constituted a clash with theatre's literary orientation (theatre's tendency towards existential and mental orientation), i.e. it was a turn towards the actor's physical and mental (but not emotional) presence in the room, which was directly perceptible to the audience.

Such a reasoning has consequences not only for the perception of the perform-ance, but also for the creative process. Compared to the idea of classical representation — in which reality is provided with a form, thus making art represent reality, but where it can also be said that reality is translated into art — the creative process of Odin Teatret often seems to go in the opposite direction. The actor creates a form that con-tains energy or presence and is shaped as information. The actor's form is a material with which the director can work according to a dramaturgical need: he can enlarge, minimise, frame, mount various materials, and rotate them like in the editing of a film montage. He can add scenography, costumes, light and sound as the occasion requires. This presupposes that the actor is able to preserve his original form (the inner and outer logic), thus creating layer upon layer: a kind of heterophony, a clash or a palimpsest.

This creative process involves a very central tendency in the theatrical language established by Odin Teatret as a cultural forum. Fundamentally, the actor and the director each work with a dramaturgy of their own that they do not share on grounds of principle. The actors also work with their own individual dramaturgy that they do not share. This means that in the relation between spectators and performance there is a tension based on something unknown. The director does not know everything about his performance and does not control the spectators' formation of meaning. Likewise, the spectators have to accept that not everything is revealed to them. As an individual spectator and not as part of an audience, one has to create one's own meaning. In a way the performance is a vacuum, a black hole that absorbs meaning from everywhere: from the actors, the director, the scenographer, the lighting designer, and from the audi-ence. It is not a question of giving shape, it is a question of taking shape. This makes heavy demands on the spectators, and no established access to the Odin universe exists.

Odin Teatret is built on bodily knowledge and technique that Barba calls the pre-expressive level, which is embedded in the training of various theatre and dance tradi-tions. These pre-expressive principles are for instance the play of opposites, isolation of body parts and movements, various techniques of obstruction, shifting of balance, principles of complementarity. During their education, the actors/dancers are intro-duced to these principles in various shapes. Although these principles are the basis for the actor's possibility of touching the audience's senses, in the finished performance they are almost invisible, hidden by the dramaturgy (the fable, costumes, make-up, light, scenography).

The actors' work demonstrations consist of an 'unmasking' of the hidden tech-nique. The work demonstration is a presentation of the technique that draws the actor and the spectator into a field of art beyond the performance. It brings into focus the heritage of the theatre and creates a spectator who is the alter ego of the director.

An essential part of the themes taken up by Odin Teatret concern destroying, reducing, scaling down or negating variety from a point of view that eventually abolishes the individual's right to say no and follow his own individual values. Thematically, there is a romantic tendency in the performances, from *Kaspariana*'s pursuit of the original, unspoiled human being to the description of otherness in *Come! And the Day will be ours* and that of strangers in *Millionen*.

There is often a romantic irony, where romanticism's longing is contrasted with the simultaneity, ambiguity and paradoxes of the Baroque.

Odin Teatret possesses a high degree of self-reflexivity through which the performances become a kind of self-definition by force of the rules and principles chosen. Several performances establish a kind of dialogic structure, for example *Min Fars Hus*, *Brechts Aske*, *Millionen*, *Talabot*.

Itsi Bitsi is an example of a performance in which the actor creates a dialogue with herself — or a memory. Iben Nagel Rasmussen had created a collection of material based on training and on her work with a number of characters from various performances. Originally, it was material for a work demonstration that was supposed to show various facets of the actor's own work. The director, however, suggested to her that she should write her memoirs about the 1960s, characterised by politics, the youth revolution, narcotics, and her meeting with the rock musician Eik Skaløe (Nagel Rasmussen 1993), who in 1969 committed suicide in India but whose music is still viable and whose song *Itsi Bitsi*, dedicated to Iben, has become a rock classic. From Iben's notes, letters, diaries and so forth a text structure was created that was woven into Iben's material. Sometimes her dance is the basis for the text, sometimes it is a contrast, comment or interpretation. In any case, there are several simultaneous, interwoven voices. Not only is it a story of personal development in which Iben finds a kind of credible 'home', a presence, in the theatre, while Eik stayed 'out there', but it is also a story about the ambiguity of the room, the doubling and mirroring of the characters that create the picture of a theatre tradition that is transcultural and not rooted in one nationality, one area or one culture. *Itsi Bitsi* of course also exemplifies a process that takes its starting point in the actor's material and later develops a dramaturgic structure and thematics. As a performance it is a kind of personal dialogue with the past, and in this sense the performance becomes a poetic memory or a personal ritual.

The experiences of fragmentation and the absence of a home can be felt as tragic, uncanny and alienating conditions to which one must become reconciled. To be homeless is not the same as to give up looking for a home and a finality as a form. One can relate to home without having a home. This loss of being, homelessness as a condition, is thematized by Odin Teatret, where identity only exists as *performance*. The scenic performance and staging creates the originality, not vice versa. The training situation of the theatre is a central metaphor in the process in which the creation of the character and the view of the stage is developed and repeated. The actor creates an impact that is a montage or construction of his or her behaviour as real actions in the context of the director and the stage. The impact only acquires meaning in the meeting with the individual spectator.

Looking at the history of the theatre, one meets a number of opposites which the theatre does not try to synthesise but which creates a dynamic complementary entity. The theatre, though autodidactic, looks upon itself as belonging to a tradition. The theatre is rooted in a social environment but at the same time is a migrant theatre. There is a professional contrast between performances in the room and the open theatre performances of the street or open spaces. The actors work with contrasts between text and movement and between soft and hard directional energy. It is the contrast between the linear linking of dramaturgy and the principle of simultaneousness. It is the balance between the theatrical irony where everything is repetitions and the pathos of loss. The importance of these opposites is that they are being developed and move in still new constellations.

The question is what traces Odin Teatret is going to leave on the theatre of the future. Will this theatre be able to create a tradition, an 'immortal dimension' that notwithstanding the mortality of the theatre can be passed on to those spectators who might never see its performances? To Barba *tradition* does not mean truths or doctrines but unpredictable connections to the future, anonymous because it works in spite of itself as an enigma, questions with no answers.

Theatre only exists in the concrete meeting, bound by time and space. The performance must admit of being repeated, not reproduced. It merely lives in the memory of the audience. According to Barba, the problem of the theatre — yet also its strength — is that in the continuous recreation of life it reminds us of mortality, of the fluctuation of life and ultimately of death. In Artaud's words theatre reminds us of the cruelty of myths. Theatre is created by a technique different from the advanced communication channels of modern society, which permit information, knowledge and expression to be communicated despite time and space, and create simultaneousness between recipients and senders all over the world.

The possibilities of Odin Teatret lie in recognising the fact that theatre creates a meeting between human beings on a human scale and that it creates direct relations in the space where a limited number of spectators must be able to see, hear and sense the actors, not necessarily the same aspects, but equally well. It is a mental and emotional space in the borderland between the reality we know and the one we do not know (or have forgotten). Odin Teatret has created a border culture or 'transient culture' in which otherness is transformed into a kind of identity that holds both originality and restlessness, presence and absence. Odin Teatret does not merely create performances, they also create a concrete culture, a space which is also a place of knowledge in relation to the technique, function and meaning of theatre; something that can be handed down and change the framing of what theatre *is in theory and in practice*, thus changing the existing theatre culture. Odin Teatret is a *network*, relations in the group and among actors, directors, theatre researchers and audiences who all have specific needs and interests in this theatre that Barba has defined as an empty ritual without any doctrines. Odin Teatret is at one and the same time a personal and an artistic project of cultural development, based on chosen dogmas and work principles.

Roberta Carreri

[**Traces in the Snow**]

Text of the working demonstration, edited in written form. All information in ( )
refers to practical demonstrations. The demonstration begins with a dance to the
music of Tom Waits' *Heart Attacks and Wine*.

This is a work demonstration, that is, a performance in which I will tell you my professional secrets. The dance that I just showed you has been inspired by my meetings with
theatre masters from the Far East — Japan, China, Bali, and India — between 1980
and 1986. I created this dance in 1990 as a part of my physical training. During my
development as an actress, my training has changed over the years, because I have gradually changed its aim according to my needs.

Since I started at Odin Teatret in 1974, I have experienced three different seasons
in my actor training. As I would later understand, the aim of the first season was to discover my presence as an actor, and to free my body from the automatisms of daily life.

The second season began when I started to develop my individual training, creating personal principles. It was also the point where I began to use the training to work
against my own clichés — the acting clichés that I had already developed.

In the third season, my training was the space in which I started to develop physical scores that already had a dramaturgical cohesion.

When I joined Odin Teatret, the group had been working for ten years. It started
in Oslo, Norway, in 1964. It was founded by Eugenio Barba, a young Italian who had
studied at Oslo University, and who later moved to Poland to study theatre. There he
met Jerzy Grotowski, and became his assistant director for the next three-and-a-half
years. When Eugenio returned to Norway, his dream was to create a theatre group
similar to Grotowski's laboratory theatre. But the first problem he had to face was that
no actors wanted to work with him: he was too young, fairly inexperienced, and had
no money to offer. So, he went to the National Theatre School and asked for a list of all
the students who had not been admitted, and phoned them. Seventeen people came to
the first meeting; after one week five remained, and only four took part in the first performance. They were young, 17-20 years of age, and they were not very experienced,
but between them, they had some basic notions of pantomime, yoga, ballet, and acro-

LIVERPOOL JOHN MOORES UNIVERSITY
LEARNING SERVICES

batics. They began by teaching each other what they knew and, using these elements, they started to put together a form of training. As we can see, Odin Teater actors have been teaching from the very beginning, and today the younger actors are still guided through their training by the older ones.

Actor training is specific to the work of Odin Teatret.

Why do we train? It is very important for an actor to have *presence*. Through physical training, the young actor/actress can *learn to be present*.

One thing that marks the difference between the actor and the spectator is the presence that the actor must have. What does it mean to be present? We are all present here now, but I know that some of you are more present than others. You, as a spectator, can let your body stay here and your mind fly away, far from this room. Me, as an actress, I have to be here, with my body and mind connected all the time. I must concentrate. It is not difficult to concentrate for a short period of time, but you must train in order to be able to concentrate for longer periods, say, three hours, if you are to perform *King Lear*.

During the first season of my training, the older actors had me work on different principles.

Work with acrobatics turned out to be basic. Every Odin Teater actor has gone through it. In learning acrobatics, your body and mind have to be connected *all the time*. If your mind leaves your body, your body will fall, and you will get hurt. So I say that the floor was my first Zen master, waking me up every time I lost concentration.

One can use acrobatic exercises with strong, fast dynamics, filling the room with energy, but one can also use some exercises from acrobatics in slow motion. *(Speaking while demonstrating in slow motion)*:

Slow motion is a principle of work that obliges me to move very slowly. I displace my weight centimetre by centimetre. I have to think with my whole body in order not to fall, and in order not to make a quick movement. *(Making a somersault in slow motion)* Now my hair will probably fall, because I cannot control it. But I should be able to control my body. I am working with the force of gravity, pushing and pulling my weight slowly. I have to know how my feet must land on the floor, in order to let me get up again without jerky movements. Standing up also has to be done very slowly. If I forget a part of my body, that part will move very quickly. Slowly... not falling... a fall of a centimetre is a fall. In order to move steadily, I have to imagine that the air gives me resistance. As if I was moving in a sea of molasses. Each action is born from what I call 'the snake', that invisible 'muscle' that runs in the centre of the body along the spinal cord. My eyes are the 'head' of the snake.

Slow motion is not only a question of speed. It is also a question of pulse. *(End of demonstration)*

We can work with different principles and exercises in the training. For instance, the acrobatic exercises are fixed. We learn them from an older actor, and they have a beginning, a development, and an end, which are fixed, so that we can teach them to other people. Or we can work within a principle, like that of slow motion. A principle means a frame of rules within which we can improvise. I can work in slow motion, improvising, not following an exercise, but the rule of moving slowly, not forgetting any part of my body.

Another basic principle that I was taught by an older actor was composition with the feet and hands.

As babies, we explore the possibilities of our hands and feet. As soon as we learn to walk — usually about the age of one — we begin to use our feet in the most functional way, as we are taught. With time, we become so skilled that we can walk without even thinking about it. This form of environmental conditioning creates the body's automatisms in daily life.

The aim of working with the feet is to find new ways, new possibilities for displacing the body in space. For instance: *(Demonstration of work with the feet)*

rounded, slow steps
making a circle in front of me with the foot
or letting the foot glide straight in front of me
or moving just on the tip of the toes
or kicking in front of me with the heel, while receding
and so on *(Continues demonstration of the work with the feet)*

And then work with the hands. The hands that we always use and never dance with. *(Demonstration of work with the hands)*

I train with the hands and feet to find a new way of being natural on stage, but not necessarily naturalistic.

Another principle that belongs to the first season of training is that of introversion and extroversion. Every part of our body can be either introverted or extroverted. This has no psychological implications; we might just as well say open or closed. *(Speaking while demonstrating):* the head, the shoulders, the pelvis, the arms, the hands, the legs. The hands can be extroverted while the arms are introverted, or introverted while the arms are extroverted. The legs extroverted or introverted. The feet usually follow the legs. I can create a dialogue between the different parts of my body, making some of them introverted, and some of them extroverted: head introverted, shoulders introverted, arms extroverted, pelvis extroverted, one leg extroverted, the other introverted, hands introverted. *(Starts moving in the space)* Or completely extroverted. Changing only one detail: the head. *(Continues demonstration of introversion and extroversion)*

After about a couple of years of work on training with different principles — like

Geronimo's hat and shoes.
Drawing: Ulla Madsen,
Aarhus, April 4, 2000

the ones I have mentioned — and participation in two performances, I created a street character. It was dressed in men's clothes, with a white shirt *(always perfectly clean and ironed),* bow tie, black trousers, big red suspenders, nice black men's shoes, and a top hat. His voice was a duck decoy. He was part of a street performance called *Anabasis.* I called him Geronimo. *(Demonstration of Geronimo)*

That was Geronimo.

After the first season of the training came the second season. It started about three years after I joined the group. After having seen my work, Eugenio decided that from then on, I could be responsible for my own work. From that moment on, my training became my own individual training. It was a moment of great freedom, but also a moment of great loneliness. Until then an older actor, or Eugenio Barba himself, had been watching my work, telling me what to do, how to do it, giving me advice all the time. Now I had to decide for myself what to work on and how to work on it. So at this point I needed inspiration. One can find inspiration by watching the work of other theatre groups, by watching performances of other kinds of theatre, or by reading books, going to movies, or looking at photography and art books.

I found inspiration for my first principle in southern France: the first principle that I created myself in my individual training. I found a book about the game of petanque ('bocce'), a game with balls. It was a book with beautiful pictures. I was really fascinated by the fact that these old men, 70, 75, 80 years old, were flying at the moment of throwing their ball. I could see in the pictures of these old men preparing themselves for the throw, that they were really thinking with their whole body, gathering exactly the precise amount of energy needed for the throw, and then throwing.

When I came back to Holstebro, I tried to create a physical equivalent to those pictures. I started to throw. I remembered that what fascinated me was that these pictures were snapshots, pictures taken in movement. So I started making 'snapshots' of throwing, freezing my movement when the imaginary ball left my hand. *(Speaking while demonstrating)*:

In order to freeze the action, I have to stay in balance. If I throw in one direction, my body will be taken in that direction. So I have to make a counter-impulse with another part of my body in order to create balance, because balance is the result of two opposite, but equal, powers. I always keep in balance on the tips of my toes. I throw in different directions, slowly, quickly, gently, strongly, with big or small movements. I can pull my arm back slowly and gently, and then throw in another direction strongly and quickly. I can start throwing slowly, and suddenly speed it up. Or the opposite: start at full speed, and then slow down. I am working on different dynamics. *(Continues demonstration of work with throws)*

The everyday physical training consists in work with four or five different principles. Now I am only showing you 2-3 minutes of work with each principle. In the training situation, we work with each principle for 20-30 minutes. This makes us meet a very faithful working companion: tiredness. We become tired. And then I can decide that to be tired means that my body has reached its limits, and that I have to stop. Or I can ask myself what lies beyond tiredness, what lies beyond my first limit? Maybe some of you have tried jogging. A beautiful morning. With a pair of new shoes, and full of good intentions, you started to run. After about ten minutes you felt how your body became terribly heavy. But, if you happened to be with a person who had been jogging for a long time, and if it happened that you liked this person, you would keep on running even if you were tired. And eventually, after about five minutes, you would experience that suddenly your body started to become light, lighter again. What happened? This is not a miracle of love. Scientifically, we can explain it by the fact that your brain has started to produce endorphin, a chemical substance that helps our body to overcome extraordinary challenges. Our brains are programmed to do this. Perhaps you have had occasion to dance for hours and hours on end, together with many other people. At the end, you may have been exhausted, but not tired. The proof is that, if your favourite number came on, you would jump up and start to dance again. And maybe you have attended a conference where you became terribly tired after 15 minutes, and maybe even fell asleep.

What gets tired first, your body or your brain? As far as I am concerned, I know that it is my brain. That is why, when I work on my training, I have to give my brain something to 'chew on'. *(Speaking while demonstrating)*:

I have to tell my brain to work with different directions in the given space, all the different directions around my body. With different speeds, fast or slow. With different sizes, a movement can be big, or it can be small. And with different kinds of energy: weak and strong. And I can also change direction, speed, size, energy, in the middle of the action. *(End of demonstration)*

After a few years of work I realized that 'physical training' was in reality mental training. People working in sports know this very well.

In 1981 I could enter the workroom and start training without effort. *(Speaking while demonstrating):* And while my body was going through the motions of different elements, apparently very precisely, I surprised myself by thinking: 'Tage and Anna are coming to dinner this evening... I should cook fish... They love fish... I should buy some white wine...' *(End of demonstration)*

When I caught myself thinking like this during the training, I realized that this training principle no longer worked for me. My body could do it without my brain being involved. After several years it had become automatic. So I had to break down the automatisms that I myself had been building into my work. For many years Eugenio had been telling me to fill the space with energies. And I always did it with big movements. From that moment I sat down and tried to radiate energy in the room with small movements.

I sat down on the floor, and I started to work with my head and arms, moving only one joint at a time, while keeping the rest of my body completely immobile. I considered the eyes a joint, too.

(Speaking while demonstrating): I can start by moving the eyes to the left, then let the head follow, or, I can move the head to the right while keeping the eyes to the left, and then let the eyes follow the head. Or I can move my eyes and my head together, but I have to decide to. I can move my arm, starting from the shoulder, and then the elbow, then the wrist, then two fingers, then again lift the arm, starting from the shoulder. Then the other arm, then the eyes, the head... and so on. What is important for me is to keep the rest of my body still, moving only one part at a time. I can also decide to move two segments at a time, but I have to decide to. It is not something that happens automatically. It is a continuous improvisation with one segment of the body at a time; always working in different directions, with different sizes, at different speeds, and with different qualities of energy. As I work with the principle of 'segmentation', as I call it, those changes are particularly important, because they help me to avoid looking like a puppet — an effect which I don't want in my work. The most difficult thing for me in this training is not to decide which part of the body to move next, but to keep the rest of my body completely still, which is unnatural. Our bodies are not used to this kind of behaviour. *(End of demonstration)*

If we think of a principle as a frame, a framework of rules that limit my freedom and oblige me to work in depth to find new ways of expression, then this principle of segmentation is the smallest frame within which I have ever worked. But it has proven very useful to me. I have worked with this principle for 5 years, and have discovered that I could use it to create a kind of theatrical 'close-up'. In film, the camera can do a close-up of an actor's hand, and the editor can later cut the film in such a way that the spectators see a hand measuring 7 metres by 4; they cannot avoid seeing it. In theatre, the spectators can always choose what to look at, and so, if I wish the spectators to look at my hand *(speaking while demonstrating)*, I keep my body completely still, lower my gaze, and let only my hand move. *(End of demonstration)*

In the second season, training became what I call 'the actor's secret garden', in which one can dilate one's power, and fight automatisms that stem from one's work: 'clichés'.

It is important for the actor to be decided. There is a difference between thinking an action and realizing it, and being one with this action. To be decided. An action, by the way, is different from a movement. A movement does not change anything in space. An action always changes something, wants to change something. *(Demonstrating)*: I move my book; this is an action. I *want* to move my book; I have a precise intention, which in English I call *in-tension*, tension inside my body. If this book were a box of beer, then my in-tension would be different. My body would prepare itself to lift it in a different way.

At times the spectator gets bored, because he or she recognizes the intention of the actor, and knows what will happen before the actor executes the action. In other words, the actor is anticipating the action. However, it is very important to realize that *in-tension* always has two levels, a physical and a mental. They are inseparable. You read the mental level through the physical. In theatre, the actor can play with his intensions to surprise the spectator and awake his or her presence. If I intend to caress you, and then, when my hand is ten centimetres from your face, I slap your cheek instead, the spectator will be surprised. But it's logical, if you are my son and have been out all night without telling me. All night long I have the worse thoughts. You come home. I am so glad to see you. But suddenly I remember how worried you have made me.

If I have to pick up something lying on the floor, but start to look above me while I squat, and only look quickly down towards what I want to take at the last moment, and gently take it, then I play ball with the attention of the spectator, keeping his senses awake. I can call the work of the actor the dance of the in-tensions.

When I arrived at Odin Teatret, the other actors were working with a wooden stick, 1.80 m long and 4 cm in diameter. They called it a 'bushman'. I, too, started to work with the bushman. Eugenio asked us to 'find the life of the object'. But what is the life of a piece of wood, if not the energy that you inject into it? We had to create with it exercises that had a precise beginning, a development (where the bushman moved because of the impulse we gave it, but not under our direct control), and a precise end. One rule was that we were always to catch the stick either precisely in the middle, or at its extremities. So when we threw the stick into the air, and we had to grab it precisely at the end, this long stick, 1.80 m, had a tendency to turn down, but we had to keep it perfectly parallel to the floor. Maybe it was easier for the men, but for me it was very hard. At Odin Teatret we have never had separate training for men and women. We always had the same training during the first years, during the first season of the training. When the training becomes individual, one can decide what to work on for oneself. After about three years, I was allowed to work with a small stick, like this cane.

(Speaking while demonstrating): It may look easier because it is lighter, but in fact it is more difficult, because it offers no resistance. So at first I had to pretend that this cane was as heavy as the 'bushman'. While working, my body would suddenly create pictures in relation to the cane, pictures that I could recognize: a bow and arrow, a sword, an umbrella, and so on. I did not first imagine them and then try to recreate them with my body. It is very important to understand that the images were gradually emerging from the physical effort, through a process that we could call 'thinking in movement'. When I recognized an image, I wrote it down. Once I had accumulated, let us say, 12-15 images, I made a montage. *(Demonstration of the work with the cane)*

(Repeating the demonstration of working with the cane, while speaking; the words in italics refer to the different functions assumed by the stick): There is a *warrior* in the forest. He hears a noise and *draws his sword*. Who is there? Ah, it is only a *lady walking* along the river *with her parasol*. And, in the middle of the river, there is an *old man rowing his boat*. He is out *fishing*. And as he *catches the fish*, he sees people *playing golf* on the other bank of the river. A young boy *watching* the small white ball flying through the air, *sees* a duck, *aims at it*, and *shoots it* with his bow and *arrow*. The *wounded duck falls* into the river. *(End of demonstration)*

The logic that I follow to link these images and make a montage consists in leaps from association to association. This kind of logic, developed during my training, is very useful to me when I work on improvisation for a performance. It helps me to create images to which I must react, and to switch from being the subject to being the object of the action. And to be able to translate the image in my body, perhaps only using my hand or my head.

I know three kinds of improvisations:

— one is the *improvisation with fixed elements*, like the one I did when I showed you my work with acrobatic exercises in slow motion: I knew the exercises, and I improvised the order in which to put them.

— the second is *improvisation within a principle*: I can do anything whatsoever, as long as I respect the rules of the principle.

— the third kind is *improvisation starting from a theme*, and working on association. We use this type of improvisation to create materials for performances.

I will now speak about the last type.

I had never performed in the theatre before coming to Odin Teatret. I arrived at Holstebro from Milan, my home town, at midnight on April 23, 1974. Two Odin actors, Torgeir and Iben, were waiting for me, and they took me to a small hotel across from the station. They came back at six o'clock the next morning and took me to Odin Teatret. An actress helped me to change into a very simple costume, and at seven o'clock we all started to work in the white room. Eugenio spoke to one actor, who then started to move in the space. After a certain time he stopped and sat down again. One by one all the other actors followed suit. And then it was my turn. Eugenio called me over and whispered to me, 'In the King's garden'. This was the theme of my first improvisation. I can still remember the beginning of it, and I will show it to you. *(Demonstration of first improvisation)*

Were I to have done the same improvisation four years later, I would have done it like this: *(Demonstration)*

Why? *(Speaking while demonstrating):* Because nobody is allowed to enter the King's garden... I am not supposed to be here... and when I see a beautiful flower and I want to pick it, I make sure that no one is watching me... and when I go to smell the flower... hundreds of small warriors jump out from it and strike me with their swords... they start jumping out from all the other flowers, too!... and they hurt me!... But then it starts to rain, and every drop of rain is a little angel who crushes the little warriors with his wings... so the rain saves me... *(End of demonstration)*

At Odin Teatret we usually do individual improvisation. Group improvisation has never been used while I have been at the theatre. Eugenio gives the actor a theme (which is never directly related to the scene he is working on), and (since 1972) while the actor improvises, another actor records the work with a video camera, given that the actor must learn his or her improvisation by heart. To learn an improvisation of about 5 minutes could take about one week. When one is able to repeat the improvisation exactly as it appears on the video, we show it to Eugenio, who sees it a couple of times and then starts to elaborate on it. Either by asking us to reduce some fragments of it, or by asking us to keep only parts of it, or by 'editing' the improvisation and creating a new montage of it, which is initially quite difficult for the actor to repeat. All those fragments from the improvisation, pasted up like that, in a different order... The new improvisation looks like a small Frankenstein, but, after a week or so, the actor manages to make it come to life again by re-establishing a stream of images within it. At this point, Eugenio can either choose to use the improvisation as it is for a scene of the performance, or call in another actor who has been going through the same process with his or her improvisation, asking us to establish a dialogue between the actions of our improvisations. Eugenio watches it several times and finds the points of contact between our actions. He may ask us to 'absorb' some of the actions, or to change their speed or size; we are now on another level of elaboration of the improvisation.

Then the improvisation is put into a context in a scene that Eugenio is working on, and in this way my actions take on new meaning. For example, we have a scene in which an evil king wants to sentence a noble young warrior to death, for which reason the heads of the church and the army are present in the throne room. The young warrior enters and kneels before the king. If I am to be the young warrior, Eugenio will make me use a part of my improvisation to enter the room and kneel down. I can take the beginning of my improvisation 'In the King's garden'. *(Demonstration)*

(Demonstrating while speaking): My slow walk, that originally was in order to cautiously enter the garden, is logical in this scene, because a man who knows he is about to die wishes to savour each moment that he has left. In the improvisation then, I looked around to be sure that nobody saw me enter. Here, I will look at those who are about to sentence me to death. And then, while I kneel, I will look directly at that general, and that bishop, who conspired against me. When I reach the floor with my knee, I will look straight at the King. In the first improvisation, I was kneeling down to pick a flower, looking to the sides to make sure that nobody saw me doing it, and at the moment of picking the flower, I heard a sound and looked straight ahead. *(End of demonstration)*

Each of the actions that you have seen is taken directly from my improvisation. I must remain faithful to each action. The action remains the same, but I change the original dynamics slightly. I must be aware of the new meaning of my actions in the new context, my new 'in-tensions', without adapting them to the point that they merely become illustrative. It is the difference between action and context that makes the action 'real'. I must not lose that tension.

Around 1982 we began discovering quicker ways to produce material for new performances. The traditional work of memorizing improvisations from videos took too much time.

We began to build simple movement scores, for instance by working in couples with a chair, and fixing the movements. Eugenio called this 'cutting out blocks of marble'. At this point, we started to speak of 'physical scores' and 'materials', and no longer only of improvisation. We also started to do improvisation 'one step at a time', as Torgeir Wethal would call it. In practice, this meant starting an improvisation doing one or two actions, and immediately repeating them. Then continuing with a couple of actions more, repeating everything from the beginning. And then adding a few more actions, and so forth.

Another way of creating physical scores (materials) that are easy to memorize is to use the words of a song or a poem as a guide. *(Demonstration of a physical score based on the song 'Dream a little dream')*

I find a physical equivalent to each word: This action corresponds to this word. The many years of training have given us actors at Odin Teatret the ability to have an

Polly Peachum's high heels.
Drawing: Ulla Madsen,
Aarhus, April 4, 2000

image in mind and simultaneously realize it physically, without necessarily merely illustrating the image.

Yet another way to create material for the building of performances is to work on the composition of the body. I compose the body and the voice of the different characters. In 1979 we put on a performance called *Brecht's Ashes*. It was based on Bertolt Brecht's life and work. I had to play three different characters: Two from Brecht's plays, and one from his life. The two from his plays were Polly Peachum from the *Three Penny Opera*, and Yvette Pottier from *Mutter Courage*. The one from his life was Margarete Steffin, who was Brecht's secretary for many years. When we began working on the performance, Eugenio wanted me to walk on high heels. And we started with Eugenio asking me to find out how Polly Peachum walked.

(Speaking while demonstrating). Well, Polly Peachum is the daughter of Jeremiah Peachum *(Walking in an extroverted and self-assured way)*. She is the very spoiled daughter of a wealthy father. We will not speak of how he made his wealth, but she is a girl who gets what she wants. She wants Mackie Messer, Mack the Knife, and she gets him. She marries him. So she is a very open girl, because she knows what she wants, and she knows how to get it. Then Eugenio said, 'Okay, and how does Yvette Pottier walk?' Well, Yvette Pottier is a whore, a prostitute. I have never seen a prostitute walk like this. *(Walks in a completely introverted way, with bent head, shoulders and knees)*. They have to show what they have to offer. So, they are very open. *(Walks in an extroverted and self-assured way)*. Not only that, but Yvette Pottier is a very clever girl. She, too, knows what she wants, and she knows how to get it. She wants to become a 'grande dame', and at the end of the play she marries a colonel. She is the only one in

the whole play who gains something from all that misery. So, she has an extroverted way of walking. Then Eugenio said, 'Roberta, you have two characters, and they walk in the same way; how can the spectators know when you are one or the other?' I said, 'Well, yes, but it is your fault. You gave me two characters who are so similar.' And he said, 'Well, let us see. Start to walk like Yvette Pottier.' (*Demonstrates the extroverted walk*). 'Right, here we go.' 'And now do the opposite.' 'What do you mean by the opposite?' 'The opposite.' 'The opposite is like this.' (*Demonstrates the introverted walk*) 'Yes, do like this. But don't forget that you are Polly Peachum, that you know what you want, and you know how to get it.' (*Exaggerates the introversion of the lower part of the body into a limp, and simultaneously extroverts the upper part of the body, focusing her eyes*)

This is how our Polly Peachum was born. In a play, many things are not written. What colour eyes does Polly Peachum have? Not written. If Polly Peachum had a little accident at birth with her hip, it is not written either. But we decided that maybe she had, that's why she walked in this peculiar way. Polly Peachum and Yvette Pottier also had two different ways of using their voices. I will now sing a song which Yvette Pottier sang, and a song which Polly Peachum sang. (*Sings the two songs as the two characters*)

In 1987, my daughter Alice started school. This is normal for a girl of six, but it made problems for me. I could not tour with the rest of the group as much as we were used to. Until that point I had been able to take her along with me on tour with a babysitter. But from that point I had to stay with her in Holstebro. So Eugenio proposed that I create a solo performance. He thought of the theme of Judith. The woman who, as the only one in the whole Bible, does not give birth, does not give life, but kills with her own hands. When we began working on the theme of Judith, Eugenio asked me to produce material that he could work on. We have not used existing plays at Odin Teatret since 1972. The interaction between the director and the actors creates the performance. The text is created at the same time as the performance. I started to work, to produce material, to fix physical scores. Eugenio gave me a book, a catalogue from an exhibition of paintings of Mary Magdalene. I looked at those pictures, and I found that some of them were still very powerful, even after so many centuries. I made photocopies of some of them. I spread them on the study floor. They were a series of pictures of Mary Magdalene with the oil, of Mary Magdalene washing the feet of Jesus, of Mary Magdalene under the cross, of Mary Magdalene in ecstasy. I started to reproduce the different poses with my body. Now I will show you what happened to the series of the poses of Mary Magdalene under the cross.

(*Demonstrates while speaking*): There was one like this; there was one like this, and one like this. Like this, from Carpaccio, like this, from a Flemish painter, and one like this, and one like this.

Then I tried to find a pulse which would help me to link the poses. I decided to let a song lead me from one to the other. To avoid spreading grease on butter, as they say in Denmark, I did not choose a dramatic song, because the images were dramatic in themselves. So I chose a lullaby, a song for children. *(Sings an Italian lullaby while executing the physical score)*

But this is a lullaby only to all those who understand Italian, not to the rest of the world. So I tried to find another song which might evoke the image of a baby in other countries as well. *(Sings the other song while executing the physical score)*

However when I showed this to Eugenio, he said, 'Good, but we can't use it, because Jesus belongs to the New Testament, and Judith to the Old. We cannot put them together'. So we decided to create a poem, a love poem, since, in our version of the story of Judith and Holophernes, Judith falls in love with Holophernes before killing him. Since, in the performance, I speak this poem to the severed head of Holophernes, the physical score was changed slightly. *(Demonstrates in character the final vocal and physical score)*

The text is in Italian, because it is my mother tongue. Since Judith is a tragic character, Eugenio thought that it would be a bad idea for me to use another language. He thought that my English, as well as my Danish, would sound too much like the language of circus clowns. So it was better to do the performance in Italian.

The voice training at Odin Teatret is based on the training that Eugenio learned at Grotowski's Theatre Laboratory. You work with different resonators: for instance the back of the head, the top of the head, the mask, the chest, and the abdomen. You use a text to work with the different resonators. A text which you know very well, and so do not have to think about. It has to be a text, but you just use it as a vocal material. We do not try to interpret this text, we do not respect the punctuation; we just speak for as long as we have breath, and then we stop and take a new breath. The aim is to make vocal actions. It means starting from the surface of my body, going out in the space as far as I can, and then going back to my body, to exactly the same place from where I started. I will give an example. *(Demonstrates the five resonators)*

Five different directions. Then I can colour some of them with my nose or with my throat. *(Demonstrates)*. Throat and nose.

Or I can start to improvise, pretending to follow a flying ball with my voice, holding it while it is moving in the space. Let us say that it starts from the floor in front of me. *(Demonstrates)*. Following the flying ball.

Or I can choose to colour my voice, imagining natural elements. For instance, I can sing a song as though it were fog, as though it were ice, as though it were running water. As though it were fog. *(Demonstrates)*. As though it were ice. *(Demonstrates)*. As though it were running water. *(Demonstrates)*

Something that has been important to me in the development of my vocal, as well as my physical training, has been the meeting with cultures from the Far East (Bali, India, Japan, and China). During several sessions of ISTA (International School of Theatre Anthropology), I had the opportunity to become acquainted with different ways of using the body as well as the voice. We have a very good library in Holstebro, where we can also take out records. In this way I am able to hear and imitate ways of singing from all over the world. Human beings are made in the same way anatomically. But Chinese sounds are very different from Danish, American sounds from Russian, Greenlandic from Pygmy sounds. This kind of research enriched my voice with new sounds.

We also make voice improvisations starting from a theme. When improvising, we use a text, sometimes mixing it with a song, and sometimes using an invented language. One improvisation theme that is very dear to me is 'In the Bazaar of Istanbul'. There you can find anything. You can have, of course, people selling, but they can be young, old, men, women; you can have people stealing, you can have people crying, shouting, singing; you can have children, dogs, cats, birds, rats, anything. The only limit is your own imagination. So now I will give an example of an improvisation starting from the theme 'In the Bazaar of Istanbul'. *(Demonstration)*

When we put on performances, we work with physical actions, texts and vocal actions. We can choose to make the vocal action follow the in-tension of the physical action. At times this also follows the action described in the text. For example, in my solo performance *Judith*, in the first monologue, when I say, 'Nebuchadnezzar called Holophernes, the greatest general of his army, and said: 'Go and occupy the territory of the rebels, and do not have mercy when you sentence them to death'.' In this case I let the vocal action, the action described in the text, and the physical action, follow each other. *(Demonstration)*

I say: 'Go', using my mask resonator, projecting my voice far in front of me, while I am pointing in that direction. Then I say: 'And occupy'. To occupy means to say: 'This place belongs to me'. So I say that with my chest resonator, withdrawing my voice closer to me, while I am pointing to the floor in front of my feet. Then I say: 'All the territory of the rebels', making a circle with the melody of my voice, as well as with my index finger. And so on.

Or, I can allow the meaning of single words to colour my voice. For example, at a certain point I say: 'She took off her widow's clothes, washed her body with water, and anointed herself with heavy perfume.' *(Demonstration)*

In this case, when I say the word 'water', I have the sensation of cold water running down my back, and this colours the way I say this word. And in this case I say, 'heavy perfume' with a thick voice, not with a thin, high voice. At another moment I say, 'She dressed in festive garments with necklaces and bracelets.' *(Demonstration)*

In Italian we have the expression 'a silver laugh' ('una risata argentina'), which means a laugh that sounds like silver. And so, when I say the word 'bracelets', I imagine them tinkling like the laughter of a young girl, and this thought colours my voice. At another moment I can choose to hold back the most important word instead of shouting it. I say, 'The elders of Bethulia decided to resist for five more days, and to surrender if, by that time, the Lord had not shown mercy on their city.' *(Demonstration)*

In this case the most important word is 'mercy', and by saying it more softly than the others, I force the spectators to make the effort of listening. Not all the words of the text are coloured, but some words are chosen to be coloured, to add a dimension to the text.

Up to now, I have spoken about technique. Technique is essential in art. But in theatre it is not what the spectator is supposed to see. As a good friend of mine once said, technique is like an iron staircase, black, cold, ugly, but necessary. Then the snow starts to fall, and the black, ugly staircase becomes white, soft, and beautiful. The snow is the performing situation, where the technique is there, underneath, but the spectator should not see it.

Now I would like to show you the first monologue of my solo performance, *Judith*. Underneath what I will do there is the work with segmentation which I spoke of before, and the vocal work with the text. In the fragment I will show you, I will sometimes be the narrator, sometimes Holophernes, sometimes Nebuchadnezzar, sometimes Judith, sometimes the guards. Everything is fixed, because the performance has a fixed physical and vocal score. Yet for me the performance is new every time I do it.

People have asked me many times how I can stand playing a performance with the same fixed score for years and years. Then I always give the example of Rubinstein playing Chopin's *Nocturne*. He is also repeating a score that is fixed, and in his case it has even been written by someone else. But I can tell the difference between a nocturne played by my daughter and by Rubinstein. He has managed to transcend the technique. What is left is the pleasure of sharing, and that is why he is able to give us so much.

As in the Greek theatre, *Judith*'s first monologue works as a prologue, telling the whole story of Judith in a condensed form. The text is taken directly from *The Book of Judith* in the Bible. *(Demonstration)*

Until now I have been speaking about the past. Now I would like to show you some of my present work. The first thing is a form of voice training that I started a few years ago, but that I feel is still in its initial stage. It is inspired by the songs of Georgian shepherds: Georgia in the former Soviet Union. These men sing with what are called 'crystal voices', not because they sing with high voices or in falsetto, but because they are able to produce a sound over their own voices *(overtone)*, like the one you produce when you rub the rim of a crystal glass with a wet finger. The harmonics they produce are very powerful, and sometimes sound like a flute playing parallel to the man's voice. Mine are very small, but I hope that you can hear them. *(Demonstration)*

And then something that belongs to the third season of my physical training. If, in the first season, the aim was to find my presence as an actor, and liberate my body from the automatisms of daily life, and if, in the second season, the goal was to increase my presence and free my body of the automatisms stemming from my own work (clichés), then the aim of the third season is still to increase my presence, but also to produce physical scores that already have some kind of dramaturgical structure. When I compose my scores, I have in mind the eye of the spectator. I will now show you the opening dance of this work demonstration, but now with the addition of a prop that will change your perception of the story. *(Demonstration of the opening dance, but with a bouquet of flowers in which is hidden a long knife, which is suddenly revealed)*

Finally, a few words that are not my own: 'The art of the actor is based on the organization of his material, and on the actor's accurate knowledge of the means of expression of his own body.' This was written by Meyerhold, the Russian theatre director from the beginning of the 20th century, and it is still valid for me.

Thank you for your patience.

Aarhus, April 4, 2000

Annelis Kuhlmann

[**Foot and Fantasy**]

Act in Shoes

From the history of the tradition of acting I have selected a basic issue concerning the way in which the creative imagination is influenced by the shoes the actor wears on stage. This problem can also imply a philosophical evaluation of the actor's creativity, but as a point of departure it is concrete. I was inspired by an interview, that Roberta Carreri, from Odin Teatret, gave around the turn of the millennium to the Danish journalist Lisbet Holst.[1]

Roberta Carreri as Geronimo (right) in Ode to Progress. *Torgeir Wethal (left). Photo: Jan Rüsz*

In the interview Roberta Carreri tells about the big pair of men's shoes she wears when playing the clown Geronimo:

> Perhaps it is the fact that these shoes wake the child in me. You know, as a child one always has to try all the adults' shoes — all the uncles' and aunts' big shoes.
>
> At all places, across cultures, languages and other possible barriers, Geronimo has inspired laughter and recognition, perhaps because he represents the child in every one of us, young and old alike. This is perhaps the reason why Geronimo is able to communicate with, amuse and entertain people all over the world, says Roberta Carreri.
>
> — This is what I found so fantastic about the character. There is a core in our soul that remains young, and this character is a revelation of that small core. I believe that it is extremely healthy to be allowed to find this particular characteristic — to be in touch with the cheerfulness of life. It is without limits. It is a spark of life.
>
> This character really means a lot to me; it has almost been a key for me, first and foremost because it is a character that very easily gets in contact with the spectators, and furthermore it is a character that I built up all on my own without any collaboration with a director.

From Roberta Carreri's interview quoted above we can see that these big shoes serve a number of different functions. The actress achieves a great deal when she is doing Geronimo's actions, and the shoes seem continuously to provoke renewed energy in the actress's actions and movements. These functions have a special impact on both the physical and the emotional sides of the actor's work.

In the history of the twentieth century, starting with Isadora Duncan's barefoot dancing, it has become increasingly common to see actors perform barefoot on stage. The barefoot actor reveals some of the outer techniques of being in contact with the ground. When the actor is not barefoot, he or she is dressed in some kind of footwear. To wear some kind of shoe does not eliminate the problem of how to stand on the floor, although the shoe apparently covers part of the problem. It is actually the opposite thing that happens: the footwear adds new problems to the old problem, i.e. how one should stand in shoes on the floor. Depending on the shape of the shoes different challenges and possibilities appear. The various sorts of footwear offer the actor a rich catalogue from which to act and with which to play.

It is my thesis that footwear on stage is a very important issue in acting. In this article I shall give illustrative examples of the shoe from the history of art, drama and theatre itself. By means of this catalogue of examples I wish to call attention to the emphasis on footwear in classical theatre references.

[Images of shoes from an unbelievable reality]

As a starting point I shall establish a horizon for the examples of footwear in theatre by calling attention to some photos taken when the Allied forces entered the concentration camps in 1945. With an exceedingly genuine sense of order, the photos show the effective recycling of things belonging to the prisoners into a suitable cynical system of the German political regime of the time: in the photo shoes are systematically arranged in piles and mountains.

The unbelievable but undeniable humiliations and sufferances and the meaningless killing of millions of Jews, Communists, homosexuals and others in the Nazi concentration camps of World War II can still be communicated to the children of the 21st century. In my context the cruelty offers its inspiration and force to the artist, and to me the fragility and the vulnerability of a creative act shape a reality in the impulse that I receive from this photo from Stutthof.

Some issues imply such a power in their appearance that once one has been hit by the cruelty of the image, one cannot keep it in one's memory without being reminded of the fragility and vulnerability of a creative act.

Shoes piled in the KZ-camp in Stutthof.
Photo: Unknown[2]

The impression I get when I look at this photo hits my sensorial experience. I am part of an act of witnessing in the year 2000. From now on the very act of putting on somebody's worn-out shoe implies a responsibility. As far as an actor is concerned, he or she shall also remember with his or her whole body that shoes represent lives in history.

To avoid any doubt, I shall immediately emphasise that I am not trying to make any sort of comparison between Geronimo's shoes and the shoes from the concentration camps. But why introduce this photo in this particular context? I shall return to this question shortly. With this photo as a memorial background, I shall present some situations where the shoe is in focus and remains a vital inspiration for performative creativity.

[Shoes from art history]

Shoes have played a major role in art history. That is, images of shoes and our visual memory of shoes are evident in the history of art. Simply recall various paintings by Vincent van Gogh: for example, *Three Pairs of Shoes* is the title of a painting he did in Paris in 1886-87.

One year later, in 1888, in the countryside near Arles, he painted A *Pair of Wooden Shoes*. And there are other similar examples created by the same artist. In these two paintings we do not directly see the feet wearing these shoes. However, indirectly, the shoes tell stories about the lives lived by the people who in the imagination of both the artist and the onlooker did wear the shoes.

In classical drawing and sculpture we find a kind of opposition to the worn-out shoe or boot. The ideal image of a naked muscular foot is famous from Michelangelo's sculptures as well as from the drawings of Willem Panneels (Cantor 1988, 231). Or consider a foot painted by René Magritte. I recall in particular the painting that shows a foot transformed into a zipped sock. To me this painting is a symbol of the paradox of an actor's working process: the actor is actor and character at one and the same time.

A contrastive reflection can also be seen in the interpretative relation between the aesthetics in the image of a three-inch Lotus foot from China and the image of the tip of a Western classical ballet toe shoe. Observing both images, we find that an unexpected dialogue on creative inspiration can be used as a consequence of the actor's creativity.

In this part of the article I have mainly included the above images of shoes in order to illustrate the art world's richness of imagination, which directly accompanies an actor's imagination and creative memory while being, moving and acting on stage.

In the following we shall approach the theatre and see how shoes are influential not only at a visual level but also at a sensorial level of perception related to the actor's creative mind.

[Shoes as a concept in space, as a mask or as a character]

At exhibitions of modern art I have seen various examples of how shoes enter the space as concepts, masks or characters. At Louisiana, the Museum of Modern Art, near Hamlet's Kronborg Castle in Denmark, the exhibition called *No/w/here* (1996) presented an installation by the artist Mona Hatoum. From 1985 to 1995 she composed an installation concept displaying a shoe on a leash following after a foot. This sequence was entitle *Performance Still* (Nittve 1996, 37).

The same exhibition at Louisiana showed about one hundred military boots in pairs, all arranged in a strictly geometric pattern. The right boot of each pair was lifted up by an invisible thread, so that it gave the illusion of a whole army of soldier-less boots frozen in the middle of a military march or a training session in collective movement. The artist — Dominique Blain — chose the title of *Missa,* meaning mass, for this installation made in 1993 (Nittve 1996, 42).

Furthermore, I saw another installation with a huge number of shoes placed as two overcrowded rectangular squares facing each other and divided by a passage of empty space. The installation was reminiscent of river banks. The image of stylised river banks immediately reminded me of the composition of the spectators' space at many of Odin Teatret's performances. Here, in my associative perception, the title could be the following: 'The audience at a performance'. The artist, Rasheed Araeen, had made his installation in 1991 and called it *A Long Walk in the Wilderness* (Archer 1997, 162). In Islamic culture, where one always leaves one's shoes outside the mosques before entering, the title on a piece of art like the one I have just described is obviously rather provocative.

[Shoes are magic]

In Denmark every child knows Hans Christian Andersen's tale *Simple Simon* (Klods Hans), where it says that an old clog can turn into a cooker with a tin handle. By the hand of the same storyteller we also have *The Red Shoes* and *The Galoshes of Fortune,* two story titles that are different in both form and content. In *The Princess and the Pea* the horrible weather and the flood of rain are described through the shoes of the wet princess: 'The water was running down her hair and her clothes, and in at the tip of her shoes and out again at the heels; [...]' (Andersen 1976, 27). In short, in the world of Hans Christian Andersen the shoe is a dramatic symbol that is magic and cruel.

Often shoes are magic in a slightly different way, like in the fairytale by Charles Perrault about *Cinderella* (Cendrillon ou La petite pantoufle de verre), where the lost shoe gives access to the prince's love. In *Puss-in-Boots* (Le Maître Chat ou le Chat Botté), also by Charles Perrault, we see the footwear as the magical characteristics that move the cat to meet unbelievable adventurous characters.

The latent dramatic tension that shoes can offer to the person who is wearing them is unique and basic at the same time. Often the shoes give the initial energy to create and maintain a character. Roberta Carreri comments on this in respect to Geronimo in the same interview as mentioned above:

> Geronimo would not be the same without the shoes from which he was born', says Roberta Carreri. 'The solid men's shoes have changed supports many times and have been resoled a couple of times. They are inextricably bound up with the theatre character.
> — Putting on a pair of size 44 men's shoes when in reality you, like Roberta, wear size 36 shoes affects your whole gait, and you are not able to do some things — other things you can do. For instance, you can place your heel on the ground and wave with the shoe in ways that you otherwise cannot.

So we can say that from a performative point of view we have the shoe in art in general and in the art of theatre in particular in order to give constant rebirth to living theatre, to reinforce the quality of energy in the actor's movements.

[Shoes from the history of drama]

The history of drama tells us that shoes have a significance which is often very sensual. The theatrical space in the written dramas that I shall use as examples here is often composed with extraordinary attention to the shoe.

In August Strindberg's *Miss Julie* (1889) 'Jean enters, dressed in livery, carrying a pair of large riding boots with spurs, which he puts down where they can be seen — on the floor' (Strindberg 1970, 78). At several places in this naturalistic 'Trauerspiel' the boots are polished energetically in a stimulating way, giving the image of an electric Eros.

In William Shakespeare's *Hamlet* (1600), when the actors have played *The murder of Gonzago*, Horatio remains with Hamlet, who metaphorically comments upon the effect of the allegorical play that was just presented:

Why, let the strucken deer go weep,
The hart ungalled play;
For some must watch, while some must sleep:
So runs the world away.
Would not this, sir, and a forest of feathers — if
the rest of my fortunes turn Turk with me — with two
Provincial roses on my razed shoes, get me a
fellowship in a cry of players, sir?

(Hamlet, III, 2)

In his comment Hamlet plays on the double code in the actor dressing up and/or adding significations to the play, here named by the actors' shoes, as if they presented a hidden paradox in the possible game. Indeed, Shakespeare's *Hamlet* has influenced many artists over the years. In 1865, the writer and painter Arthur de Gravillon (1828-99) rewrote the clowns' scene in *Hamlet* in one of his illustrated books, *A propos de bottes*, so that Hamlet no longer speaks to Horatio while watching Yorick's skull, but meditates on his shoe. Arthur de Gravillon made the following comment on his idea:

> When you think of all this in the right way — that the head is nothing more than an unworthy and clumsy piece of footwear that parts with the soul in order to rise to heaven freely and easily — would it not be possible then to say that old and greying death is also a good cobbler who excellently works with the senses? (Bredow 1976, 93 — my translation).

In this respect Gravillon transfers the intellectual perception of the world from the head to the feet. The transfer does not result in a mere caricature, but in an unexpected perspective of perception, that is, from the feet. One might say that here this image of opposite perceptions becomes a parallel to text and subtext. The feet perceive from a position below the lines. Shakespeare's works offer other examples of how shoes play a definite role. There is a brilliant example of the shoe as a symbol of a character in a monologue; the lines are said by the clownish character Launce in *The Two Gentlemen of Verona*:

This shoe is my father;
no, this left shoe is my father;
no, no, this left shoe is my mother:
nay, that cannot be so neither;
yes, it is so, it is so, it hath the worser sole.

(The Two Gentlemen of Verona, II, 3)

Of course, we are witnessing Launce's witty word game in the quoted passage above when sole and soul finally merge as homonyms. This effect gives animated shoes with relationship to the actor's personality.

Finally, in Samuel Beckett's *En attendant Godot* from 1952 the shoe as a theme practically becomes a leitmotiv. There is constant dialogue about taking shoes on and off in the play. The sujet is not only a simple grotesque representation, it is also an experiment, full of hope, which in the case of theatre concerns a *horror vacui* and a longing to redeem the playful character. This experiment involving longing is severely rehearsed, as if Estragon were taking part in an eternal rehearsal:

> Vladimir: [...] (Estragon with a supreme effort succeeds in pulling off his boot. He looks inside it, feels about inside it, turns it upside down, shakes it, looks on the ground to see if anything has fallen out, finds nothing, feels inside it again, staring sightlessly before him.) Well?
> Estragon: Nothing.
> Vladimir: Show.
> Estragon: There's nothing to show. (Beckett 1965, 11)

Similarly, later in the play, in answer to Vladimir's critique of him walking barefoot, Estragon mentions that Jesus Christ did the same and that his whole existence is built on this comparison. Finally, the following day, when — at the same time and the same place — nothing has changed, they cannot figure out whether Estragon's boots really do belong to him. The colours are no longer reliable and the space tricks them. Estragon is not present. He is represented by his boot — together with Lucky's hat the only object present in the two acts of the play: 'Estragon's boots front centre, heels together, toes splayed' (Beckett 1965, 57).

At this point I shall elaborate on the signification of the boot in Beckett's universe. One has often wondered who or what Godot was supposed to be. Who did Beckett have in mind when he wrote the play? Beckett was once asked this question and gave the following answer: 'If I knew, I would have said so in the play' (Esslin 1976, 43).

I suppose that many readers have tried to figure out whether Godot was just a nickname for God. In that case Vladimir and Estragon's waiting is existential and can be directly interpreted as waiting for God. Martin Esslin mentions the discussion of an etymological link between Godot and God. This interpretation is perhaps valuable in an associative reading of the play in English, and Beckett actually did translate the play into an English version, *Waiting for Godot*, in 1955, and as an Irishman he could of course play with the English language. However, Beckett originally wrote the play in French, in which language the allusion to God in connection with Godot is not obvious.

I am not advocating a philological analysis but rather the physical space of the concept of 'Godot'. If we insist on the question of the identity of Godot in a French association, an interesting associative context appears. Two images very close to each other in this context give possibilities for a new interpretation. To the French reader the association of sounds in the word Godot recalls the words *godillot* and *godasse*. *Godillot,* which contains the repeated 'o' as a vocal image, like in Godot, has the neutral semantic signification of a delivery for the army. In informal language a 'godillot' is a military short top boot. 'Godasse' is just a popular word for footwear. The suffix of 'godasse' ('asse') is characteristic of pejorative semantic values. This means that we have an associative space of rigour and everyday pejorative values attached to poor Godot.

The associative imagination affected by the name of Godot referring to a boot underlines the role that the boot plays throughout the play. Godot is absent but the boot is present. The understanding of the universe of the play in relationship to the physicality of the characters emphasizes the world as a circus inhabited by clowns, as seen in the situation with Lucky's monologue. When, like in the passage quoted above, Estragon examines the boot, it is a variation of the previous situation in Beckett's text, where Vladimir examines a hat in the very same way. So we can see a similarity to the clown scene at the grave in Shakespeare's *Hamlet*, where Yorick's skull is taken for a boot.

A parallel example would be the little shrimp of a vagabond with a hat, a stick and big shoes turned outward (Charlie Chaplin). In the representation of the silent movie his gait reminds one of the staccato rhythm of the tottering child who has just learnt to walk.

The very signification of the shoe for the actor is prominent as a durative inscription in the history of drama. But also in the history of the theatre we have seen some examples that each in its own way pays special attention to the performative character of the shoe.

[Shoes in theatre performances]

I shall finally draw the attention to specific shoes in three particular theatre performances. In Odin Teatret's performance *Kaosmos* (1993-98), the young bride from the village (Tina Nielsen) shows her small silver-plated shoes from very early childhood to the Mother (Roberta Carreri), who is looking for her child that has been abducted by Death. The Mother refers to *The Story of a Mother* by Hans Christian Andersen, but the silver shoes were, as far as I know, Tina Nielsen's, from her own childhood. Traditionally in Denmark the children's very first pair of shoes, which were silver-plated, were kept as a souvenir of the child and of childhood. The information about these silver shoes belonging to Tina Nielsen's personal childhood is evidently not revealed to the audience. But as stimuli the shoes add a sensorial memory of lost childhood to Tina Nielsen's artistic presence. The silver shoes represented an actress and a character at the same time.

In *Mythos* (1998-), in the final blue-lighted image of the performance, we witness reminiscences of our civilisation as if it were preserved in an aquarium at an exhibition. As such, the last revolutionary, played by Kai Bredholt, is represented by one of his boots. The character of the last revolutionary has become a fragment of intact garbage at the bottom of the river, with the audience, in keeping with the classical theatrical space of an Odin Teatret performance, sitting on the banks of the river witnessing in a way him-/herself watching. The spectator has become a double.

The third and last example of the shoe's significance in a theatre performance is taken from Jerzy Grotowski's 1962 performance based on Stanislaw Wyspiański's *Akropolis* (1904). In the performance special clogs were used with the purpose of underlining a special wooden sound in the rhythm and the way of walking in order to call to mind prisoners in a concentration camp. The sound and rhythm of the actors' movement in the wooden shoes remind me of the imaginative sound of the movements of mechanised skeletons. And this sound image recalls the sound of a floppy marionette. The stage had been raised so that the actor's feet were at the level of the eyes of the audience (Barba 1991, 121). This made the audience experience the sounds and movements of a brutal story of the past as composed infernal music.

These examples show that the footwear used on stage can not only have a strong impact on the spectator's experience, but definitively also on the imaginative force of the actor. In a literal sense the footwear generally leaves traces, and in a figurative sense the footwear leaves very specific traces. As I see it, these specific traces are strong enough to hit the spectator's sensorial life experience.

Now, I have presented a survey that shows through various examples from the field of fine arts, from performances and from the history of drama that the appearance of a shoe or a boot on stage is to be taken explicitly. The shoe is an immediate sign of the performative possibility in the play — seen from the actor's 'point of foot'. Let us now take a look at a model of apprenticeship connected to the idea of acting implied by the wearing of a shoe on stage.

[The shoe in theatre education]

At about the same time Roberta Carreri joined Odin Teatret in 1974, the etude with shoes was introduced at the State Theatre School in Copenhagen, which had opened in

1968. Until then the Danish acting schools had only existed in close connection with traditional theatres, themselves imitations of the *théâtre Italien*. The teaching at the State Theatre School had been a kind of copy of the master's apprenticeship, but the school did not protect any specific style or method. Today the State Theatre School is still primarily based on the so-called pedagogics of experience of the individual student.[3]

For a period of more than twenty-five years, shoes have been part of an educational concept formed as a specific etude for the first-year students at the actors' school in Copenhagen. The etude is still practised, and one of its major purposes is to provoke the student's dramatic and creative imagination in a narrative course.

The etude begins when each student is given a pair of shoes and told the following: 'Here is a pair of shoes ... Work with them'. The shoes are not specifically theatre shoes, but shoes that have been worn and have served as footwear.

The actor can handle the etude by wearing this shoe, feeling it from the inside. This means that foot and fantasy are working together. For the person wearing the shoe, the important thing is that the shoe becomes a mask in relation to the actor's work with a character. But the shoe can also become a psychological character that is scrutinized intensively, worked with, and seen from the outside.

In sum, the shoe can be *1)* a print to be left on one's feet, so that it immediately influences one's physical postures and movements; *2)* a mask, and *3)* a character. Finally, the shoe can be perceived as a symbol. The shoes may be said to have the following functions: they

a) constitute a character when an actor is wearing them.

b) form a symbol.

c) appear as pars pro toto (footwear changes significance: for instance, after having worn a pair of boots, one then puts them on a table and they turn into a pair of big altar candles). The shoes now represent the character but with new associative imagery, underlined by the gestures of the actor; they

d) are footwear.

One might wonder whether this etude can be done with an overcoat. Yes, this is possible, but a coat does not give one the same kind of impulse as shoes do. A shoe is formed by a person's weight, and when the actor puts on the shoe, he senses it with his whole weight. To maintain the opposition, by its weight the coat has an impact on the actor. It is furthermore a fact that shoes that have been worn speak much more strongly to us than other articles of clothing.

This etude is originally rooted in the question of what a mountain of shoes represents. And this question refers to the reality behind the photo from the concentration camp in the beginning of the article. A single shoe can tell its story, and a pair of shoes their stories. But what kind of story can be told by a mountain of shoes?

The shoe itself can become the narrator. The shoe can undertake a development in the work of an actor. The shoe can help the actor to develop his or her imaginative creativity when working with a character. The shoe can help the actor to improve his or her emotional and physical memory. In this case the shoe can be perceived as a provocation consisting of latent stories with an inner/outer development.

To sum up, the shoe etude is about the actor in relation to narration. When practised, certain conditions for this shoe etude are given. A central idea is to find *a third way* through the outer/inner working process. The shoes are always concrete. This means that in the actor's dramatic shaping there are no supplementary questions of who, how, when, where or why to ask in a naturalistic way, as an actor might ask a character. But there are questions regarding the imagined reality of the persons who wear or did wear the shoes. The shoes are concrete objects liberated from their own biographies.

In the etude the actor's intentions are implicitly only acceptable as action. This means that no explicative comments such as spoken director's notes like: '... the shoes are shabby because of the hard work she had to do at the factory ...' and other sorts of settings or 'bad excuses' for a lack of imagination in the actor's actions are accepted.

A set of game rules and conditions for the etude and its solution was developed. There are often three persons in one group. Each one can only say what he sees. He or she is not allowed to judge, verify or falsify the others' work. Only the single student wearing the actual pair of shoes can know and judge whether his or her communication, or what he or she thinks he or she is communicating, works.

[Shoes in idiomatic expressions]

Another source of the actor's creativity is obvious in the linguistic context of shoes. I am thinking of the surprisingly great amount of imagery and the many idiomatic expressions that contain shoes as symbols in order very often to build a metaphorical level for understanding what can be said only with great difficulty. I shall name a few examples here to give an idea of the wealth of material we can find in the imagery.

The Biblical saying 'Take off your sandals; the place where you are standing is holy ground' (Exodus, 3:5) can be applied to many of the stage artists from the end of the 19th century up until today. The barefoot dancers, mostly identified with Isadora Duncan as a pioneer, and actors training barefoot like in Grotowski's exercises illustrate this saying. Of course I am not pretending that this proverbial saying is directly taken as epitaph for actors and dancers. However, the attitude towards the theatre space as something sacred and intended for holy actions done by holy actors is noticeable in an outstanding tradition of theatre ensembles in the twentieth century, where the professional ethical aspect of entering the space of the stage is done with as much humility as if the artist were entering a temple.

'When the shoe creaks, it is said that the person wearing the shoes has not yet paid his shoemaker'. This saying was applied in drama by Anton Čechov in 1903-4, when he wrote the comedy *The Cherry Orchard*. Soon after the beginning of the play, there is the first director's note: 'Yepikhodov comes in carrying a bunch of flowers. He wears a jacket and brightly polished high boots which make a loud squeak'. (Chekhov 1964, 146). The clownish character, Yepikhodov — also known as 'twenty-two misfortunes' (or Simple Simon, as it says in Ronald Hingley's translation) — gets most of his physicality as a character in the stimulus from his shoes. They form much of his physical awkwardness and turn him into a clown.

[Final remarks]

The evidence of how shoes in various areas of the arts exercise a particularly insistent influence on the spectator's nervous system is the main theme of this article. The initial statement above by the actress Roberta Carreri tells in the most basic and bare way a very long and complex story about some essential issues in an actor's creativity in action or movements in the space of the stage. It is obvious that the big pair of men's shoes goes well with a character like Geronimo, who is a clown. But the actress could have built these shoes in such a way that the inside of the shoes corresponded to the size of her own feet. She did not. And there is a good reason for not doing so. By wearing big shoes on small feet one can revive the sense of being a child in a grown-up's shoes. This sense is connected to the sweet playfulness of being an actress or an actor. It is obvious that Roberta Carreri arrives at a specific naive sense of joy from the impulse of the child in big shoes. As we know, this naive joyfulness can be very fruitful for communication with an audience, especially because on a mimetic (fictitious) level the actor/actress is liberated from troubles belonging to the world of grown-ups. But at another level the naive feeling on stage is also a specific distancing technique for the actor. The world is open and non-naturalistic at this level, and it is pure in terms of actions. That is, the shoes provide a certain freedom in the acting and in the interaction with an audience, whether on the streets or in a building suited to theatre activities.

The very essence of acting from the big shoes one is wearing is often accompanied by the effect of walking or moving in a clownish way. This is also true in Geronimo's case, and it suits him well since he is a clown like the ones we know from the circus. The shoes somehow let the action avoid automatism. There is a demand for a special effort and every action seems to be constantly rediscovered. The action is reborn in each new position.

From the artist's point of view, when every physical action and movement is to be rethought, recreated and redone, the allusion to the child learning to walk his first steps becomes very evident. At a metaphorical level this is a parallel to the actor's knowledge about his or her skills and craft. In the actor's creative birth of a new character on stage, each and every character actually has to learn how to take its first steps as though it were the very first time.

At a methodological level these first steps correspond to the first steps in the childhood of an actor's artistic biography. In other words, the scenically concrete and almost naively seductive construction and reconstruction of an artistic childhood becomes present in the growing process of the actor's creative work. The immediate love of the actor's profession that appears in the clownish presence apparently corresponds to a sincere undercurrent of the satisfaction of creativity in an artistically erotic way.

Notes

1. At http://www.forum.kvinfo.dk/forum.asp?PageID=48888 on the internet the interview with Roberta Carreri was published under the title *Milleniumshoe*.
2. It has not been possible to find the person who took this photograph. If somebody should own the copyright of this photo, that person is requested to contact Aarhus University Press.
3. I thank the Danish theatre director and pedagogue Eva Jørgensen for providing me with information about the practice of this etude.

References

Andersen, Hans Christian 1976. 80 *Fairy Tales*. Translated by R. P. Keigwin. Odense: Skandinavisk Bogforlag, Flensteds Forlag.

Andersen, Hans Christian 1985. *Fairy Tales*. Vol. 3. Translated by R. P. Keigwin. København: Reitzels Forlag.

Archer, Michael 1997. *Art Since 1960*. 180 illustrations, 74 in colour. London: Thames and Hudson.

Barba, Eugenio and Nicola Savarese 1991. *The Secret Art of the Performer. A Dictionary of Theatre Anthropology*. London and New York: Routledge.

Beckett, Samuel 1965. *Waiting for Godot. A tragicomedy in two acts*. London: Faber and Faber Limited.

Bredow, Barbara (ed.) 1976. *Shuh-werk, Aspekte zum Menschenbild*. Kat. Nr. 32/1976, Berlin: Kunsthalle Nürnberg am Marientor, München.

Cantor, Rubens 1988. *The Drawings of Willem Panneels*. Vol. II, Copenhagen: Department of Prints and Drawings, The Royal Museum of Fine Arts.

Chekhov, Anton 1964. *The Oxford Chekhov*. Vol. III. *Uncle Vanya, Three Sisters, The*

Cherry Orchard, The Wood-Demon. Translated and edited by Ronald Hingley, New York, Toronto, London: Oxford University Press.

Esslin, Martin 1976 (1961). *The Theatre of the Absurd*. Revised and enlarged edition. Middlesex: Pelican books.

Nittve, Lars et al. (eds.) 1996. *Nowhere Louisiana. Louisiana Revy*. vol. I, 36, no. 3, May, Copenhagen.

Strindberg, August 1970. *Pre-Inferno Plays. The Father, Lady Julie, Creditors, The Stronger, The Bond*. Translations and Introductions by Walter Johnson. Seattle and London: University of Washington Press.

LIVERPOOL JOHN MOORES UNIVERSITY
Aldham Robarts L.R.C.
TEL 0151 231 3701/3634

Frans Winther

[Odin Teatret and the Music]

[Time and theatre]

A viewer in the first row looks at his watch, and the actor on stage despairs. Something must be wrong. The viewer obviously will not let himself be seduced, and has decided to escape from the spell cast by the performance, and return to the technically measurable time of the outside world — so-called reality, where clocks rule, digitalizing time, splitting it into countable bits, and hence making us believe we are in control.

Therefore, the actor should take off his own watch and leave it behind in his dressing-room when he goes on stage, so that he does not invoke this technical sense of time in the minds of the audience. In the theatre, it is the performance that should play with time and with the inner clock of the audience. Carl Åge Rasmussen, the Danish composer, says in his book *Is Time Audible* that: 'In fact the ear senses time far better than space; our ability to locate sound in space is weak and uncertain, but our ability to locate it in time is a precision instrument ... Music is the only proper language we have on time.'

[Sound and time]

In the world of the theatre, music is a finely-tuned instrument that we can use to play with time, and music — in the sense of sound organised in sequences — has always been part of the performances of Odin Teatret — and a phenomenon to which the theatre takes a very dedicated approach. The actors use vocal effects, stage requisites, and all other available tools to create a variety of sounds, which are incorporated into Odin's performances on an equal footing with text, light, images. And, in the course of time, the actors have learned to play a number of musical instruments: Else Marie Laukvik plays the accordion, Iben Nagel Rasmussen the charango, Tage Larsen the violin and trumpet, Julia Varley the trombone, etc.

Odin uses songs — both well-known and unknown ones, and sometimes just snatches of them — with the intent that they create associations in the minds of the audience, who may not actually know the song, let alone understand the lyrics. A morning song should conjure up special images of the early morning; a fragment of a wedding song should bring the union of the lovers to mind. It may not always turn out like that in practice, but that does not really matter. The magic emanating from the song may not allow of one specific interpretation, but it nevertheless adds significance to the overall performance.

The use of voices is especially interesting; Odin has developed a number of techniques, ranging from chords bordering on classical lyrical singing to birds' cries, whispering, and guttural sounds, which meet the need to create a unique sound universe; a universe which can invoke the image of beauty or terror, and which, so to speak, is the personal voice of the theatre.

In more recent performances, the music has relied more closely on professional musical conventions, as people with a professional musical background have been attached to Odin. Kai Bredholt is a street musician, Jan Ferslev is a rock musician, and the author of these lines grew up with classical music at the Northern Jutland School of Music.

[The processes of the music]

The processes by which music originates at Odin Teatret split roughly into the following categories.

1) *The music of the actor.* Drawing on his own work on his voice, body, and stage requisites, the actor improvises an acoustic score that may take the form of a song, a fragment of a tune, a rhythmical figure, a pattern of sound, and various combinations of these elements. At a later stage of the process, the actor adapts the score for a specific performance. He will most often do so in collaboration with the director, but he may also work with other actors, musicians, or the composer.

2) *The music of the musician.* A tune is improvised and given its final shape, supported perhaps by a harmonic pattern, a sequence of chords. Or, conversely, an interesting sequence of chords — a cycle — could form the basis of a tune. This could take place by a collective process, where one musician will compose the cycle of chords and another will create one or more melodies based on the cycle. Or, a new harmonic pattern, new chords, may be attached to a tune to change its character or make it more interesting. The same may be true of rhythmical elements.

3) *The music of the composer.* Very often, the composer will have a set assignment to carry out. He receives a text and is asked to write music that suits it. He then reviews the text carefully and, already at this stage, a spontaneous musical idea arises, which is put to the test at the piano and written down. In recent years, the music has been written on a computer, which makes it possible to produce legible sheets, and not least, transpose and write individual parts quickly. Most often, the full company will then set to work on the music. The composer must therefore take into account that the music is intended for a theatre where viewers sit on two sides of an oblong stage and at a highly varying distance from the actors. Those sitting on the left may hear Julia Varley and Iben Nagel Rasmussen best; those sitting on the right will hear Jan Ferslev, and those at the far ends will hear Kai Bredholt. Therefore, all voices must have the quality of a first voice. Since each will hear something different than other viewers, each part must function on its own with the others as accompaniment.

4) *The music of the director* is a montage of elements, encompassing the three techniques just mentioned, and songs from various countries, which the director has come across, and which have inspired him and 'created associations'. Songs which the actors must rehearse and adapt to their own voices. And which the composer must set about arranging and adapting to the rest of the music, and possibly orchestrating.

[The music of the music]

Over the last ten years, work on the music at Odin has become more focussed on what might be called the music of the music. Witness the fact that the music is included as a separate point on the theatre's credit list. The music is now to a greater extent handled by people who were engaged in musical activity before joining Odin Teatret. This is the process I am familiar with myself, since it coincides with the period during which I have worked with the theatre as an ensemble.

The following sections describe how the music is built up and integrated into Odin's performances. I shall use the performances *Kaosmos* and *Mythos* as examples to illustrate this.

'Kaosmos'

In the changing rhythmic patterns of *Kaosmos*, a number of tales are combined into a whole, with affinities to both the Yugoslavian tragedy and the collapse of popular cultures in Europe. *The Story of a Mother* by Hans Christian Andersen, and *Before the Law* by Kafka are interwoven with the poem, *The Seventh*, by Atilla Youssouf.

Picture four girls sitting in the grass in front of Odin Teatret; the sun is shining, and they are singing an old Spanish procession song about the Virgin Mary. Isabel Ubeda is teaching a song from her homeland, Spain, to the other three. Somewhere in the shade, the composer is listening, fascinated, first and foremost preoccupied with the constantly changing beats. A rising movement in five-eight time, unfolding and changing into a seven-eight time, and finally settling into a calm quadruple time — difficult to put to music.

The director decides that this very tune is to be incorporated into the work in process, but the company does not entirely agree on how to deal with the structure of the tune. The rock musician prefers it to be fitted into a normal sequence of twelve beats; the street musician is more used to changing beats from his work with Eastern European folk music, so rich in rhythmic variation.

The Seventh

Then, the poem *The Seventh* by Attila Youssouf crops up. The director suggests that we try to adapt the tune to this poem. In practice, we opt for a two-way process, where both the tune and text are adapted until they form a whole. I first draft a text that very nearly fits the tune, and we then go on to refine the entire material further by singing the song over and over again. In the end, this leaves us with a tune which fits in well with the lyrics, and which has been made even more rhythmically complex: 'Slår du dig ned på denne jord, da skal din mor, bringe dig til verden syv gange.' ('If you settle on this Earth, then your mother shall give birth to you seven times.'). Jan Ferslev improvises a parallel fifth voice; Julia Varley rehearses it, and we add it to the basic melody.

At a later stage, the composer takes this melodic structure along to his workshop and adds a third-based lower part, which is rehearsed by Kaj Bredholt. The director suggests that we add a little contrasting line in major, at the end of the song. Finally, I compose a short chorus: *Den syvende skal du selv være (The Seventh shall be yourself)* as a classical three-part movement that finishes off the song. We then combine all the elements and write them down. Voilà: the song is complete. An instrumental introduction is improvised later on, and the song is used as a sort of leitmotiv during the play.

Before the Law

For Kafka's text on the man who waits before the door of the law all his life, and who is told only shortly before he dies that this door was made especially for him, I have composed a four-part movement that has been handed to the actors as sheet music. We can use this work process, as those who can read music help those who cannot. But it is a rather onerous process. The music is more complicated than the musical material the actors normally work on. It appears inorganic, so the voices are only slowly incorporated. The complexity that normally evolves at later stages of the process, as one layer is added to another, has been built into this movement right from the beginning, and needs extensive rehearsing.

The music has been composed in phrases. This means Julia Varley can alternate with the choir; she recites the text in a language the audience understand, and the choir answers her, singing the same text in Danish. In the final stages of the process, we split the whole movement into four parts, which are introduced at various points of the performance to counterbalance *The Story of a Mother* by Hans Christian Andersen, which, contrary to Kafka's story, is about going through the door of the law, into death, in quest of love and the beloved child.

The Story of a Mother

The mother first manifests herself through a popular Japanese tune, *Cherry Blossom*, played by Iben Nagel Rasmussen on the flute, and Kaj Bredholt in the upper register of the accordion. They are accompanied by Jan Ferslev on the ukulele, paraphrasing the figures he has developed over the German folk tune, *Ach du lieber Augustin*. To this web is added a contrasting melody to a text by Lorca, sung by Isabel Ubeda. A melody I first wrote more or less according to counterpoint rules, with *Cherry Blossom* as cantus firmus. However, the director found that the notes of my counterpoint ought to be longer, while those of cantus firmus should maintain their value. That would have caused the counterpoint to break down.

Somewhat annoyed by this, I further added the last phrase of *Before the Law*, 'He Won't Live Much Longer', which very well described my feelings for the director at the time. So the early versions came out rather odd. But something strange happened. As time went by, the individual elements came to make up a whole, and, as Joseph Fux wrote as early as 1725 in his book on counterpoint: *Gradus ad Parnassum*, '... why should I be doing so at this time when music has become almost arbitrary and composers refuse to be bound by any rules and principles, detesting the very name of school and law like death itself'.' We had hardly reached 'Die nie erhörten Klängen', but a sort of complexity that functioned in the theatrical context.

The River of Time

In *Kaosmos*, a variety of sounds — popular songs, the door-keeper's magical shovel monochord, the banging of a door, cloth being ripped to pieces, the sound of an old clock — form a symphonic structure that lasts for an hour and twenty minutes. At that point, viewers and actors descend into Heraclit's river, the river that you can descend into only once, because the forward movement of time keeps changing its course, so that the next time you descend, it will be into another river. But the performance itself can create the illusion of the same river, because the performance appears to be the same night after night, and because of the floating condition of time.

'Mythos'

The river of time also flows through the performance of *Mythos*; it unites with the stillness of the ocean in the sound of the stones that are pushed around to produce the sound of ocean waves, or the sand of the beach, the hiss of the star plunging into the ocean, the wind above the waves. In the beginning, before the performance had found its final shape, the sound of the stones annoyed the audience. It was a disturbing element that drowned the dialogue or singing of the actors. It was not until after we had worked on it for quite some time that the recalcitrant material yielded and turned into a kind of music of coincidence. Music constantly balancing on the brink of chaos, because the thousands of stones of different materials, shapes, and weights can never be forced to behave in exactly the same way each time, and because the white noise they make also balances somewhere close to chaos. Yet, chaos has been brought under sufficient control to represent the actual sound of the ocean, a sound that is both reassuring and threatening at the same time.

The Ocean of Overtones

An ocean of overtones produced by the actors floats above the murmur of the ocean of stones. One of the challenges the company had to meet when rehearsing Mythos was that all the actors had to learn to sing overtones. Overtones are very precisely defined, and represent, contrary to the stones, a high degree of organisation. They can be measured and read, but it takes quite a lot of skill to sing them. Overtones are the barely audible secondary harmonic tones that accompany the primary tone of a person, and they make it possible to distinguish between the various vowels of a language. If one develops the right technique, it is possible to make the overtones come out stronger than the primary tone. They sound like a clear, true, flute tone coming from an indefinable position in the room. That is why they come to represent an ocean of overtones in the play.

The Revolution

One of the themes at the heart of Mythos is the wreck of the twentieth-century dream of a just society, and a number of the old revolutionary songs were taken off the shelf and dusted off for the play. The soldier marches, singing 'Brothers, let your weapons flash …', until the song is drowned by the overtones of the ocean of time. The *Internationale* crops up as a leitmotiv; it refuses to die, and plays itself over humanity so devastated and lost. These tunes have not been changed much, but have been allowed to stand as they are, in the midst of the manipulated sound of stones, overtones and polyphonic songs.

Medea, Cassandra and Daedalus

Iben Nagel Rasmussen, as Medea, performs songs that she brought to the play herself. The director handed her a number of texts by Henrik Nordbrandt, the Danish poet, which she adapted to tunes she had written herself or heard elsewhere. Similarly, Roberta Carreri and Julia Varley compose their songs by adapting texts to music that they provide themselves. This leaves it to the composer to organise the songs, working with the director. He must find a key that fits in with the rest of the performance and, in this context, puts the songs to a thematic treatment. Roberta Carreri has based several of her songs on reconstructions of early Greek music, to achieve an archaic tone that suits the mythological character she represents. Naturally, no one knows what the music sounded like in ancient Greece; after all, our musical notation is only a thousand years old. But, by combining some of what Pythagoras wrote, for instance, and the music known from that part of the Mediterranean, we get an impression of the music. We coupled that music with new texts, and that is how a number of Cassandra's songs in *Mythos* arose.

Orpheus

Some of the songs in *Mythos* are texts by Henrik Nordbrandt, set to music by Jan Ferslev. We have given the songs the titles, *Little Morning Prayer*, *The Road Sign of the Dead*, and *Each of One's Fishes*. They have been given a flowing rhythmic accompaniment performed on a South American armadillo guitar. The composer has added upper and lower voices to the songs.

Did I Sail the Seas

A little tune emerged spontaneously as Torgeir Wethal and I were working on overtones. The other actors learned the tune, and texts were added. Then, Eugenio Barba introduced a text by the Turkish poet, Yunus Emre, that had been translated by Henrik Nordbrandt, and I was asked to adapt the text and melody. Later on, I added counterpoint parts, so we ended up with a long piece of music that plays while carved-off hands are being placed in patterns on the stones, and a merry five-part love song is performed. The love song can be heard from all angles, because each part has a quality of its own that is complemented by the other parts; this is very much like a prism, which can also be seen from all angles, but radiates light in different ways, depending on the location from which you look at it.

[From Kaosmos to Mythos]

As Odin has moved from *Kaosmos* to *Mythos*, it has also moved from extensive use of popular songs towards music created directly as part of — and for — specific performances. Odin now allows the music more scope to live a life of its own, on its own terms, but the music does not escape the regularities of the theatre. 'Each time has its time and its music; time passes through the ears. And the music has room for remaining in motion, much like the eternal circulation of the pointer on a dial.'

Translation: Martin Torp Larsen & Anne Kirstein

Elin Andersen

[A Doll's House]
Odin Meets Ibsen

The actors *Roberta Carreri* and *Torgeir Wethal* have asked themselves about whether their experience from working with Odin Teatret can be translated to other forms of aesthetics. For example, to a (an approximate) naturalistic style that at first seems to be much more than merely distant from the aesthetics they have cultivated throughout the years with Odin Teatret. Furthermore, they have chosen a scene from a text that throughout the 20th century has been the very essence of naturalism on the stage: Henrik Ibsen's *A Doll's House* from 1879. They have chosen to base their work on the very last lines, copies of which they distribute to the audience from the original in Norwegian (Wethal's background) and in an Italian translation (Carreri's background). They read as follows (Ibsen 1961, III, 4):

NORA	… I can at any rate free you from all responsibility. You must not feel in any way bound, any more than I shall. There must be full freedom on both sides. Look, here's your ring back. Give me mine.
HELMER	That too?
NORA	That too.
HELMER	There it is. …….
NORA	Well, that's the end of that. I'll put the keys down here. The maids know where everything is in the house — better than I do, in fact. Kristine will come in the morning after I've left to pack up the few things I brought with me from home. I want them sent on.
HELMER	The end! Nora, will you never think of me?
NORA	I dare say I'll often think about you and the children and this house.
HELMER	May I write to you, Nora?
NORA	No, never. I won't let you.
HELMER	But surely I can send you …
NORA	Nothing, nothing.
HELMER	Can't I help you, if ever you need it?

NORA	I said 'no'. I don't accept things from strangers.
HELMER	Nora, can I never be anything more to you than a stranger?
NORA	(*takes her bag*). Ah, Torvald, only by a miracle of miracles …
HELMER	Name it, this miracle of miracles!
NORA	Both you and I would have to change to the point where … Oh, Torvald, I don't believe in miracles any more.
HELMER	But I *will* believe. Name it! Change to the point where …?
NORA	Where we could make a real marriage of our lives together. Goodbye! (*She goes through the hall door*)
HELMER	(*sinks down on a chair by the door, and covers his face with his* hands.) Nora! Nora! (*He rises and looks round.*) Empty! She's gone! (*With sudden hope.*) The miracle of miracles …? (*The heavy sound of a door being slammed is heard from below.*)

Why not choose a scene where the dramatic element is in play, where the 'Italian' is in the foreground such as for example Nora's tarantella dance dressed as the Neapolitan fisher lass. Why this down-to-earth but fateful final scene where the role playing and subtlety are apparently completely gone and they are speaking in 'clear text'?

To this question the actors respond that they simply started at the end. And this is not such a bad idea, considering that Ibsen himself often began here. His first notes on *A Doll's House,* for example, began with an idea for a contemporary tragedy.

Before I devote myself to their work on the scene I must take a detour. For, however matter-of-fact the actors go about choosing their starting point, we cannot avoid the fact that it is precisely this final scene that has made *A Doll's House* controversial. Both as literature and as performed drama. It has given rise to a certain amount of speculation as to what kind of drama *A Doll's House* is and what kind of a woman Nora represents.

Is *A Doll's House* a comedy with the wrong ending: a divorce instead of a marriage? (Kott 1980). Or is it a tragedy with Nora as a Greek heroine of modern vintage? (Northam 1960). When she leaves the doll's house wrapped in her black shawl, she steps into a melancholic exile where there is nothing left but the hope that a miracle will put an end to it. Or maybe it is a love tragedy, or at least a love drama, namely the swan song for a courtly love illusion from which both she and Helmer under pressure go (Bredsdorff 1985).

No way, will others say. Nora, with her rhetoric of emancipation and her break from the doll's house here in the final scene, was and still is an ideal for female emancipation (Templeton 1989). She comes to represent a liberated utopian force in the women's movement. Nora's concern is not feminism, but humanism, still others will say. Ibsen does not send her out into society completely at random. She has been given the best ballast a person can have: autonomy. She has been given the capability to distinguish essential things and the courage to think and believe in things other than that which is accepted. She is an emancipated individual in the modern existential sense (Østerud 1994).

These are but few of the interpretations to which the final scene in particular has given rise in the Ibsen literature.

[A question of credibility]

But the final scene has also created problems in the stage history of *A Doll's House*. The world's first Nora was a Dane named Betty Hennings. At the time of the premiere of *A Doll's House* at the Royal Theatre in Copenhagen, she was the very image of a late-romantic bourgeois school-girl ideal on the stage. Coquette, but chaste and totally unaware of her erotic charm. It is precisely this child/woman image with which Ibsen wished to settle accounts in *A Doll's House*. But Betty Hennings played Nora according to the classic romantic type of role in which she was educated, i.e. as the *ingenue*, keeping her childlike nature until the very end of the performance, opposite a just as full-blooded late-romantic actor in the role of Helmer, namely, Emil Poulsen. The world premiere of *A Doll's House* naturally reached just as much backwards to the 19th century romantic idealistic stage tradition as forwards towards the 20th century realism that did not yet exist on the stage. It was not completely off the mark when Strindberg called Nora a romantic monster in the preface to *Giftas*, his parody on *A Doll's House*, in 1884. The Russian theatre pedagogue Konstantin Stanislavsky has more than anyone else become the theorist and practitioner of naturalism throughout a life-long career that began in the 1890s. It was not, however, until after World War Two that Stanislavsky's more extensive work on actor training and the actor's creative work on his or her role became known in Scandinavia and gained influence in the educational programmes for actors. Before then we could not speak of the creation of a tradition of psychological realism, and certainly not an ideal of interpretation based on Stanislavsky's complex unity of scenic theory, method and acting. At the same time it is to this ideal that *A Doll's House* and other contemporary dramas by Ibsen have been connected. The aim is not only to create a richly faceted portrait of Nora and her co-actors, but also a psychologically realistic and credible portrait. This necessitates in particular the creation of a logic of psychological development from the first scene to the last, so that Nora does not end up merely as the dramatist's mouthpiece or as a purely idealistic figure of emancipation. The secret is thus to portray Nora as the very same Nora while she at the same time also becomes someone quite different; to make the Nora who, like a skylark, chirrups and frisks through a number of role plays and lies to get what she wants, harmonise with the woman who breaks away from her previous life and leaves her husband and children. In the course of time dramaturgists, producers, interpreters and the like have made many attempts to create this coherence for the actress who seeks psychological consistency in the character. This is probably most successful in productions that concentrate on Nora's inner tensions, which is what Ibsen does in the text. In moments of solitude she exorcises her desperate anxiety for Krogstad's disclosure:

> Candles here ... and flowers here. — Revolting man! It's all nonsense! There's nothing to worry about. (I, 5)
> Rubbish — nobody's going to come. I mustn't think about it. Brush this muff. Pretty gloves, pretty gloves! I'll put it right out of my mind. One, two, three, four five, six ... (II, 1)

And her anxiety grows into desperation and thoughts of suicide as Krogstad penetrates deeper and deeper into the idyll of *A Doll's House*. She is no longer afraid of her secret about the loan and forgery being discovered, for she sees it as a heroic gift of love: the money meant that they could travel to the South and that Helmer's life was saved. At the same time she is certain that Helmer will step forward and take the blame and put his whole professional career at risk. And this thought is at once wonderful and terrible. Such a testimony of love she can only repay with her own life. Her desperation culminates when Helmer has gone in to read the fatal letter from Krogstad.

> NORA (*gropes around her, wild-eyed, seizes Helmer's cloak, wraps it round herself, and whispers quickly, hoarsely, spasmodically*). Never see him again. Never, never, never. (*Throws her shawl over her head.*) And never see the children again either. Never, Never. Oh, that black icy water. Oh, that bottomless ...! (III, 3)

When Helmer accuses her instead of being a hypocrite and a liar, she realises that she was on the point of committing suicide for all the wrong reasons. It is this rude awakening that is to motivate her *anagnorisis,* which has even been called a paradigm shift (Ibsen 1985). The portrait of Nora that masters the balance between the acting, coquetry and desperate anxiety and thus wins the spectator's sympathy can count on the spectator the rest of the way. Even if Nora does 'outdo' herself in insightfulness and activeness in the finale.

It is this type of consideration that arises and resounds the moment the actors take possession of the text. To create a *tabula rasa* is hardly possible with a text such as *A Doll's House*, no matter how selectively one works with it.

[Dialogue in space]

They begin memorising the lines in a neutral fashion, Wethal in Norwegian and Carreri in Italian. They mark the course of Nora's definitive farewell: First her liberation, when she returns the tokens of their union and marriage, the ring and the keys; then a hasty dialogue in which Helmer makes his last attempt to make her stay and Nora consistently refuses; again, it is a question of the *miracle of miracles*, but merely as a discarded illusion that still manages to infuse new hope in Helmer, and finally the famous boom from the door being slammed. At this point they put aside the text and begin improvising a series of physical actions that are to result in a physical score for the part. One could speak of an approach to Stanislavsky's *method of physical actions* that he developed in his training of actors in the 1920s. In short, it entails improvising independent physical actions arising from the situation surrounding the role, not as an illustration of the lines and always within the universe of the role. They arise out of the unity of the role. Carreri, from now on 'Nora', and Wethal, from now on 'Helmer', work parallel but separately with these scores. It is characteristic for them both that they create a picture that motivates the individual action. 'Nora', dressed in a 1950's coat and carrying a handbag and an old-fashioned sports bag, practises walking as though — she comments — she is 'on thin ice', 'out of her depth', 'traipsing through mud' with a 'heart as heavy as lead' and a 'cool head'. All the while 'Helmer' sits somewhere else in the room, dressed in distinguished brown trousers, an open waistcoat and a tie. Using a minimum of bodily expression he improvises a 'Helmerian' life story in reverse, from old age to the middle-aged bank manager, back to the young man and finally the boy. This directly refers to Helmer's situation. For this is certainly a great shock to Helmer: the moment when one's life stands still or flashes by in a second. 'Helmer' suggests this physically. However, as opposed to Nora, Helmer does not understand what is happening. The sensitive person that he *also* is, he is completely destroyed. This at least seems to be the idea behind the illustrations of actions with which 'Helmer' is working. 'He uses form to keep his head above water', Wethal comments, and practises a 'skylark song' out of tune, only moving at a short radius from his chair. At one point he tears the script into pieces and is going to burn it on the floor(!) but returns to the chair and to his point of departure. He continues the minimalist, suppressed expression, vacillating between a stiff body and a voice that breaks off when he holds his loose tie to his mouth during the line '... can I never be anything more to you than a stranger?' 'Nora' occupies a larger space and has little by little integrated voice, physical actions and text using this space. She stops in front of the imaginary 'Helmer', puts down her sports bag, lifts up her hands and looks at her wrists 'as though they had just been released from handcuffs', catches sight of the ring and takes it off during the lines about full freedom and the exchange of rings. 'Nora' says that she gives him the ring like 'a dead skylark'. She then takes the keys out of her handbag while she 'gazes around at the things she's taking with her, smells the atmosphere of the home'. She removes herself rhythmically during Helmer's attempts to keep contact, bends her knees a little when speaking of the children. She returns and falls to her knees in front of him, bows her head and says: 'Ah, Torvald, only by a miracle of miracles'. She gets up resolutely during the following exchange, 'I don't believe in miracles any more', takes both bags and leaves with a short goodbye.

They act through this exchange many times, still back to back and with the other as an imaginary co-actors. But they do this synchronously, and explain their odd form of dialogue as a means of occupying a larger space before turning to face each other and acting together. They do this at the end, with perfect timing. This time we hear the boom of the 'door' slamming behind Nora and witness a short sequel with Helmer. Left alone he starts to light his cigar but the match goes out.

[Action images]

Roberta Carreri and Torgeir Wethal underline time after time that they have not worked with the scene for very long and that it can turn out very differently. But their method is obvious enough. We can thus — without being mutually bound — reason about the possibilities that might arise in their work in respect to a hypothetical staging of *A Doll's House*.

In a more traditional staging, the actor works on acquiring the text mentally, so that she understands its meaning and feelings, and physically, so that the words become her own. It is the text in the actor that decides which expression the role will have in the end. This is a working method that has lead to many excellent results. Carreri and Wethal go a different way. They also work close to the text and as a rule closer than is usually the custom in Odin Teatret. But they insert a metaphor between themselves and the text, an image that they can transform directly into a physical action on which they can continue to work. The metaphor springs from the text, the text is reconnected to the action, and new actions for the text appear in this exchange. This can create a certain tension between the physical actions and the words and can give new and unexpected plays on meaning if they succeed in integrating thought, idea and feeling as well as the physical in their acting. Odin Teatret's actors reluctantly speak of feelings but willingly of technique. At the same time they play to an extreme degree on the spectator's emotional identification with the feelings expressed in their productions. Also here, at the level of the work-in-progress, where everything is still on a back burner, one can sense that through their scores they especially seek access to emotional layers in their roles. When 'Nora' imagines that she is handing a dead skylark to Helmer instead of a ring, she gives this gesture a special degree of ambivalence. This is adapted to the basic physical attitude of ambivalence she practised at the beginning: 'to walk as though on thin ice, with a heart as heavy as lead and a cool, clear head'. With her method, the stage is set for her to undauntedly play a seldom seen Nora in this the final scene. For even the best renderings of Nora, which brilliantly master the balance between the coquette and the desperate Nora until the turning point in Act III, often end by being too composed and too unambiguous in their liberation at the end. Here we glimpse other possibilities. The same is true for 'Helmer'. For him the stage is set for an emotional vulnerability that is seldom seen in the newly appointed manager at the joint-stock bank. It seems as though they are on the trail of some contrasts in the text that are not usually given the opportunity to surface.

[Reversed comedy]

The problem is of course that it is not only Nora who experiences an immense turning point in her life, but the whole drama that reverses itself most emphatically. From being a comedy with an intrigue based on cheque forgery and blackmail from Act I to the middle of Act III, the drama loses its interest in this type of thriller effect and becomes a serious drama with a thesis of emancipation. It is a collision of genres for which the perspective of realism cannot really make room. But on the other hand it is interesting. The Polish critic Jan Kott is very much aware of this type of collision in Ibsen (Kott 1980). In *The Wild Duck*, for example, the characters in a bourgeois comedy are set to perform a tragedy. And of course it goes awry. In *A Doll's House* Ibsen turns the sign of tragedy and comedy around. Here the total disintegration of a marriage and the wife's departure from the home turn, for the first time in the history of drama, into the happy-ending of a comedy. In the comedy and the tragedy alike it is the *recognition scene* that leads to the final resolution of the conflicts in a climax. A brother and a sister recognize each other beneath their masks in the Elektra tragedies. In the mistaken-identity comedies spouses recognize each other in this type of scene. But in the recognition scene in *A Doll's House* the husband Helmer becomes a stranger to Nora, a stranger with whom she no longer can stay under the same roof. Kott latches onto the *tarantella*, the spider's dance that Nora is to dance disguised as a Neapolitan fisher lass at the masked ball. In folklore this dance symbolizes the intense flaring up of life just before death. And this is how Nora experiences it in the scene where she practises the tarantella under Helmer's instruction and to Dr. Rank's accompaniment while Kristine looks on open-mouthed. She dances more and more wildly and does not hear Helmer's remarks until:

HELMER	But my dear darling Nora, you are dancing as though your life depended on it.
NORA	It does.
HELMER	Stop, Rank! This is sheer madness. Stop, I say.
	(Rank *stops playing* and Nora *comes to a sudden halt.*) (II, 7)

In the comedy — in Shakespeare for example — the disguise often symbolizes a time of disorder, a time of sexual liberties and purely momentarily *lost* identity. But what happens here? Helmer sees a new Nora during the dance, a Nora with a new and frightening identity. Here the disguise does not hide an identity as it normally does, but reveals it instead. Again the reversed sign of a comedy and the most important according to Kott. In his eyes, the tarantella is a Dionysian dance that makes the rhetoric of emancipation fade. And he brings forward the suggestion that it is this new Nora that Helmer fears and will no longer allow to stay in the doll's house. A point of view that deserves careful consideration. And it may give a lopsided twist to the drama if it is followed through to its logical end, because it shifts the relation between Nora and Helmer too markedly.

[Or melodrama?]

But we can elaborate Kott's idea about sudden changes of identity instead of focussing on the demand of logical development in the realistic tradition. This is at the same time a point of view that agrees with new readings of *A Doll's House* in the 1990s (Østerud; Aslaksen 1997). Nora and the drama transform in a flash, as we have seen. So do the other characters. Instead of persuading the pure villain of the drama (Krogstad) to give up his blackmailing, his friend and helper Kristine Linde proposes to him. This in turn causes Krogstad to suddenly change from being a cynical blackmailer to a repentant sinner, even though he is as far from reaching his original goal of restoring his middle-class standing and respect as he ever was. 'How things change!' Kristine exclaims (III, 1) when he, happy, leaves the drama. And we must certainly agree with her. As far as I know, Helmer's changes have never been understood as anything but expressions of pettiness, hypocrisy and self pity. In Act III he maintains yet again that he will risk everything for Nora's sake. And then goes in to read the letters while Nora waits, terrified. Suddenly he flings open his door and stands there with Krogstad's letter in his hand and shouts: 'Nora!' — and all hell breaks loose: 'All these eight years ... this woman who was my pride and joy ... a hypocrite, and a liar ...' (III, 4). When the next letter arrives, in which Krogstad abandons his blackmail and returns the IOU, Helmer tears it open and exclaims with a shout of joy. 'Nora, I am saved!' (ibid.). Shortly afterward he tears both letters and the IOU into pieces. Naturally, his performance of this gesture here is deep irony on Ibsen's part, it belonging in another ritual, namely, the one that was supposed to be an expression of love, by which Helmer would take upon himself the responsibility for forging the signature. But his reactions are not really any different than those of the others. He reacts to his feelings spontaneously, as do the others to theirs.

In reality, the meaning of the great fluctuations, the unmotivated changes in direction, the letters and the tokens hardly belongs in a moderate naturalism, but rather in a mystical, allegorical drama or maybe best of all in a melodrama. The doll's house can of course by no means become a pure allegory or a naive melodrama. But it can undoubtedly pay to increase the volume of melodramatic feelings and changes in its meeting with the irony of the modern world. This would strengthen the contrasts in the drama rather than reconcile them as has traditionally been the goal. But maybe under this changeableness a Nora and a Helmer can come closer to a mode of existence and the condition of varying identities that seem to be the prerequisites for life in our culture here at the beginning of the 21st century. Maybe such a staging of *A Doll's House* could be a project for Odin Teatret. The theatre that has no more shrunk from melodramatic acting out than it has feared the irony of conflicts.

Odin Teatret in
A Doll's House in Aarhus
April 5, 2000:
Torgeir Wethal as
Helmer and Roberta
Carreri as Nora.
Photo: Jan Rüsz

References

Aslaksen, Kamilla 1997. Ibsen and Melodrama. In *Nordic Theatre Studies*, vol. 10, Gideå. 36-50.

Ibsen, Henrik 1961. *A Doll's House*. Translated by J. W. McFarlane in *The Oxford Ibsen* vol. V, London: O.U.P.

Ibsen, Henrik 1985. *Et Dukkehjem*. Translated by Thomas Bredsdorff, Copenhagen: Gyldendal.

Kott, Jan 1980. Motsatserna hos Ibsen. In *entré*, no.5, Solna.

Northram, John 1960. Ibsen's search for the hero. In *Edda*, Oslo.

Templeton, Joan 1989. *The Doll House Backlash: Criticism, Feminism, and Ibsen*. Wisconsin: PMLA.

Østerud, Erik 1994. Henrik Ibsens italienske karneval. *Visualitet og teatralitet i 'Et Dukkehjem'*. In *Masken som repræsentation* 1994, edited by Jørgen Østergaard and Charlotte Engberg, Aarhus: Aarhus Universitetsforlag.

Østerud, Erik 1997. *A Doll's House:* Ibsen's Italian Masquerade. In *Nordic Theatre Studies*, vol. 10, Gideå. 23-35.

Klaus Hoffmeyer

[Directing Shakespeare]

It was a great inspiration to watch the two actors (Tage Larsen and Julia Varley) from Odin Teatret working with *Othello*. Through the seemingly irrelevant physical gestures accompanying the text, they were able to eliminate a great many of the problems that I would have had to face, confronted with the usual psychological approach. With Odin, there was no previous analysis, no intellectual starting-point — there was a kind of innocent jumping into action, which might save a lot of time spent on dry discussions about 'why' and 'what'. Having admitted to that, I will start in my corner — the opposite corner — and I will do so without too much repentance, since I have spent some of the best rehearsals in my life working with Shakespeare.

One of the reasons why I went into theatre has to do with Shakespeare. But that's the case for many people. At any rate, I am determined to do all his plays before I die. The great advantage of Shakespeare is that everyone can join in the discussion of his work. He apparently liberates everyone. Intellectuals are, on the subject of Shakespeare, suddenly freed from their intellectualism, for Shakespeare is the poet at once belonging to 'fine art' and appealing to the people. We always assume that Shakespeare's plays had a wide popular appeal. They were, as we know, performed in a theatre where ordinary people stood in the stalls and watched. And we have a romantic idea that they threw tomatoes at the stage whenever they got bored. Everything the intellectuals find missing in the theatre of today — that people throw things at the actors — was found in Shakespeare, side by side with great poetry.

So all the fine ladies and gentlemen sat up in the boxes and flirted with each other, while the 'simple folk' stood down below with their tomatoes, as we theoretically can relive it in the rebuilt Globe Theatre in London. But when one actually reads Shakespeare, I often wonder how this noisy mob could have been quieted by the opening monologues. This fall, we put on *Love's Labour's Lost* at the Royal Theatre in Copenhagen. One of Shakespeare's earliest plays, called in Danish: *Kærlighedens Kværulanter*. Let us imagine that a wildly noisy audience is standing, tomatoes at the ready. In comes an actor and says:

Let fame, that all hunt after in their lives,
Live register'd upon our brazen tombs,
And then grace us in the disgrace of death
When, spite of cormorant devouring Time,
Th'endeavour of this present breath may buy
That honour which shall bate his scythe's keen edge,
And make us heirs of all eternity. (*Love's Labour's Lost*. London: Routledge 1990)

This is the first 15 seconds of the first speech in the play. A modern audience would ask to have it repeated. It is so complicated and full of information that one must either assume that the audiences of the time were brighter and quicker in the uptake — or that the tomatoes had already begun to rain on the stage.

Several of his plays begin with a monologue of that type. And that makes me doubt that this author really was so 'popular' in the ordinary meaning of the word. But he had the ability to give people, who may not entirely have understood the lines, a clear understanding that this has got to do with life and death.

Anyhow, I found it important to stop the action after this initiating monologue; so we let the actors ask one another a few questions about what the hell this was about, and after that they started all over again, but now the monologue was a bit more comprehensible, not so condensed. The point is: We cannot take it for granted that Shakespeare just moves, like some heat-seaking missile, automatically striking home to the audience of today. So we started by literally opening the text, splitting up the blank verse for a moment.

One of the reasons for making a dilemma of Shakespeare's opening monologue is that it has always fascinated me how Shakespeare is able to bring chaos onto the stage. He is able to bring the theatre close to a state where that which is clearly structured, stops being structured. There are breakdowns and mental collapses in all his works, and the temptation of playing him, I often think, is that, from one moment to another, that which one has just come to believe in is demobilised. I remember that we once tried to put music to one of his songs, in a performance I put on 20 years ago, and it was quite simply impossible for a composer to move as quickly as Shakespeare. As soon as he had positioned a melody, Shakespeare's language had moved somewhere else. That is to say that we are dealing with an utterly vibrating, maybe fundamental element of theatre, moving so quickly that only an actor can keep up. Only a work process prepared, on a second's warning, to give up the battlements just captured, can keep up.

That was the knowledge we used, when we demobilised the text at the beginning of *Love's Labour's Lost*, and let the actors ask each other what the words meant, and among other things, explain what kind of bird a cormorant is. Which made the audience realise that the whole stuff was actually to be debated. The language itself was open to debate, as it is, in reality, everywhere in Shakespeare. The poem mirrors the language, takes a position on the language; all his figures are linguistic talents in one way or another, capable of turning the language topsy-turvy. I shall return to the question of language later, when I again return to *Love's Labour's Lost*.

But at the moment I would like to take something up that I, at least, have had in my 'baggage' with regard to Shakespeare. I am referring to Artaud, whom I translated to Danish when I was still practically newborn. The book is called *Le théâtre et son double* (The Theater and its Double).While Brecht was, and is, part of the common intellectual baggage, Artaud is still so little known that one can with impunity be an observer of the theatre without having read him. I don't believe I know very many people who have read his book. It was published in French in 1938, and I translated it in 1967. And in it he writes, in a chapter titled 'No More Masterpieces':

> One of the reasons for the asphyxiating atmosphere in which we live [...] is our respect for what has been written, formulated, or painted, what has been given form, as if all expression were not at last exhausted, were not at a point where things must break apart if they are to start anew and begin fresh.
>
> We must have done with this idea of masterpieces reserved for a self-styled elite and not understood by the general public; the mind has no such restricted districts as those so often used for clandestine sexual encounters.
>
> The masterpieces of the past were good enough for the past; they are not good enough for us. We have the right to say what has already been said, and even what has not been said, in a way that belongs to us, which is immediate, direct, corresponding to present modes of feeling, and understandable to everyone (*The Theater and its Double*. New York: Grove Press 1958, 74).

As an example, Artaud uses Sophocles' *King Oedipus*, who makes use of 'a manner and language that have lost all touch with the rude and epileptic rhythm of our time'. Characteristically, the recent debate on the molestation of the classics in Denmark: 'Who owns the classics?' has gone on without any knowledge of the Artaudian and surreal tradition of modern theatre.

But I was very early absorbed by the idea of avoiding the well-known works, trying to outwit Shakespeare, sidetrack him, derail him.

The first thing I dreamed of doing, really dreamed of, back in the sixties, was *Titus Andronicus*. I even had a poet translate the whole play, after which I realised that I had no qualifications whatsoever for doing it. I had a vision of the actors leaning lazily against empty walls, and a whole pool of language would hang out of their mouths. And it would be punctured by totally mad, brutal physical actions that would completely derail and destroy the language they used. I realised too late that the necessary actors did not exist. Not yet. I had no access to the theatre I needed, or it had not yet been invented.

One of the reasons that I was taken by *Titus Andronicus* was not just that it was unknown. It was one of Shakespeare's first and most brutal pieces, which the humanistic Shakespeare-tradition may possibly have disregarded because it thinks that Shakespeare became wiser, since, of course, he became a humanist. So he left off the brutal stamp of his predecessors, and instead we saw the noble Shakespeare, who speaks his unforgettable lines.

At the same time, one turns on the television or opens the newspaper, and is struck by the epileptic rhythms surrounding the murder of Kennedy, where he is killed, and then his murderer; after which a third is murdered — exactly like the central scene in *Titus Andronicus,* where one of the two quarrelling parties serves a meat pie for friends and relations, after which they explain that the guests have now eaten their own relatives, whereupon there are four murders in a row. Before Kennedy, that kind of action was something one might not have thought appropriate in a proper theatre. Four murders in a row is a considerable number. But that is why this play had to be performed — the combination of the order of the language and the disorder of the action.

The first Shakespeare play I came to do was *As you like it*. It has an incredible, unpredictable action. At first glance, it may seem as if it is a fantasy more than a drama. It is a play that would hardly be accepted by a dramaturgic reading committee today. Because it is too wild; there is too much parallel action, too much disorder, and too many distractions. In drama today, we look for rationality, coherence, speed, and immediate recognition, because we are so inspired by television.

My main idea at that time was to look for the original physique of the drama. That is, not its spirit, but its body. Artaud again. My point of departure was the knowledge that the play was originally open-air theatre, and we were now to perform it in the Ålborg Theatre. How could we then shape the distraction, the disturbance of the text, so people didn't just sit there saying: 'Oh, yes, this is the famous text, *As you like it*, that we more or less all have in our baggage — it's one of his masterpieces'. I was now possessed by the desire to refute a masterpiece. I thought: If they sat in the open air, there must have been constant distractions. Gulls flying past, noise from the nearby inns, playing fields, and whatever else. There must have been some type of distraction, more or less similar to that of the classic Greek theatre, which was also open air theatre; and it must have resulted in a whole different way of listening than we know from our day's concentrated theatre, which easily becomes literature with a thin layer of theatre-varnish, because the text is taken for granted, and in a way just needs to be delivered in an agreed-upon language. So what we did was, quite simply, to interrupt the action at certain points, by having the actors run down among the audience and start selling things to them. A major part of the action is in the woods, and I had decided that it probably was a wood near Shakespeare's birthplace, Arden, close to Stratford. So we simply sold refreshments and a map of Arden Forest, so the audience could follow the geography of the mental digressions of the comedy.

There was a certain amount of controversy with the actors, since they were being forced to interrupt at the culmination points of the action. Obviously, Shakespeare would never have done that. So I knew very well that I was looking for trouble. But the purpose was to impose a destruction, a distraction, which would place the audience in a new relationship to this text. They were, in a manner of speaking, to fight to be allowed to listen. They were not just to hear it. One may call these methods externalities, but the interruptions actually did shape a renewed responsiveness, because people were forced to struggle to keep Shakespeare. They could not take him for granted.

I remember that the manager of the theatre was against the idea, and tried to talk me out of it: 'We don't understand that kind of theatre up here, north of the Liim Fiord'. I realised that there are many hidden borders in this country, but it helped that we were sold out for three weeks.

The set designer and I had another idea: we started in a traditional stage setting, with painted back cloths, just like the old days in the theatre; among other things, there was a gold frame on the back cloth, with a traditional landscape, which was thus hanging on the wall in the court of Duke Frederick, where the action, of course, begins. And at the shift from this scene to the woods, a whole prairie-wagon — one like you have in cowboy movies, when they ride across the plains — came through, simply ripping open the painting, as it, with a crash, drove directly onto the stage. The theatre painting was smashed, in favour of a more plastic and three-dimensional construction on stage. The wagon then became the starting point for the rest of the action.

Again an attempt to break with a kind of harmony, and giving the audience a more direct, physical idea of what it means to quit home — to tear something down, in order to emerge to something else.

One last thing I remember from that production was the epilogue, which had always irritated me, where the heroine, in a beautiful costume, comes out to the audience and says:

> I charge you, O women, for the love you bear to men, to like as much of
> this play as please you; and I charge you, O men, for the love
> you bear to women — as I perceive by your simp'ring none of you
> hates them — that between you and the women the play may please.
> If I were a woman, I would kiss as many of you as had beards that
> pleas'd me, complexions that lik'd me, and breaths that I defied

not; and, I am sure, as many as have good beards, or good faces,
or sweet breaths, will, for my kind offer, when I make curtsy,
bid me farewell.

These lines are Rosalind's, who in the course of the play has been disguised as a man, and now returns as a woman, — a shameless plea to the audience to thank us for the evening by clapping. And there we have a charming creature, usually one of the theatre's greatest actresses, who has spellbound everyone all evening, flirting for that applause. We had to prevent that; so after she had been casually dressed in boy's clothing all evening, she was now dressed by a chambermaid in the whole Elizabethan formal dress, so she became more and more prim and stuffy and destroyed and stiff, while she spoke her last lines. Thus vanished every trace of charm from them, except just the last bit you cannot take away from Ann-Mari Max Hansen.

Shakespeare is so sturdy that you can positively smash him, and he will still be Shakespeare. I will not take a position on all the post-modern stuff that has now appeared. I don't think there is any advantage in systematically interpreting everything into our times. If you ask me, I think it's a form of poverty. But there can be periods, and there were at that time, both in your own life and that of the theatre, when it is a necessary form of art to paint a moustache on Mona Lisa. It may be necessary because we have simply become blind and deaf to both Mona and Lisa. In any case, I do hate seeing masterpieces being taken for granted. I am still infected by Artaud on that point.

(After a review of *Macbeth* (The Danish Theatre, 1982) and *Comedy of Errors* [*Förväxlingar*, Malmö Hipp, 1995], Klaus Hoffmeyer returned to *Love´s Labour´s Lost*).

I began by saying that Shakespeare can apparently free us all. Everyone can refer to Shakespeare, and say: 'Now look: *He* did theatre the way *I* think theatre should be done.'

But the question is whether Shakespeare was *so* uncontroversial? *So* popular? I have seen *Hamlet* 8-9 times in Denmark. Each time, the critics suffer a kind of mild short-circuiting of the brain, for each time, they write: 'At last, a Hamlet just like you and me.' They are so relieved that the old monstrosity of a play communicates, that the theatre has again become popular, so they can keep their jobs, that they forget that they wrote the same thing last year and the year before. But I am not sure that Hamlet is just like you and me. Perhaps Shakespeare wrote the play because Hamlet is not like the rest of us?

To return to *Love's Labour's Lost*. It seems to have come as a chock to us all that this little-known play, bristling on all sides, appeals to quite a large audience. Maybe precisely because it bristles — bristles with language, and words, and nonsense. It is all talk, and there, the play somehow hits the spot in the year 2000, in studio-host paradise.

It's not just that the language is beautiful and fantastic and full of fantasy, but it is also a language that wreaks havoc on itself. It is a language that the characters use, either because they are so much in love that they must continuously talk about it — or because they are unable to love, but can only talk about it.

I think it's Beckett who has a sentence: 'It is not enough for them to have lived; they must also talk about it.' — That is very much what happens in this play. They talk and talk for want of better. Again, we have the doubleness: Shakespeare is famous for his language, but he also puts the language on trial. He uses it as a kind of barricade or barrier between the characters and the life they live.

I think it was important to get the actors — and many of them were very young — to try to take this language to themselves and make something of it. But for exactly the same reason, at the beginning of the performance, we immediately tried to make it clear to the audience: 'This is a play about language.' By breaking the lines to pieces, and, so to speak, distributing them to people. And letting the actors stand and scratch their heads, and speculate: 'Are we saying this, or are we saying that?' And the interruptions that took place in the course of the performance were of the same type. An attempt, at two different moments, to make the language belong, and make it homeless. That is, take it to us, and then throw it away. I think it is almost always a question of finding the motion of the material that makes it fun to work with Shakespeare — but also madly difficult. Because in reality, the actors, as some English actors can, were to make this language sound completely natural. And it is not natural, as you could hear in the opening monologue quoted above.

I think that the knowledge that language can function as a derailing is something that we should have been able to take with us from the theatre of the absurd. A knowledge we should have brought with us from all of modernism; and that is where Shakespeare's earlier plays may suddenly have a potential: the language does not just translate the psychology, but the language is precisely what the play is about — that is what makes the play interesting to do right now. The elusive and somewhat faithless relationship to all psychology, inherent in language, and consequently, in the characters.

These are some of the viewpoints that I find missing in the recent theatre debate on why and how the classics should be done. Maybe a certain amount of amorality is lacking in those who have taken part in the debate — a little knowledge of Artaud, of modernism, of theatre? Because you can begin to do theatre in whatever corner of the world you want. But you can't do it, if you take anything at all for granted. Least of all the text.

Morten Kyndrup

[**Mythos**]
Text and Performance

A dedicated admirer of Henrik Nordbrandt's poetry. This is how I would characterize myself without hesitation. I am the kind of person who has bought every book Nordbrandt has written over the past 20 years, preferably on the very day of publication. I have read his poems over and over again, above all as a reader or user, i.e. for private reasons and out of sheer joy. Very seldom and only parenthetically have I written about Nordbrandt's poetry on a professional basis.

I am also a great admirer of Odin Teatret's work over the years. Of course that love has been practised more irregularly — a theatre performance cannot just be taken from your bookshelf whenever you feel like watching it. But Odin Teatret has given me many great theatre experiences with its breathtaking bombardment of the senses, at one and the same time self-contained and insistently addressing. Odin Teatret is indeed apostrophic theatre. It is theatre in terms of theatre and is what I have elsewhere called a theatre of heterophony.[1] I shall return to that below.

All in all: An Odin Teatret performance based on Henrik Nordbrandt's texts ought to be the artwork of my dreams. Perhaps best compared with sleeping with two beautiful women at the same time, which is said to be the dream of any man.

I must admit that it has not been as easy or simple as a happy dream to carry out this work in reality (and the dream about the two beautiful women probably would not have been either). The combination of Odin Teatret and Henrik Nordbrandt is neither unproblematic nor self-evident. Already the fact that Henrik Nordbrandt's art is poetry and Odin Teatret's art is theatre makes it difficult: We are dealing with diverse art forms and thus with different fundamentally aesthetic strategies. Also taken individually, however, there are pronounced differences between the aesthetic strategies and constructions of their respective artistic expressions.

In order to understand these differences and their interplay it has been necessary for me to distinguish the perspectives. To begin with I shall outline a couple of features of text and theatre and representation in general; then I shall briefly characterize Henrik Nordbrandt's poetical universe by way of a couple of examples so as to outline its aesthetical distinctiveness; subsequently, I shall discuss the text of *Mythos*, and, finally, I shall deal with *Mythos*, with the performance as a whole including the text and a comparison with Henrik Nordbrandt's aesthetic universe in order to uncover and discuss differences and similarities.

[Theatre and texts]

By and large there are two different types of relationship between text and theatre.

One is the relation you find in so-called traditional theatre. Here the relation between text and theatre is what might be called Platonic. The texts always exist prior to the theatre performance (fig. 1).

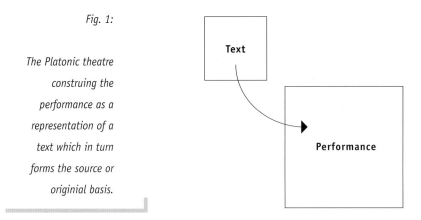

Fig. 1:

The Platonic theatre construing the performance as a representation of a text which in turn forms the source or originial basis.

The performance is the 'representation' of the text, it becomes a version 'of' this text (among other possible or perhaps real versions). This brings about an understanding of the text as something which is present 'before' the performance also in an ontological sense, of the texts as something more original, more genuine, as something possessing a more primary existence. This understanding engenders a certain mode of reception. Because a text like that, one would think, stems from an idea, from an author's idea. The mode of reception thus takes the form of a decoding, of a reversed genealogy. On the basis of the performance, you go backwards through the texts, the idea, the author in order to reconstruct some sort of original meaning, often assuming the shape of an estimation of intentionality. In the case of *Mythos* this understanding or mode of reception may be construed as in fig. 2.

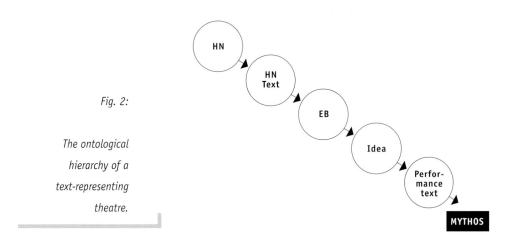

Fig. 2:

The ontological hierarchy of a text-representing theatre.

We have a poet, Henrik Nordbrandt, who has written a number of texts; one day Eugenio Barba encounters these texts, and on the basis of this encounter Barba has an idea and creates a text which results in the performance *Mythos*. In that sense *Mythos* is a representation of Henrik Nordbrandt and his poems. It is a version of them, so to speak, and consequently the relation between the poems and *Mythos* is understood as a relation between original (Nordbrandt) and interpretation (Barba, Odin Teatret, the performance).

But there is also what one might call non-Platonic or non-representing theatre (fig. 3).

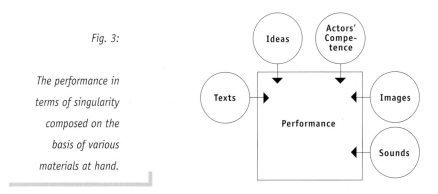

Fig. 3:

The performance in terms of singularity composed on the basis of various materials at hand.

111

LIVERPOOL JOHN MOORES UNIVERSITY
LEARNING SERVICES

Here the text is a part of the performance in terms of material on a par with any other kind of material: artistic techniques, the actors' individual competencies, ideas and intentions both on the micro and the macro level, pictures, sounds and so on and so forth. This material is indeed to some extent present before the performance; but here 'genealogically before' does not mean 'ontologically before'. By no means does material which comes into being during the working process have a lower status than that which might have existed before.

This understanding of theatre sees the performance as a singularity. Not as something which is the representation of something else, of something which comes after something else, which is a version of something else. No, the performance is what it is: itself. But furthermore it is above all a singularity *doing* something, something which points *forward* to its own competence and doing, rather than backwards to what it might *be*.

Roughly speaking, this is a distinction between supreme being as opposed to supreme doing. Whereas the pole of being is associated with something authentic, something pre-existing, with some transcendental being to which expressions refer or in which they partake, the pole of doing is linked with reception, with impact, with the view that the act of signification is singular, an acknowledgement of it as an act of engendering something. Whereas the pole of being refers to ontological hierarchies, the pole of doing gives birth to rather pragmatic hierarchies.

These basic types do not exist in pure versions. Furthermore, it is important to emphasize that they exist both as modes of understanding and as modes of creation, i.e. as types of reception and as types of artworks. Moreover, they may be mixed. Works conceiving themselves as primarily referring to being may be acknowledged against themselves, so to speak, in their singular doing. And vice versa. This may result in disastrous misunderstandings and of course in deliberate misreadings with fine perspectives.

Before turning to Nordbrandt I shall close this section with just one remark: In its aesthetics Odin Teatret is an eminent example of the 'doing type', of non-text-representing, non-Platonic theatre. Should one try to construe Odin Teatret as a text or intentionality-representing theatre, one would be wrong.

[Henrik Nordbrandt's texts]

What characterises Henrik Nordbrandt's poetical universe? This question cannot of course be answered exhaustively in just three words. I shall only point out three different, important issues which will subsequently be exemplified in a couple of Nordbrandt poems. These three issues will hopefully suffice for this purpose.

The first issue addresses the levels of metaphors and it deals with what might be called their ontological entangling. The second issue addresses the peculiar constructions of enunciation of the poems. And the third issue deals with the concrete wording of the poems, especially metaphors and the mutual linkages or bridges.

The first example is 'Eftersomre' (late summers), from *Udvalgte digte* (1981).

Eftersomre

Jeg kommer fra eftersomre af udefinerlig melankoli
lange som klavertimer i fraflyttede forstæder
hvor facaderne ikke længere kan bære husenes mørke
og folk er blevet gengangere i deres egne øjne.

Hvor østenvinden hærger gårdene som en gal mand
der skraber sine knogler rene med en rusten kniv
og falder om på jorden med en lyd som Mongoliet
og hver solbeskinnet mur afslutter et helt århundrede.

Hvor blå aftener synger tomme brønde gennem hjertet
og hver skygge er en faldlem i et kirkegulv
og hvor jeg indhenter min ventende skikkelse på hvert hjørne

og går videre, lidt trættere, tynget af et nyt tab
uden at vide helt præcist, hvad jeg kommer fra
eller hvad det er, jeg har søgt så meget, at jeg har tabt det.

I shall now briefly illustrate the first issue and the levels of metaphors. The poem starts with an 'I' situated at a sort of level of reality (b1) related at first to another level of late summers (b2), which is then compared with piano lessons (b3) in empty suburbs (b4). From here the b4 level, the suburbs, is elaborated until finally compared with a mad man (b5) collapsing, in turn linked to Mongolia (b6) before turning back to the level of the suburbs (b4). Now this level continues all the way up to the last line but four, where the elaborated b4 level is suddenly linked to the level of reality (b1). Suddenly the 'I' becomes a part of a level of metaphor which itself was the picture of a picture of a picture. At this level the 'I' ends and the poem's point is revealed. As a reader you do not spontaneously note anything strange about this entangling of the levels. The significations of the levels of metaphors are discretely being rotated into each other. But strictly speaking there is a kind of ontological short circuit between the levels, a sort of anacoluthon of being, one might say. This very figure is incredibly fundamental to Nordbrandt's entire aesthetic universe. Different worlds with different references within different logical orders are being forced together. The speaking I penetrates all levels, all worlds, has them at its disposal, so to speak.

This is also apparent in the other poem 'Midsommerdigt' from *84 digte* (1984).

Midsommerdigt

Hvis havene i dette øjeblik er blå
og sletterne flimrer grågult

går den tungeste tid til gengæld
hurtigst i platantræets skygge.

Torvene sover i middagsheden
som døde heste med benene i vejret.

Brøndene sover i sletten.

Kun et sejl langt ude på havet
viser, at verden bevæger sig.

Fra platantræets mørke krone
falder små ting ned på mit bord.

Jeg gider ikke samle dem op.
Man skal ikke føje unødig vægt

til sit eget fald. Det er tungt nok.

Here, in turn, the 'level of reality' is transformed into a picture, into metaphor, through the movement of the poem from the great perspective of the outer world — the seas, the plains — by way of the a-logical or oxymoron-like linking to the time in the shade of the plane tree ('on the other hand'), on to a series of flapping pictures (squares like dead horses, wells asleep), and finally to its flamboyant zoom in on the 'I' that is falling and the screaming litotes of the last sentence: Heavy enough.

It is a common feature of Nordbrandt's poems that they lead us around in striking references to the world, basically establishing a grand or vertiginous opening that is sooner or later suddenly switched off by the flap of a closure, offering monstrous linkages accepted by us as a matter of course.

Nordbrandt's poetic universe is distinctly hypotactical, i.e., it plays with the problematics of superiority and inferiority, with the relation between primary and secondary levels, with levels being metaphors for other levels that in turn engender new ones. This is anything but a flattened out ontology; this is rather an almost vertiginous ambiguity. Further, there is a touch of idleness in the poems, a sense of something being said different from what is actually being said, not in terms of a parabasis of irony or sarcasm, but precisely in terms of uselessness or powerlessness. At one and the same time there is something ostentatious, i.e. something demonstrative, challenging, something like 'I will' in the exposition of the poems, yet on the other hand something distractedly averted or casual, a sense of 'I will not' or 'cannot' do this. Both these features are found in one and the same voice. It is inherent in the very intonation, at one and the same time signalling that it intends to say everything and that it will not and cannot do this anyhow — by means of which it may actually happen to do it.

The poem is a link from a here and now to something much greater. The poem is for and by one and only one voice. It works in various scales by means of various levels of metaphors and various orders of being, but always in only one voice.

There is nothing Platonic or representational or referential in Henrik Nordbrandt's aesthetic universe. The access is fixed by the presence of the speaking I, whose apotheosis is at that very moment the point into which the poem is flapped together. To a reader that moment of the poem is his or her moment. The enunciation is evident and pure. This is thought of and said by someone; indeed, this is recited. The poems are clearly in an addressing mode and they are singular. But they themselves contain their own signification. They claim no other or greater being than the one they might engender.

[Mythos and the text]

Mythos includes cuts from Henrik Nordbrandt's poems. Cuts in many shapes, some comprising several lines, others consisting of single words. We even find passages composed on the basis of different poems. This means that all the characters in the performance *Mythos* recite Nordbrandt's words among other things. Now, does that imply that the text of *Mythos* is like a Henrik Nordbrandt text? Does that imply that the characters are some sort of Nordbrandt voice in the same sense as the voice in a Nordbrandt poem? Without hesitation these questions may be answered with a clear No.

The similarity between the aesthetic universe of Nordbrandt and the text in *Mythos* is only present in connection with one of the three issues above, namely, that of the single words. These, however, are abundant and many of them of great beauty. And they certainly imply examples of Nordbrandt's linking of metaphorical levels or enunciative twists or dialogue directly from Nordbrandt's poems.

Aesthetically, however, they are used in a completely different way here. The words and the linkages are recited by fictional characters placed within a fictional frame with its own time, its own concerns, and its own supreme aesthetic strategy. This means that each and every expression is just an expression among other expressions; that is, each expression refers to and plays along with the other expressions of the performance. Consequently, the words become much more concrete and much more referential (within the fiction). In other words, a kind of de-symbolization or de-metaphorisation takes place, because each individual expression also refers to something outside its own self-containing context, yet within a supreme aesthetic construction. It is not like that in a poem. In a poem the expression inside the poem refers merely to itself; and besides this, of course, forwards and backwards to the world. However, this is a different matter.

Now, does this mean that *Mythos* is a poor representation of Henrik Nordbrandt's work?

A question like this is extremely leading. The answer might be yes insofar as this is Nordbrandt cleared of Nordbrandt. But the question is a bad one because this is *not* a 'representation' of Nordbrandt's texts. This is a use of Nordbrandt's work within another autonomous aesthetical intentionality. We shall return to the precise proceedings of this use, including the question of use contra misuse.

Before we do so, however, there is reason to point out that Odin Teatret is engaged in a dangerous business when cutting up Nordbrandt's texts and inserting them in its own text. One thing is that real Nordbrandt connoisseurs have very concrete problems. The reason for this is that the single cuts evoke quite precise associations to those poetic spaces of Henrik Nordbrandt from which they are cut. These associations can hardly function as anything but 'noise' for the *Mythos* reception; they simply do not fit into the aesthetic universe because each individual expression is linked to other aesthetic intentions. This of course only applies to connoisseurs who recognize the original affiliations of the single words.

But to that problem is added another: Since the use of the Nordbrandt texts is so overtly advertised, a great part of the audience may be expected to view the *Mythos* text and the performance as some sort of representation of the Nordbrandt universe, as some sort of interpretation of Nordbrandt, cf. the Platonic theatre above. And at this point I am not so sure that Eugenio Barba's clear denial of such a view (e.g. in the programme really helps.

Something similar is true for the use of the myths. Already here it is easy to expect that *Mythos*'s rendering of the myths might be some kind of representation, might be some new interpretation of the big truths or experiences *behind* the myths of Oedipus,

Sisyphus and Medea, respectively. As if the performance were positioning itself above the myths, so to speak, were mastering them. And it is also evident here that in fact nothing could be further from the truth. This is not what *Mythos* does. But what does it do?

[Mythos as performance versus Nordbrandt's poetry]

On a previous occasion I characterized Odin Teatret's aesthetics of expression as heterophonic — as differing from polyphonic aesthetics, which comprises several voices in a hierarchical order that might be construed as organic, and as differing from homophonic aesthetics, in which one voice takes the melody and is properly accompanied. In Odin Teatret's performances one hears several voices simultaneously — also literally, of which anyone can convince oneself by listening to a performance. In an Odin Teatret performance there are at one and the same time several expressions and several sounds and several lights, several symbols, several levels of metaphor, several significations all intrusively insistent and basically situated paratactically side by side in an almost vertiginous simultaneity. Both extremely present and totally unsurveyable. The latter is marked in the very mounting of the stage contra the audience: There is literally no possibility of a central perspective, no point-of-view surveying it all. Each and everyone simply sees the performance differently, i.e., actually sees a different performance.

Mythos does not refer to myths or for that matter re-interpret them — just as the performance does not refer to or re-interpret the poems of Henrik Nordbrandt. No, *Mythos* unfolds the myths 'forward' in and by its expression, not as a reference backwards but as a presentation. The myths are being recreated at that moment. This means that from this point the weight of the myths in the past is created, from this point the occasion for their existence in the past is given and not vice versa. The myths are above all addressing us in the theatrical now. Thus, what we witness is the coming into being of the myths, their re-appearing coming into being, one might say, addressing us at this very moment. *Mythos* is an apostrophic theatre, one might say; everything in the signification converges into the 'you' element of the enunciation. It all hits exactly me in the heterophonic presence of the performance.

Back to Nordbrandt: *Mythos* uses Nordbrandt's words in foreign service, so to speak, in a different aesthetics. Diverging aesthetic strategies are indeed the point here. Comprised within a roughly outlined binary antipole it might be put like this: Odin uses a heterophonic voice as opposed to Nordbrandt's homophonic voice, although the latter is extremely advanced as regards its enunciation. Odin Teatret has a paratactical structure whereas Nordbrandt's structure is hypotactical. Odin Teatret works with a horizontal lay-out, i.e., it offers a number of doors which are open and available for access at one and the same time. In contrast, Nordbrandt's lay-out is a vertical one, there is one door, which is the door offered by the voice and which then leads you into a labyrinth of roads (and doors). Odin Teatret is theatre, even theatre as theatre. In contrast, Nordbrandt is poetry, and even poetry as poetry. No intermediating convergence is to be found. As a matter of fact, there is such a thing as poetic theatre. But Odin Teatret does not make poetic theatre. And there is such a thing as theatrical poetry, but Nordbrandt's poetry is not theatrical poetry. In short, these aesthetic universes are totally different.

On the other hand, there is certainly a level for similarities, as mentioned in my opening remarks. That level is above all connected with the question of the place and mode of the significations coming into being. Both for Nordbrandt and for Odin Teatret the crucial point is in front of the works: in their doing rather than in the being to which they might refer, in the myths engendered rather than in the myths represented. The privileged instances are not the persons behind the doing, not the ideas, not the texts, not the myths, not history, and not the intentionality. In both cases the aesthetics applies to the place where signification is born: in the spectator, in and by the doing or the saying of the work as presence, as itself, as becoming-present, if you like. Not as a sign for or a representative of anything pre-existing, more original or more real.

This is, one might say, a statement which Odin Teatret and Nordbrandt have in common: Reality is here: reality in terms of the aesthetical constructions — not necessarily in terms of referential statements of this or that part of these constructions. Or, in other words: the metaphysics of Odin Teatret and Nordbrandt is not one referred to or invoked. It is one which is raised here and now. In so doing it may hardly be a metaphysics at all. On the other hand, this may be the reason why it ends up being one.

This profound kinship makes it nonsense to talk about any misuse of Nordbrandt's texts in Odin Teatret's performance. It is true that Nordbrandt's texts are not used in accordance with themselves. The aesthetics of Odin Teatret is not congenial to that of Henrik Nordbrandt. We are dealing with bits and pieces of text lifted out of their aesthetic context and thus out of their original function and placed in another aesthetic context of construction and thereby given a new function. The very same bits of text simply signify something else in the specific context of Odin Teatret.

And so what? one might ask. Does that matter? Nordbrandt's texts are simply used as material, as a part of the world at hand. Actually, precisely like the myths, like the gravel of the scenography, like the voices of the actors; indeed, like the individual actors' whole complex of competencies. All that is material too.

Henrik Nordbrandt's personal attitude to Odin Teatret's use of his work would probably be indifference. Why care? Not Nordbrandt's poems but his words are being used. One might be content with that (or not), but one would not have to call anyone to account for that. *Mythos* uses a lot more than mere words: pictures, music, movements, objects. And, in conclusion, allow me to repeat this: Within this heterophonic theatre the text holds no privileged position whatsoever. The text is not the key, it does not hold a monopoly on the meaning. It is just one column among many others.

The text of *Mythos* has elements of great or strange lingual beauty here and there. Thanks to Henrik Nordbrandt among others. But certainly this performance also contains flashes of other elements of great, strange and monstrous beauty. And basically these other elements have nothing to do with Nordbrandt's text. To the extent that they do at all, the connection exists merely and directly at the level of the material. That is certainly no little thing. But from there to 'everything' the distance is in all respects immense.

Note

See: Itsi-Bitsi som tekst. In *Ilden i glasset. Performerens levendegørelse af tekst og partitur.* Edited by Erik Exe Christoffersen and Tina Lauritsen. Aktuelle teaterproblemer 32. Århus 1994; Institut for Dramaturgi, Aarhus Universitet. Re-printed in a revised version in *Riften og sløret.* Essays over kunstens betingelser (Aarhus University Press 1998).

The opening scene of Mythos. *'Relatives' from left: Torgeir Wethal, Frans Winther, Roberta Carreri, Jan Ferslev, Tage Larsen (sitting), Iben Nagel Rasmussen, Julia Varley, Kai Bredholt. Photo: Jan Rüsz*

Julia Varley

[**Dramaturgy**]

according to Daedalus

The Daedalus who allows me to make these considerations on dramaturgy is the character I play in *Mythos*, the production by Odin Teatret presented for the first time on the first of May 1998 in Holstebro, Denmark.

A long time before the theme of the production was known, and also before I was informed of the character I was going to play, Daedalus had begun leading me into the labyrinth.

A music tape had arrived by post from Brazil. It was a gift sent to me by a spectator of another performance, *Kaosmos*. On one side of the tape were a few sonatas by Villa Lobos and on the other a concert that used bird songs and jungle sounds as a starting point for developing a chant interpreted by a woman. I had always liked Villa Lobos, and the music inspired by nature also attracted me; the female voice was similar to my own and offered me subject matter for research. I listened to the tape so often that its sounds began to sink into my system.

I knew gold would be my colour. I had found a gilt feather in a shop in Holstebro and I had bought it. Showing it to the director, I had said that it was an element for the next production. I don't know why I knew this.

Dramaturgy, according to Daedalus, could be described as a seductive path, which seems mysterious from a distance and along which one inevitably gets lost. This path obliges us to defy closed roads, to turn back and start the journey again. It makes us meet difficulties and monsters. Once within the labyrinth, the main preoccupation becomes finding the way out, how to arrive at the end and conclude the process. The red thread provided by a plot, a theme, or of the life of a character is continually breaking. As the steering logic seems to disappear, we have to continue to simply move forwards or backwards. When everything seems lost, a new clue appears that prompts us to keep on marching.

The actors and the director do not always have faith that what is being built will have an effect on the spectator, but this result becomes important only when one is near the exit. It can happen that also the spectators immersed in the labyrinth recognise what they have explored only a long time after having passed through the experience.

I have defined for myself the actor's dramaturgy as the instrument that helps to organise a scenic behaviour, the logic with which actions are chained together, and the technique to do real actions in a world of fiction. The actor, trained to be without divisions between body, mind, imagination, senses, feelings and reason, acts physically and vocally to affect the senses of the spectator. During the process of creating the performance, the order of importance and priority of the different phases of fulfilment of the actor's dramaturgy changes depending on the actor, on the stage of development of the work, and on the point of professional evolution. The building of presence, the creation of scenic behaviour through improvisation or composition, repetition, the interpretation of a text or of a character, elaboration, the repeat performances — each of these phases has its own dramaturgy for an actor.

But in this article I would like to consider dramaturgy in more general terms, rather than in those of an actor. I would like to enter the complex dramaturgical logic of a performance, *Mythos*, but from the limited point of view of only one of its characters, Daedalus. The first step is to find the entrance to the labyrinth.

While travelling in Bali, I was fascinated by the flowers that adorn the statues and the costumes of dancers, and by the richness of colour of all the decorations in the streets, temples and villages. In the tropical regions of northern Australia a little later, while crossing a bridge over a swampland, the enormous variety of sounds and songs of birds and animals had impressed me. I listened to them and tried to repeat them: impossible. Those sounds reminded me of the Brazilian music tape. As I continued my journey, I started to mix the sounds of imaginary birds into my attempts of producing harmonics with my voice.

I had learnt some rudiments of harmonic chant technique a month earlier, during a workshop with Michael Vetter, a German who was Stockhausen's musician collaborator. The workshop had been organised in Turin by Vincenzo Amato of the Cooperativa Il Mutamento, and announced on the newspaper of the Italian Invisible Theatres. Michael Vetter was a name I was familiar with. Fifteen years earlier I had found a record of his in the library that had kept me company for a long period during the morning training hours.

My interest in harmonic chant had arisen after having listened to a recording of music from Mongolia. It seemed to me that I could hear the sound of a high whistle together with a male voice, even if the presentation on the cover of the record explained that it was the double song of only one person. I could not understand how it was possible to emit such a sound. I searched for other references, and so I came to know about

Tuva singing, David Hykes and his Harmonic Choir, and Michael Vetter. Later Vetter's music remained as a background accompaniment to my physical training, and the harmonic chant disappeared like many other acrobatic exercises that I absolutely did not manage to do, while I followed other roads to grow as an actor.

Chance — and the interest in their movement — made me read the newspaper of the Invisible Theatres. Chance — and the decision to have some time without engagements, in order to regain contact with my dreams without having to chase a pre-arranged schedule — resulted in my being free for the three days of the workshop. Chance — and curiosity — made me sit at the table with Michael Vetter and his assistant Natasha Nikprelevic, during the lunch break and ask them if they wanted to come to Denmark and how much it would cost. I wanted to share the experience of that workshop with my colleagues at Odin Teatret. The workshop had enriched me; during the work I had discovered a new vision of sound and text, and I thought that it could be interesting for my colleagues as well. Chance works for us when we help circumstances. By chance we find the point of departure.

I wanted a character that would be of 'nature' and not of 'culture'. I worked a whole night preparing a costume composed of a carpet of flowers. I was afraid that the flowers would wither before showing the costume. I only managed to prepare two shields of pink and yellow daisies that I placed on my back and chest. I had painted my mouth black in a thin shape to reproduce the image of a beak. Waiting outside the room where actors and director would meet for the first time, I was embarrassed and excited. A poncho covered my suggestion of a costume, so that it would not be revealed before entering the space that had been prepared secretly during the previous two weeks. We had all been informed that in the next production we would work with the poems by Henrik Nordbrandt, a contemporary Danish poet, and that the theme would be the burial of a myth. The men of the group knew their characters: Oedipus, Thersites (the cowardly soldier of the Iliad), Orpheus, Prometheus and Guilhermino Barbosa (the rebel soldier that marched for 25,000 kilometres in Brazil together with the Prestes brigade).

I, too, turned to stone when I entered the room and saw the scenic space prepared by the director together with a stage designer and one of the actors: it was a Zen garden. Nothing was alive in there and everything was grey. The space was icy and very powerful. We sat on the benches around the combed gravel and the stones placed asymmetrically and perfectly, while the director spoke. Amongst other things he gave the women the names of their characters. I should be Clytemnestra, and the others were Medea, Cassandra and Smyrna. One by one, all the actors started to improvise, moving in the space, using what they knew about the characters as reference. My costume of real and colourful flowers was completely out of place.

Whatever movement the actors did in this landscape of stones was excessive. It was as if the presence of the actors was too much. The director usually found a difficult starting point that would force us to find new solutions, but it seemed to me that this time he had gone too far. I felt dispirited: I was a long way from the Balinese and Australian tropics, and I was cold. The next day I came to the rehearsals with a woollen suit and a fur hat, and the following day with a leopard skin coat. But my courage and my defiance finished there.

Months of technical and building work followed. We moved towers and stones, we tried out light effects and floors that could withstand the trampled gravel. Every experiment demanded hours of preparation in order to clean the room by making heaps of gravel on the edge of the space using spades and wheelbarrows, only to then redistribute the pebbles again. Clouds of dust were raised. During the rehearsals we wore masks over our mouths and labourer overalls. We asked ourselves how long our lungs could last. We ordered various kinds of gravel to test its colour and solidity. We washed the gravel and passed it through sieves. The men of the group were active, fascinated by having to solve technical details, while the women — alarmed, as well, by the weight of all the elements used — often observed all the activity from the benches.

I must confess that the Greek myths did not captivate me much, and the figure of Clytemnestra did even less. I would have preferred to have a male character, so as to take distance from Doña Musica's habits, from the long black dress and high heels this character wore in the previous production. One of the actresses left the group and by doing so changed the balance amongst the characters: now there were fewer females who had committed a crime. Therefore, the director proposed that instead of Clytemnestra I should play Daedalus. I immediately recognised the possibility of flying like a bird and of translating the theme of the Greek myths into the natural world I was interested in, and I accepted. Smyrna had disappeared; with time, Prometheus became Lucky from *Waiting for Godot* and finally Sisyphus; from a certain point onwards Thersites was called Ulysses, without this changing anything for the actor who interpreted that character.

In the meantime, after having worked in Holstebro with Michael Vetter and Natasha Nikprelevic, with the Vietnamese musician Trang Quang Hai, and with four musicians from Mongolia, each morning the actors worked with harmonic chants and adaptations of fragments of Henrik Nordbrandt's poems to Mongolian melodies. We wanted to create a 'mythical' sound which came from another world, a non-human timbre, and to sing with a rhythm that would urge us to dance.

I studied all the information I could find on Daedalus, and I decided that instead of simply representing the character, I wanted to present the context in which Daedalus belonged. Instead of following the logic of a character, my personal dramaturgy in the performance, and consequently the materials I proposed during the rehearsals of *Mythos* referred to all the situations and people with which Daedalus had contact, even indirectly. The labyrinth, the Minotaur, the god in the likeness of a bull that emerges from the sea, Pasiphae, Ariadne, the thread, the betrayed love, Theseus, the quail, the machine for the coitus between woman and animal, the jealousy between artisans, the mechanical dolls, the string in the snail, the power of Minos, Icarus' flight towards the sun, the journey to Sicily and Sardinia, the melted wings, the island in the Aegean Sea, the spring dance…: these were all elements I referred to and that I wanted to present in synthesis through my Daedalus. I wanted to play a context and not a character.

One day, a spectator of *Mythos* surprised me by asking why I played a man using a high-pitched voice. I never thought of Daedalus as man or woman, but as the builder of the labyrinth, a worker and parent. In the centre of this context of the myth of Daedalus I found the Minotaur. The thread would give me orientation. The most typical visible attributes in all images of Daedalus and of his son Icarus were wings.

I built my own Minotaur. To depict a leg I used a long rain stick bought in Colombia that I painted gold; a white rabbit skin was the body; a big hand with lean fingers sculpted by a Balinese artist from the root of a tree represented the head and horns. I hung a golden rope on the horns. Different references came together in this composed object: there was nature in the form of the sound of rain, the wood evoked the construction of the coitus machine, the white fur of Zeus, the cut hand and crown were the attributes of power. The supernatural and mythical being, neither man nor animal, was also inspired by the sculptures I had seen in Turin's Egyptian Museum.

In a haberdashery shop in Utrecht in Holland, I bought metres of golden string in different sizes and width, and a long roll of rooster feathers. In Korea I found a small bell-cup with a cover that resonated harmonically. I first wrapped twenty metres of string into the cup, and then let it unravel freely so that it magically fell on the floor following a tangled itinerary. I sewed the roll of feathers in a V shape and found a way of attaching what looked like wings to my arms. In this way other references and ideas were transformed into tangible elements: the bond between Ariadne and Theseus, the shape of the labyrinth, the harmonics, the hidden secret, the constructed wings, the bird, and once again, the colour gold.

With these props I worked to create some scenes.

I was in Amsterdam with the director visiting the Museum of Van Gogh, one of my favourite artists. At the exit we came across four Asian men who were playing and singing in a nearby square. Their clothes helped us identify them as Mongolians. They had a strange string instrument that could neigh like a horse, and a kind of mandolin. The songs followed the pressing rhythm of a gallop and the 'whistle voice', the harmonic chant, that alternated with a low and soft growling voice, could be clearly heard above all the music. One of the men, making use of majestic gestures, at times declaimed texts in which one could distinguish the words 'Chingiz, Chingiz Khan'. He was the one with whom we tried to communicate as he spoke a little German and Russian. His name was Palamshav Childaa. After many telephone calls and meetings with their local hosts, and having put pressure on the Danish Embassy and Home Office in order to receive an immediate entry visa for them, we managed to get the whole group to Holstebro. They immediately charmed us with their generosity, cheerfulness, and musical and vocal ability. In five minutes they learnt the melody and text of a Danish song, while we needed a whole week to manage just to approximate the rhythmical variations and the vocal effects, and to write down on paper some lines of their song about the Altai Mountains.

Palamshav was also a dancer and one day he showed us some folk dances from Mongolia. I saw a bird fly. The movement of the arms and the steps that augmented in pace, in fact represented the daily actions of people who ride, use a whip and lasso, go hunting and hold reins. But the fast lifting and lowering of the shoulders, and the arrow that hits a bird that refuses to fall, seemed to me to be the essential movements of flying. That would be Daedalus' way of moving.

I recorded some dances on video and then, helped by the image of an always smiling Palamshav, for a month I devoted myself to learning the steps and movements of those dances from Mongolia, accompanied by the driving rhythm of their music.

While working with Michael Vetter and Natasha Nikprelevic, one day we improvised for a long time using only one word. It was really incredible to discover the huge variety of possible ways of saying the same thing. I worked with the word 'minotaur'. Later, the Minotaur also became a central element of the performance, but not in the form of the stick that I had built, nor as simple text, but as the long snake of goats' hooves which had been hanging over the space since the beginning of rehearsals. With Vetter, I had discovered that a whole world to explore can be found within a word and a syllable, and that it is possible to sing harmonic melodies that would be difficult for me even with a normal voice.

The director had given me three texts; one of them was composed of fragments of poems by Nordbrandt. I tried to apply the harmonic chant technique to the words. For one text I used an extremely high-pitched voice, where my harmonics were limited in number, but stronger. In another text I used the lowest and most relaxed voice I could reach, and in the other I interrupted the words with sounds of birds using the harmonic effects of some positions of the mouth and tongue. I had fun improvising for a long time, mixing the sounds of birds, monkeys and frogs. I let the director listen to these improvisations refusing to fix them into a finished vocal score. I wrote other texts myself starting from what I had read about Daedalus. The other actors of the group, especially the Scandinavians, concentrated more on Nordbrandt, and then presented some of the poems they liked most.

Many of these texts disappeared completely or were reduced in length, even to the extent of keeping only the vocal articulations that change the harmonics in the voice. Other texts were added; some of these I worked on by grafting them onto a montage of Sephardic songs, the Jewish songs from Arab Spain.

It was difficult to reach a coherent musical dramaturgy in the performance and overcome the fragmentation of the different melodies from Mongolia, Corsica, Sephardim, which were added to the original compositions of our musicians and the vocal improvisations of the actors. The sound of the gravel, which created the 'sea' or the 'labyrinth', helped us find this unity.

The first idea for the costumes came from two glossy jackets that the director had bought in an expensive shop at the airport of Santiago in Chile. These were shown to us together with objects such as a deer cranium and lama foetuses that he had found during a travel across Bolivia and the north of Argentina. In other shops in Utrecht and in Italy we bought evening dresses, coats, hats and wigs. Two sets of skirts and jackets had been sewn for me while I stubbornly continued to follow my own image of a crafts-man dressed in overalls and gold to create my costume. Only when I managed to com-plete my own suggestion by adorning it with many metres of the string I had found in Utrecht, were the trousers and golden jacket finally accepted.

In fact Daedalus' costume is what is left of an enormous amount of work around the labyrinth. Starting from the idea of the tangled itinerary of the string that fell out of the Korean bell, I had suggested a labyrinth made of rope held at the extremities by some of the actors, that would serve to pull Guilhermino Barbosa into the mythical landscape. I imagined that this labyrinth came from Daedalus' mind, and, to make this idea concrete, I made a hat of plaited rope that slowly freed itself from my head in the shape of the labyrinth. Many metres of rope were necessary to make this labyrinth. I had to add other plaited string, wrapped around my neck, to the hat and, to help me find the point from which I should start unfolding, I hang the extremities of the string on the stick that was my Minotaur. The technical solution, and the preparation that the many metres of cord required, kept me busy for two or three hours a day for many weeks. The rope should not only form the labyrinth, it also needed to divide into four parts to capture and pull Guilhermino Barbosa, like a wild animal to be tamed. Moreover, if the labyrinth made of rope was used towards the end of the performance, it also needed to be introduced earlier. Therefore, besides the scene with the tangled string that I worked upon with another actor on the base of an Italian *tarantella* song, I also tried to create an extended spider web and a rain of strings from the centre of the scenic space.

From one day to the other the director got rid of all these scenes. The string and cords no longer existed in the performance. They were left only in Daedalus' costume, to make the hat and the decoration around my neck and at my wrists, and to pull off Guilhermino Barbosa's clothes and boots.

During the rehearsal process I had created the rope labyrinth and the other made of the tangled string that fell to the ground, while another actress had suggested the image of the animal captured by cords, and the clothes instantly pulled off. Yet another actor had designed a labyrinth in the gravel, by allowing the red carpet to appear from underneath it with the help of the snowplough that we normally used to clean the space at the end of rehearsals. The carpet permitted the string lying on the ground to be seen better than the gravel did, and consequently I had to dig a labyrinth following the path of the string. When the string finally disappeared from the general montage in the performance, what was left was the labyrinth drawn by the contrast between the carpet and the gravel. My Minotaur stick then became the sceptre of power and Daedalus' building tool, by adding a small spade and a fork at the opposite end of the sculpted hand. The hand was placed directly on top of the rain-stick and the white fur, now redundant, was taken away. The drawing of the labyrinth later also transformed into Guilhermino Barbosa's tomb, and the sceptre became the element that guides the ritual that wants to change history into myth.

I arrived at the end of the rehearsal process with the feeling it was not worthwhile to work hard. All the scenic material that I had spent hours, days, months to develop had been cut away, while the scenes I had proposed without engagement and just as a transition or as a solution to changing my position in the space, remained in the montage. I consoled myself by thinking that the wastage could be used to build another performance in which strings could have the main role, and by maintaining some of the work of composition in my way of walking and dancing.

Two years later, during a meeting with the actors, the director explained that all my efforts, which he had considered as mistakes from the beginning, had allowed him to discover the dynamic structure of the performance. I could be satisfied: even though my actor's work had disappeared, I had contributed towards the building of the dramaturgy that was useful for the performance as a whole.

I believe also that the wings I had sewn for Daedalus helped to change the dramaturgical direction of the performance. They were beautiful and I absolutely wanted to introduce them into the daily 'run-through', even though the director insisted that he wanted to save them for a final scene. I did not trust that this would happen and I knew that the material that was not used in the rehearsals would soon be forgotten. Therefore, I persisted to the point of disobedience and during each 'run-through' I would introduce the wings at a certain point. I kept the feathers rolled up in my arms as if they were a child, then I unwound them to show them and put them on. Also this prop was technically very difficult to master: the transformations always took too long and at times I remained caught up in a tangle.

With Daedalus' wings, Icarus, the son, appeared, and slowly the mythical figures' criminal action that had been central at the beginning of the process started moving towards the relationship between these characters and their children. Idealism, the hope for a better world, the struggle to change reality and the future, were made visible through sons and daughters: children who had been killed, sacrificed, put to death, forgotten, placed one against the other. The cry of the parent who searches for Icarus, the scene I created to present his fall into the sea, of which only the song was kept, the bird movements I had learnt — all this contributed to making the sons and daughters visible. And one day Icarus' wings were put on Guilhermino Barbosa. In this way, another knot was formed in the performance that brought together not only the destinies of Medea, Oedipus and Daedalus, but also that of the Brazilian soldier who marches to safeguard honour. It was as if all the characters of the performance met in the labyrinth from which they tried to escape in flight to reach the sun, armed with wings of wax. The parents, those responsible, would survive, but what would they leave as legacy?

I absolutely had to go to Crete, where Daedalus had built the labyrinth. The performance was nearly finished so the journey would not have given me concrete elements to use in the montage, but I felt that it was my duty towards the character. I had to see the labyrinth, the place where it is said that the Minotaur was shut in, where the wife of Minos had made love with the white bull, the uncontrollable god.

It was strange to arrive to the island at the same time as German tourists and see the bars and restaurants called by the names we knew from the work on our performance: Mythos, Labyrinth, Minotaur …

I searched for the traces of the labyrinth in Minos' palace and in the other Cretan palaces. I did so, not so much from observing the position of the walls, but from the Mediterranean landscape, the objects locked up in the museum and the signs that the dance steps and rituals of the past could have left on the stones. I discovered the power of matriarchy in the rooms of the priestess, in the colours left on the walls, and in the statue of the woman with naked breasts holding two snakes in her hands. I perceived the laborious passage to patriarchy in the upside down bull-horns, in the battle between religion and politics, in the extremely well maintained bodies in the paintings. The artistic value and magic were to be found in the daily objects exhibited at the museum, in the dolls and toys, in the jewels, vases, and small cups in clay, that had been crafted with care, time, and artisan insight. The quality and variety of each of those fascinating objects of the past rendered terribly evident the abundance of mediocrity with which we live today, despite the paraphernalia modernity makes available. I could recognise the value that we try to give to our work when creating a performance at

Odin Teatret in the perfect irregularity of the form and decoration of the small cups, in the attention to detail, and in the simple imperative of the object. Visiting the museum, I had the impression that, in that distant past, art was an integral part of daily life.

Spring was just starting to show itself, as I toured the island in a rented car with Dorthe, a painter friend. The dolphins, the blue and turquoise colour, the consistency of the stone in Crete were both 'nature' and 'culture'. That which had been created by human beings had the same congruity as the sea, as the trees on which the first flowers were appearing, as the sky, as the rocks and the wind. The big coin with indecipherable signs, exhibited under glass in one of the rooms of the museum, manifested the fascination of that which cannot be grasped: the attraction of the labyrinth. In Crete I became aware of the secret that Daedalus had taught me: dramaturgy starts with the capacity to explore beyond that which is evident, with the attention and care for details.

In *Mythos* the story represented does not evolve in a logical way, with relationships of cause and effect between the characters, but rather it jumps in contiguity from one character to the other.

One scene starts when Ulysses gathers the amputated hands in heaps around the stones, while a blue light blinds the spectators like the glare of the sea. Ulysses says: 'Of the sea from last summer only the reflection of the sunset is left. Of the reflection only the faces and of the faces only their waiting.' Daedalus cries 'Icarus!' and throws himself over the hands, as if in search of his son amongst the waves of the sea. All the characters sing: 'The sea … in front of us … full of secrets …' while Sisyphus accompanies the events with his violin. Orpheus and Oedipus pass through this landscape of stones and amputated hands. As he continues to rake the hands on the gravel illuminated in blue, Ulysses comments: 'I am afraid that I am a house inhabited by many people who never tire of going round at night sweeping, and that dust fills my body instead of blood.' Cassandra sings: 'I see a child on the seashore'. Daedalus picks up a feather from underneath one of the stones and sings: 'The weight of your skeleton tells me every night the height of the mountains I fly over in my dreams' and then, seeing the winged soul of Guilhermino Barbosa carrying his own lifeless body in his arms, he cries startled: 'Icarus?!' While Guilhermino Barbosa continues his march, Cassandra warns: 'You taught him the art of flying. You didn't teach him the most important thing: the art of falling.' Daedalus embraces the winged Guilhermino's knees and says: 'Cursed be the impatience which has filled your pockets with sleepless nights and dreams that scream like a child being born.' Guilhermino frees himself from the embrace to continue advancing undaunted. Daedalus picks up the feather: 'I saw a child on the seashore. Ulysses, I thought it was mine. He shook his head as if to say: don't use me once again in your dreams.' The feather falls to the ground accompanied by the sound of a sad twittering. Daedalus kneels to bury the feather in the gravel, while Oedipus laughs scornfully: 'Blind yourself. Tear out your eyes so you will see history only in the light of your memories.' Daedalus leaves while uttering a lament of bird sounds. Ulysses uncovers the feather with his feet, picks it up to put it in his hat as a decoration, and tells the spectators: 'In Italy they are smarter. There they eat the small songbirds so they don't wake you early in the morning, and above all don't shit on the cars!' Daedalus looks upon Medea in terror, as she advances with two lama foetuses visible on her shoulders and Orpheus sings: 'I call out to love and despair, to madness and insight. I call out to her everywhere where I have not been.' Medea strangles the foetuses, buries them in the gravel and abandons them: 'Be naked small children, and calm. This is the guest we awaited so impatiently, you and I, the guest who soon will separate us and take us home to ourselves.' The scene finishes with Ulysses who enters with the rake to add the foetuses to the heap of amputated hands.

The characters remain isolated in their torments and in their world, but they participate together to build the story of the performance that simultaneously concerns and transcends each of them. If I only follow Daedalus' point of view, I could interpret the scene as the search for Icarus after his fall into the Aegean Sea, and I could recognise in the big stone the island where Theseus stopped, or where Ariadne was abandoned. But during the performance I do not think of this, even though it can be interesting to discover other meanings in what happens around me through my actions. I could see Icarus' soul in the soldier with wings, the anger of the gods at the human longing to fly in Cassandra's predictions, the alternative to exile and running away from Crete in Oedipus' choice of blindness, the interlocutor for the parents who refuse to understand in Ulysses' shrewdness, the corpse of the son vanished in the sea in Medea's foetuses, the victims of the ideals of my youth in the amputated hands, the fallen Wall of Berlin in the stones, or the infinite illusions for a better future in the gravel.

The story of the performance passes from one character to the other through a work of montage and simultaneity: Cassandra warns at the same time as Daedalus is searching, Orpheus and Oedipus are passing through the space, Sisyphus is playing, and Ulysses is raking. In this simultaneity of actions, the spectators do not necessarily orient themselves, but the director must know how to follow the different threads that merge in this assemblage of apparently diverging directions. The director's logic does not follow a linear course, but it moves in a contiguity of territories. The passage from one closed corridor to the next is opened up by details in the story, which can even be single words, objects or light effects: Ulysses mentions the sea in his text, Daedalus searches for his son Icarus in the sea, Icarus flew as a bird, the soul of Guilhermino has wings like an angel, Cassandra speaks of the art of falling, the feather falls, Ulysses amuses himself with the image of birds who let their dirt fall on the cars ...

The simultaneity and montage are believable when they are built on an organic relationship between the actors, and not necessarily because of a psychological logic between the characters. The organic, living — and not psychological or logical — relationship follows the principles of action and reaction, instead of the normal dramaturgical construction based on cause and effect. This relationship is not only established through the ways of looking and an exchange of lines, but it is a dialogue of actions and impulses that needs a long time to develop, especially when it happens between solitary characters like those of *Mythos*.

The organic logic is dictated by a continuous reaction of impulses between the actors, by a complex linking of physical, vocal and musical actions, and by a constant between the actors and the space in which they move. When Torgeir (Ulysses) finishes the text and the blue lights turn on, the accompaniment of Jan (Orpheus) changes tonality to start the collective song about the sea. Julia (Daedalus) cries 'Icarus!' and Torgeir starts to rake, Iben (Medea) and Roberta (Cassandra) continue to sing, Frans (Sisyphus) plays the violin with another rhythm, and Jan (Orpheus) and Tage (Oedipus) enter the space. The thud of the stone falling silences everyone; one hears only the fine vibrato of the violin and a whispered text. Roberta sings after another call to Icarus, Kai (Guilhermino Barbosa) advances to the rhythm of the song and the last note provokes Julia's fall and the embrace of Kai's knees. Kai starts walking again and Julia picks up the feather from the stone, and, in the dark searches for the stream of light to illuminate it, while directing her attention towards Ulysses, who stands at the opposite side of the space. After the feather has fallen and it has been covered with the gravel that makes a sound like waves on the seashore, Tage starts his text. Julia turns towards him and follows the rhythm of his words with small impulses of her body and the sound of birds. Meanwhile Torgeir waits for the precise moment in which the text ends, to suddenly leave the stone on which he has been standing in a precarious balance to slide towards the feather and take hold of it. The sudden arrival of Torgeir makes Julia stand up, and the rhythm of her exit corresponds with Iben's entrance.

Through this precise rhythmic modulation of actions and reactions it is possible to allow meanings and stories to appear. The director discovers the narrative thread to present to the spectators by working on what we call the organic level of dramaturgy, on the microscopic and continual elaboration of tiny details. The actors' material and actions, the relationships and new contexts that are created during the process, indicate the path to follow to find the way out of the labyrinth, and these have sensorial and interpretative consequences for the spectators and the performance.

Daedalus looks from a distance upon one of the scenes I like most in this creation of meanings by contiguity. Ulysses has just finished commenting ironically on the revolutionary song of Guilhermino: 'And if the hands are yours, what they do is also yours.' when Medea, calling for her children, appears with her hands red from blood. Daedalus is in the dark; nobody sees him as he is shaken by the movements of the Mongolian dance.

It is the spectators who must fly away free of the story, the characters, the montage, the dramaturgy and of the performance itself. Ariadne's thread, that leads the eyes of the spectators through the scenes with the invisible power of actions, must disappear.

Entering a labyrinth, getting lost, meeting the unknown, finding an exit, feeling liberated, flying away, these are experiences I could call archetypal, belonging to the imagery each of us owns. For these kind of experiences myth still has a function: it is a common recognisable reference. Daedalus has helped me understand the dramaturgy of *Mythos* and to accept that the Greek myths can be useful in speaking about a contemporary myth.

Each of the spectators should be able to enter a personal labyrinth through the performance, in which they can identify what they have believed, and perhaps still believe in, their own experiences, histories, myths, ideals and dreams. Daedalus has persuaded me that also nowadays we are able to fly, even if our wings will melt in the sun. But after all is it so bad to fall into the blue Aegean Sea?

Translated from Italian by Julia Varley
with thanks to Gilly Adams for reading the translation

Mythos. *Julia Varley (Daedalus) and Frans Winther (Sisyphus). Photo: Jan Rüsz*

[Act II] *Text & Performance*

Iben Nagel Rasmussen

[Fragments]
of an Actor's Diary

In Aarhus April 2000 Iben Nagel Rasmussen gave a technical work demonstration on how to develop the performance, *Itsi Bitsi* from 1991 and onwards together with her fellow actors, Kai Bredholt and Jan Ferslev. To start the demonstration she shortly said:

> I want to start with a question, that you probably will raise anyway, a question I have got ever since we started playing *Itsi Bitsi*. And the question is: 'Isn't it terrible to be confronted with Eik's life after so many years?'
>
> If you loose a person, that has been so near to you, then it is not something you are suddenly confronted with ten, twenty or thirty years later. It is with me all the time. It is not a sudden: 'O, God, there is Eik!' and I suddenly remember the terrible things at the moment I perform. It has followed me since Eik died — I can't separate it from my life. So giving words to that experience has not been traumatic, on the contrary it has almost been a release to share it with other people.

The following article about the creation of *Itsi Bitsi* has been published in *Open Page* #2, March 1997 around the theme *Theatre Women Lives*.

[Vienna 1989]

We are on tour with Odin Teatret's performance, *Talabot*. Every morning I walk to the theatre to 'train'. The training consists of preparing scenes and fragments for a new production. I have asked Kai (Bredholt) to participate as a musician. He plays the accordion, sings — is my boyfriend — and is not connected to the theatre. For a long time I have wanted to develop physical scores/actions in relation to music. In my suitcase I have a tape he has recorded. Some of the songs are about the sea. At the end of the tape there are sounds of sea and waves, a recording we made at the beach the evening before I left. I still do not know what the theme of the new production should be. Perhaps it has something to do with the sea and with a drowned person.

I have a recurring nightmare: two minutes before the performance starts, my costume is un-ironed and it is not even the right costume, it belongs to another show. The public is waiting, my lines are not right and the props have either fallen apart or are wrong. I want to use the nightmare's logic in the new work. I want to mix together costumes and characters from earlier productions.

[The training room]

It is half past seven in the morning. It is quiet here and the room is empty, apart from a chair with my costumes and props. The morning light flows in through a window. Where shall I begin? I tie the two ends of a long coloured elastic bandage to the training room's door-handle. In my mouth the bandage becomes a bit. I try to move forwards. The bit/elastic bandage stretches, it becomes so long that it nearly fills the whole room. This image gives me associations of scenes I played in the streets a long time ago. I imagine that the bandage will later be held by Kai. Right now I can hear the sound of his accordion from the tape-recorder, playing a Jewish melody which expresses longing. The space opens up and I slowly remember as if in a dream: the towns and places we passed with our parades, Odin Teatret's and my own youth. Street after street, rooftops, balconies, cornices. I remember the position of the drumsticks I played with, how my body stretched out, ran and cringed; the cries — mute now — to the people in the street and houses, or to the other parade characters with drums, trumpets and stilts. We had so much power, and used it, in the wild flight towards ourselves. I fix my actions (my score); I write it down in a notebook and draw a sketch of how I could imagine Kai placed. Tomorrow I will repeat the whole thing.

Jan (Ferslev, musician and actor at Odin Teatret) has recorded a guitar composition of his on another tape. Jan is also on tour, but he is not supposed to be in this new production. Together we had fixed a part of my physical actions with his guitar playing. Each little fragment fits with a melody line: closeness, tenderness, sensuality. The actions are soft and delicate, containing an inward sweetness so different from the outgoing strength of the elastic bandage scene. I hardly move in the space. It is a small body-poem with guitar accompaniment.

I choose the Japanese fan amongst the props on the chair and put on the tape with the sound of the sea. The score with the Japanese fan is of an earlier date, its rhythm is more dramatic, and its movements change from slow panning to fast strokes and turns with the fan. I have used this score before, on the street, together with the lamenting sound of a bagpipe, but never in a formal performance. The sound of the waves rocks and colours the physical actions, as if the whole scene happens on the sea. Sound and action feed each other, but still it is as if something is missing. I choose to use a text from an earlier production, expecting it to be changed later for another, related to the yet unknown theme.

I still use the nightmare's logic: characters, costumes and situations that mix together.

My 'story' begins with an old man. His steps are unsteady; he leans on a stick with a dragonhead. The old man knows and remembers everything: my own life and my characters from earlier productions. He speaks with a hoarse voice from under a big black hat that covers most of his face.

In what for the moment is the last scene, I return to the drowned person. From the tape-recorder, Kai sings about a ship and a loved person who has disappeared. The drowned person is a doll made of costume pieces and the parade character's mask. It lies on the floor under a transparent violet cloth. I slowly move the cloth up and down. With some good will, thoughts could be led to water.

I repeat the sequences, one after the other, with only the pauses necessary to press the tape-recorder's on and off buttons. Something is taking form, without any proper text and without the theme being defined.

[The theme]

Back at the theatre in Holstebro I show Eugenio (Barba) the chain of sequences. 'We must find a theme!'— he says — and proposes *Oedipus at Colonus*, a classical play about the old Oedipus reaching the end of his wandering and of his life. I am absolutely not stimulated.

During the summer holidays Kai and I continue to work. We develop the montage, placing Kai within it, and once again show it to Eugenio, who repeats that also this new assembly leads his thoughts towards *Oedipus at Colonus*. Eugenio must have noticed my expression, because after thinking a little, he adds: 'But one of the scenes, when you have the bandage in your mouth and move following the accordion music, could also be a memory from your own youth, your travels and your relationship with Eik in the sixties'. (Eik was my boyfriend before I entered Odin Teatret, he was a beat-singer and poet; he committed suicide in India in 1968.) Suddenly the key lay in our hands, a space opened up and something resonated in all three of us.

But is it possible — I ask myself — to talk about Eik, drugs, the sixties in a theatre performance? How can it be at all possible to talk of something which is so closely woven into my own person without becoming banal, pathetic, sentimental or much too direct and personal? I am aware of the danger.

As a point of departure we use the already existing scores performed by the characters which belong to my past as an actress: the Shaman — from *Come! and the Day Will Be Ours;* the white character from the street parades; Trickster — a magical creature, somewhere between Harlequin, an ape and a juggler, from the performance *Talabot;* Kattrin — Mother Courage's mute daughter from the performance *Brecht's Ashes.* The characters and their actions are accompanied by music and song. Nothing has much to do with Eik, except the drowned person who could be associated with his death. A person suffocated and foundered by a pressure so violent that it pulls the rudder out of his hands like a force of nature.

Eugenio is nine years older than I, and has not been through the same experiences. He would like to know more, and he asks me to write about my life with Eik and about that time in the sixties.

[The text]

The story must be told, but which story? I have tried many times, and each time I've said to myself: no, even if I don't speak a single untrue word, it is not the right picture of what happened. And then I gave it up with a feeling of impotence towards the words, those words which were so important in my relationship to Eik, which sometimes were the relationship. When I started at Odin Teatret and moved to Holstebro in 1966, it was as if this bridge of words collapsed between us. Eik died ... I was told one New Year's Eve in Saunte. On New Year's Day I walked hand in hand along the beach with Torgeir. It had snowed. The air was white and quiet. Without Eik and without words.

We are in Stockholm with *Talabot.* I am staying in a big apartment together with Torgeir Wethal (actor at Odin Teatret). There is snow and sleet outside. Every morning I sit at the writing table in the sitting-room. A long letter starts to take form, it is written to Eugenio and Kai — who does not know about that period in my life either. I write:

It was in the darkness that I met Eik for the first time, during the campaign for nuclear disarmament in 1961. It was night. We had been out to stick up posters. We had both been taken by the police. He quacked a lot, but was rather unimpressive. A weed with red hair.

We were a small group who met each other on the Holback march — artists, workers, intellectuals, students. What did we believe in during that time when we marched day after day, or when we lay down for twenty-four hours in front of the city hall? We believed that it was meaningful.

We were heading towards a new open society. Away with weapons. Forward with fellowship and warmth. The post-war political ice was melting. We were so many, and we breathed and breathed on that glacier to help it give birth. And it did give birth — to the flower children, to folk music, to beat music, to new ways of dressing, to new words.

Eik and I lived together. We could have up to ten people in our room and bed. We read, talked, listened to Bob Dylan. Eik wrote and wrote. He wrote all the time I knew him: poems, novels, articles, letters.

I don't remember any precise reason why the politics faded into the background. Had life in Denmark become too easy for us, with a lot of words and meanings which were no longer rooted in something real? Was it the journeys or the drugs which started to change our way of looking at the world and life?

The journeys placed our lives beyond what was secure. We had never experienced hunger before, never lived without a roof over our heads, frozen in the night, never made our way with a guitar and hat to collect money at the French Riviera, in Italy, in Spain.

On board the boat, with a thousand stars above us, Eik pointed into the darkness and said: 'Iben, Africa! We are away from the tidy, the cold, the calculating, the mediocre. We are away from Denmark'. Eik played and I collected the money. Desert … in the villages, desert … in the towns, desert … Morocco, Algeria, Tunisia, Libya, desert … The Bedouins offered us goat's milk. Eik received continuous offers concerning my person. The towns were dirty, the museums far too big. We sat in hitch-hiked cars and saw the descending sun colour sky and earth in the same colour. Egypt, Lebanon, Turkey, Greece. I was pregnant. We played in the bars, in the streets, to get money for that terrifying abortion where I saw God's face without love, like a distorted image of myself. The summer was almost gone. I longed for the North — for rain, clouds, wind, snow. 'I hate the thought of the coming autumn in Denmark', said Eik.

We travel to the north of Sweden, to Umeå. The snow lies half melted in big mounds. It is icy and slippery on the road and pavements. People fall over easily and suddenly, breaking bones and hips. We are taking part in a festival. My hotel room is small, but there is space enough for my typewriter. We have some days off. The others leave in small groups to visit the Swedish landscape, while I have decided to stay in Umeå to write.

I sit down to finish my long letter, and in the evening I carefully go out in the dark to listen to Northern singers' and musicians' concerts in churches, theatres or community halls. There is a great distance from the daily life in Umeå to the world which is slowly reappearing through my words in the hotel room.

... We lived with the blind rolled down in borrowed apartments. We chewed amphetamines from spoons. We fixed morphine and Dexedrine. The abuse turned us to crime: we broke into the chemist where we also took the money from the cash till. We sat and messed around with our own or someone else's veins to get a shot in. The veins on the arms and the hands were destroyed. Then we changed to the legs or the feet, the most unthinkable places on the body. It could take half an hour to come through the vein — desperate minutes until the blood, like a little thin snake, trickled into the pump and then mixed itself with the liquid in the syringe.

When LSD came to Denmark we got hold of some capsules. It was the meeting with a divine world, wonderfully beautiful and sometimes ferocious.

Eik was taken by the police again, so was I. This time I got probation.

Eik went to Kuwait, Baghdad, Teheran, where he begged for money for a typewriter. I went to Istanbul, Athens, Israel ... 'If I could talk ... if I could talk ... if I could talk', I said to myself in the mountains in Eilath.

Through the window I can see the Swedish flag flapping gently against a pale winter sky. The letter is reaching its end, nearly one hundred pages. I am nervous about delivering it.

Back in Denmark I dig out Eik's letters; it occurs to me that they have waited many years just for this moment. I had put them away in a big folder; they fill nearly twice as many pages as those I have written myself.

It is a very big package with texts Eugenio has taken with him in his luggage to his summer house in southern Italy.

[The rehearsals]

We have asked Jan, who had composed and played the guitar piece, if he wants to take part in the performance. He has said yes.

Jan belongs to my generation, and has been through many of the same experiences. He falls in easily with the sixties' music, both Eik's own songs (that Jan knew from before), the song about Eik for which my brother Tom had composed both music and text (Jan worked with Tom many years ago) and the Doors' themes Kai had chosen for the first montage.

> There are dark forces which blind you, and there are dark forces which give you insight. We are led by dark forces — to where? — we don't know.
>
> (Eugenio Barba's text, used in *Itsi Bitsi*)

When Eugenio shows me the text assembly, first of all I am shocked. Can it be possible? He has not used Eik's letters, nor any of the other poems I had given him. All my lines (monologues) are taken from what I wrote on tour. I had never imagined my writing should be used for anything else but a reference for the story.

The scene with the elastic bandage is put together with the text which tells about my meeting with Eik, about our political activities and travels. It follows the same thread of associations I had, working in Vienna. The scene is the same, Kai's music is the same, only the text is different and it fits well. But what about the part with Jan's guitar music? The soft, gentle actions are put together with the description of my experiences with drugs, a nasty and ugly reality in complete contrast with my own associations. But it takes me only a little time to understand that this is exactly how it should be. Only this way, with such a distance between the physical expression and the text, is it possible to speak of such an experience.

My personal history is woven with the characters I have played earlier. I already knew it, but never before had it stood out so clearly: most of my roles — Trickster, the Shaman, the white character — contain an element of the dimension, of the magical expanded consciousness, we searched for with drugs.

> When we got in contact with drugs, we thought that a revolution of the mind was just around the corner. For some, the drugs were a game, for others a form of escapism, for others again a way of meeting 'God'. But without us knowing it, the means became the end. The drugs which should have served as door openers, became door closers. Some were on the wrong side when the doors started to shut.

[The performance]

Trickster sits on the long wooden box with his back to the public. An umbrella is fixed to his back with the shade turned upside down, full of paper snow. Through the eyes in his mask I can see his red gloves. The spectators start coming in. My breathing changes. Most of all I fear for the text, what if I should not remember it? What if I get stuck? The light in the room is turned off. Only the white sheet on the floor, and part of the wooden box, are lit. When Jan has finished his musical monologue, I/Trickster must jump in. In this position, it is practically impossible to imagine the transformation. The performance is a different experience, like jumping out with a parachute, hoping it will open.

Cue. I jump. Trickster turns towards the public: hands, feet, jump on the box, down from the box, the snow flies out of the umbrella when I move. Each hop or turn of the body means the snow falls in a certain way. It must land precisely to cover the whole stage area. Not in lumps, but free (how much time we used to find the right mixture of heavy and light paper). Jan plays and sings, with a low voice now, while Trickster repeats the words of the song.

> Eik came to say farewell,
> We'll meet again some day.
> A journey without its equal
> Begins for me at sunset.
>
> Then we said goodbye
> And wished him good luck,
> And stood a time in silence
> While he travelled to another continent.
>
> They found him one evening
> On the jungle edge where the soil is red.
> In a ragged yellow kaftan
> With nothing else, he was dead.
>
> The room became so quiet
> Nobody could speak a word.
> All conversation was stunted
> The snow fell so quiet outside.
>   (From my brother Tom's song about Eik)

The performance flies. Trickster becomes Iben, who says that Eik's story must be told. Iben changes to the Shaman, who tells of the dark forces which lead us.

Jan and Kai follow and lead by way of the music; at times they break in to comment or to support. We get to the elastic bandage scene with the text about travelling. I am dry in the mouth. The parade character resurrects without the drum, its white costume hangs loose in front of my own body. It is attached at my neck and hands with elastics, like a doll cover. When I move, it looks like a strange puppet-on-strings. The mask is just beneath my own face.

I cannot see that the performance flies, I only feel the wind that twists and carries me. At times the wind becomes a storm that throws me around. I am about to capsize, but I don't. I hold on to each little detail in the text and action. I recognise them, perform them and am steered by them. It is the same as during rehearsals, and at the same time completely different, the details vibrate in another way. Close to the end of the performance, I have transformed to the mute Kattrin from *Brecht's Ashes*. She stands on top of the box, which is placed upright, and cries out her warning to the town of Halle and to the auditorium. With deaf and dumb gestures, she hits two pieces of iron against each other. They give a resonating sound, which reminds one of church bells.

The box falls; Kattrin says:

> When you make me happy,
> I often think, now I could die,
> Then I would be happy until the end.
> When you then get old and think of me
> I will look just like today,
> And you will have a sweetheart who is always young.
>   (Bertolt Brecht)

Kattrin drops her hands and Iben tells the spectators:

> ... Eik died, twenty-five years old, in India on the border with Pakistan in 1968.

Jan and Kai start gently playing Bob Dylan's *Blowing in the wind*. Iben takes Kattrin's costume off, she picks up the props and pieces of costume from the floor and puts them back in the box. She puts on a 'private' woollen jumper over her black lace dress while I speak to the audience.

> Eik once wrote to me: 'One should speak cautiously, because words are fragile, crumble between the lips and will express nothing of what we feel and think'. But isn't it like that anyway: only words exist, have always existed and will always exist. If Eik could see us now, would he be able to recognise the little flame which I try to protect, and which speaks in the characters I perform: that which others call theatre?

I have shut the box. Only the white mask and a hypodermic needle are left on the floor. I speak directly to the mask. No, directly to Eik:

> You walked into the jungle dressed in a yellow loincloth. You carried the poison and your eternal notebooks. You may have sat down to write the letters for us at home. You don't sound sentimental, or dramatic, more like the letters we read together by young men condemned to death by the Germans during the war. You have fallen over in the grass; you must have been in terrible pain. Sky, grass and trees must then have become a wheel which turned around, over and through you ... and you have then heard an old woman sing.

No tape-recording of water, no drowned person covered by a transparent cloth. No Kai who sings about a loved one who has disappeared. But at the same time it is all there, like an underground current, a deep echo. I do not think of it, I do not want it; the current is present in the same way as the wrinkles around my eyes and the lines on my hand.

A long journey has ended and a new one can begin. We are ready to go on tour with the production that is about and *is* my life, at the same time. We call it *Itsi Bitsi*, an affectionate name Eik gave me, and the title of one of his songs. Jan and Kai sing it in the final scene. *Teeny-weeny* — it could also be the play, in which everything fits into a box that reveals a microcosm of life, words and characters when it is opened. My own life as a private person, as actor and as a woman.

Montevideo, Hotel Carrasco, October 1996
Translated from Danish by Julia Varley and Nigel Stewart

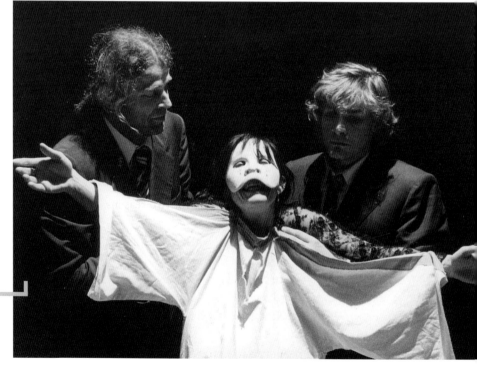

Jan Ferslev, Iben Nagel Rasmussen and Kai Bredholt *in* Itsi Bitsi. Photo: Poul Østergaard

[Act II] *Text & Performance*

Svend Erik Larsen

As Time Goes By ...
[**Theatre and Memory**]

... a case of do or die!
The world will always welcome lovers,
— as time goes by.

[Memory is complex]

The first few lines of *Itsi Bitsi* (1991) go as follows: 'My name is Jan. Now I am an actor. Before I was a musician. I was five years old when I started to play ...'. Shortly afterward, the actor actually starts singing. There is a triade here of theatre, memory and acting; this is the subject of my paper.

Recall, retain, recollect, remember, remind — we have many words for that strange capacity of ours to reshape what has been lost to time. These five synonyms, taken from a longer series, show the complexity of the process. The roots of the words cover different dimensions of the shaping process: *-call* points to voice and language, *-tain* relates to holding or grasping by the body, *-collect* means to unify, especially by reading (*-lect*) or understanding, and, finally, *-member* and *-mind* both refer to the mind. Their identical prefix *re* — refers to the *again* of the process, the past made present. This is what is going on: by means of language, mind and body we, once more, reach back to make the past timeless, and in doing so we try to understand it as a whole.

I begin by underscoring this complexity for two reasons. First, because the most common word for the human activity we are dealing with, *memory*, basically refers to *mem-* or mind, to what is in the mind, to the mindful, and reduces memory to a primarily mental activity, not an activity that embraces all dimensions of our lives. This reduction is common in our culture: memory concerns first of all, and most often solely, the mind. Second, because here we are discussing memory as part of theatre, which cannot memorise anything without taking into account the process in its entire complexity.

The complexity of memory can nevertheless be approached in two ways. First, memory can be taken as a compound of different aspects taken one by one: the mental process, the linguistic, the corporeal, the spatial and so on. Complexity, then, is just the sum of two or more of such dimensions, all with the same content conquered from the past, only expressed in different ways. From this point of view the simple version of memory as mainly mental is sufficient, but maybe a little poor without other dimensions added. Like a tune played on a flute and blown up by a symphony orchestra may be the same, but still...

Second, and more importantly, memory can however also be conceived as a contradictory phenomenon that therefore, to be memory at all, requires several intertwined dimensions. Media such as the theatre that inevitably and by their very nature work with memory as a complex and irreducibly multifaceted phenomenon offer the only genuine approach to memory. In this perspective, the simple version of memory as purely a matter of the mind is not just too simple, but misleading if not erroneous. A fish without water is still a fish, but it will die. That the complexity of memory is essential and not accidental will be the position sustained in this paper.

[Memory is paradoxical]

It sounds so simple: memory transgresses time and makes the past present. Without losing its essential identity, a slice of experience is transferred from one time zone to another. 'I remember my first day in school as if I were still there,' one might say. Therefore, the classical debate on memory from Plato onwards focussed on repetition. In memory we repeat our otherwise inaccessible ideal origin in God's mind because we possess the inherent capacity to do so. The empiricist tradition from the 17th century, which in all other respects contradicts Plato's idealism, takes over the argument that memory is a transfer in the mind of an identical content from past to present. The mind is a blank whiteboard, a *tabula rasa,* on which perceptual experience leaves its marks in such a way that they are always the same. In that capacity they may be remembered or forgotten but are not influenced by the process unless, of course, by mistake on the part of the memorising mind. When idealism and empiricism basically take the same stand vis-a-vis memory, it becomes very difficult to indicate a new position.

Søren Kierkegaard nevertheless does away with this argument in his treaty entitled *Repetition* (1843). Instead of defining a third position he points to a contradiction inside the idealist argument and *eo ipso* also in the empiricist one. Kierkegaard's rejoinder to idealism is that it grounds any new knowledge on inward reflection on something that is already in the mind, either as the image of an original idea or as the image of an experience. This cannot be true, he claims, because this conception overlooks the fact that memory is an existential category that relies on our being bound to time. Repetition is not a way of getting hold of the past as a content independent of time, but a way of reorganising the present on the basis of the past and thereby placing us in time. This process makes the present something genuinely new and changes the perspective of the past. Memory should not be looked upon from its content but as the transformative time-bound process it unfolds.

Of course, Kierkegaard is not Freud. He does not go into the psychic elements of this process but rather explains the paradoxical logic that makes it a process in a couple of astute remarks, for example: 'Repetition and recollection are the same movement, except in opposite directions, for what is recollected has been, is repeated backward, whereas genuine repetition is recollected forward' (Kierkegaard 1983, 131) and 'The dialectic of repetition is easy, for that which is repeated has been — otherwise it could not be repeated — but the very fact that it has been makes the repetition something new' (ibid., 149). What is new about memory is not that it distorts the content, but that the paradoxical process requires the memorising subject to re-experience the memory simply because of the fact that the subject evolves over time. Memory does not safeguard the past from the destructive process of time; quite the contrary: it reinstalls us in time, the time of the subject. Memory is always represented indirectly by and for experiencing subjects, and therefore, by the very process of representing, every representation — be it a story, a jerking movement of the body, a mood that is struck, a whiff of a particular smell, a moment of a performance — adds something to the memory that it did not have before, making it exist on new conditions. It is a process of renewal, not of maintaining. As Henri Bergson says in his book on memory to which I will return, *Matière et mémoire* (1896), the present *is* not, it *happens* (Bergson 1903, 162).

This is the paradox of memory: you cannot renew without memorising. How should you otherwise know that you renew anything? And you cannot maintain things from the past without changing them. How could you otherwise move them from one context to another? So, the paradox of repetition or memory as laid down by Kierkegaard demonstrates that memory is process before it is content, that its focus is actual time not past time, and that the way it is represented is as crucial as what is represented. That is why a simplistic view, even on its own grounds, cannot hold, but the complex one I outlined above has to be sustained.

[Memory is double]

Memory proceeds through a series of reduplications. I shall point to three areas — communication, consciousness and representation:

1) *Communication:* We can be *reminded of something* that voluntarily or involuntarily seeps into our mind or can be traced in our bodies, but we can also *remind somebody of something*, force somebody not to forget certain things or to do certain things. Here, older discussions on memory, especially in rhetoric, underlined a basic opposition between the passive and active, or the natural and artificial, aspects of the mind.

I think another aspect is more important, namely, that memory is hereby seen not in relation to its intimate roots, but first of all in respect to its degree of communicability. Even when the most intimate memory is recalled it is reshaped so that it has the potential of being communicated and thus shared with others. That is the driving force behind Freud's use of dreams, free associations and so forth: memories of your individual past only work when they have been told, thereby, via a communication, returning to you as something by which you can recognise highly personal if not existential aspects of your own life. Memory will always have to be viewed as communication, or at least as a challenge to our forms and media of communication. It is forced upon us as something to be interpreted, and at the moment a recollected interpretation is also made possible. This is the meaning of memory as recollection. Memory has to be externalised before it can be internalised as yours, not the other way round.

2) *Consciousness:* This leads us to the next double aspect, that of *conscious* and *unconscious* memory, both in the process of being reminded and in the process of reminding somebody else. We know, and I guess actors know it more than most of us, that learning by heart your own words, gestures and movements and those of the other actors is a process to be learned through training (as the ancients did in the courses on *memorial artificialis* in the schools of rhetoric). This process is a mixture of conscious and unconscious elements — although we do not know entirely why it works, associative links are activated for the individual person during the training, and once learned we are able to recall many of the elements simply by partaking in the flow of the performance rather than in consciously singling out every one of its details. Those of us who are not actors or musicians know it from driving a car, bicycle key codes and telephone numbers. We do not remember as bodies or as minds, but as subjects.

When we wish to remind somebody of something the double structure of consciousness and unconsciousness is also involved, making — as Kierkegaard said — any repetition a new phenomenon. We have no waterproof means of controlling whether the essentials of a message are conveyed, and if they are we cannot ensure that something else does not slip through as well, and that it does not come to occupy a stronger position than the features we consider to be essential. In being reminded of something by us, the receiver may be carried away by a detail that makes something else surface for this particular person that may even contradict what we have carefully formed — the unwilling laugh or cry is well known.

When I was asked to present this paper, the name *Itsi Bitsi* did not remind me of Eik Skaløe, but rather of the popular hit *Itsi Bitsi teeny weeny, yellow polka-dot bikini* from the 60s. And when, finally, I was brought on the right track, the first thing that came to mind was my son's third-year high school paper on Herman Hesse's *Der Steppenwolf* and the rock band *Steppeulvene* and the lilac-coloured peaked shoes he brought back from Turkey after a high school excursion. Being fairly disciplined, however, I am able to keep such memorial flows in the background and focus on the topic at hand. But they are inevitably there.

You could not control my memorial processes, just as I cannot control yours now while I am writing. But when we control ourselves, as I have done in preparing this paper, it is because memory is not only communicable, it is also dialogical: we actively adjust our memories in accordance with the situation in which we are dialogically engaged — whether open or closed. Digressive memories are therefore not only disturbing fringe phenomena, they actually motivate and drive the dialogue so that we may focus our memorial attention. This is what happens during a performance. Kierkegaard's emphasis on memory shaping the present can be made more precise: it shapes our present as communication and dialogue.

We know from religious and mythological contexts that this dialogue opened by digressive memory may be regarded as dangerous on a collective level, and from Freud that it is dangerous on an individual level as well. Therefore, different forms of controlling the digressions have been tried out. In Freud, by a therapeutical process embedded in a theory so that our cognition and will may guide the process. In religion it happens in a conceptual framework of warnings, monsters and wonders. Instead of triggering norm-breaking individual impulses, often of libidinal characters, a good deal of phenomena were interpreted as signs or reminders from the gods to make people repress their own remembering. Monster literally means reminder.

Today, when most of us believe it an essential aspect of our existence to be confronted with or also reminded of involuntarily remembered and unpleasant elements of the individual and collective past in order to be able to deal with them and thereby be able to remind ourselves and others of basic facts of life, it is crucial to shape such dialogues in open forms and media that respect the complexity of memory. Theatre is one such form.

3) representation: In literature it is a paradox that the most *intimate feelings*, the most unheard-of experiences, the most individual conditions for artistic creativity have to be moulded in a language and thereby submitted to the conditions of a *shared system* of symbols and meanings. The same holds for memory, which is often used in literature to exemplify the paradox of literary creation as such — Dante, Cervantes, Goethe, Proust and Musil, to name a few. Therefore, the delicate and constantly shifting balance between what can be communicated and what not, what enters into a dialogue and what is kept out, and what belongs on which side of the threshold of consciousness, is a process which to a large extent is determined by the means of expression used. Even the most private memory leaves traces readable by others. Therefore, it paves the way for a dialogue where those traces are developed by words, gestures, bodily appearances, movements, and so on. What is represented is not the memory as content, but the tight rope-walk of its interpretability.

[Memory and the senses]

In his dialogue *Paradoxe sur le comédien* (ca. 1769), Diderot deals with this very balance as a problem of theatrical representation. *My name is Jan. Now I am an actor.* It has often been held that Diderot's main interest is to highlight as sharply as possible the opposition between the actor as a consciously used system of signs and the emotional individual being who carries the sign. The paradox is that the more deemotionalised the individual, the more successful the actor in creating emotions in the spectator through his use of signs. Here, the individual's memory, which is not controlled professionally during training and rehearsal, will impede the spectator from being reminded of anything.

One moment of sublime transparency in the acting, when the individual person behind reveals his feelings and thus becomes interchangeably blended with the actor, is obtained at the price of ruining the whole performance. The comedy on stage is not to be confounded with the comedy of the world, as Diderot tersely remarks. An actor is not a bad actor because she or he forgets their life experiences, but because they forget their part, he notes. If an actor has a passionate relationship to an actress and they are performing together, the value of the performance may increase — but only if the actors are mediocre (Diderot 1994, 311, 323, 336). 'In cold blood' is the formula for Diderot's theatre.

In order to work, memories also have to be transformed from personal ones to depersonalised theatrical resources. One cannot play oneself except as another. If one is a miser and plays Molière's *L'Avare*, one does not play at all. The author added something new to reality by the characters he created, but nothing is added to what Molière already did or to reality by one's performance if one is already a miser (Diderot 1994, 337) This very process of adding something new to reality by playing oneself as another is brought on stage in *Itsi Bitsi*, not just the results of the adding.

There are, however, two points often overlooked in Diderot. First, for him the paradoxical tension only drives the actors' performance. In contrast, Diderot seems to regard both author, spectator and reality in a rather static manner; only the actors are dynamical figures because of the paradoxical working conditions of their profession. But if we add to the author's work, as Diderot claims, he is both used and transgressed, is both part of the play and outside it; and the audience is not just observing and receiving what the actors set out to do, but has to activate memories, cognition and emotions of their own triggered by the drama; and reality becomes something that *is* not but rather *happens* where we are. In short: the paradox enlarges both the author and reality and therefore also changes the role of the spectator. The paradox comprises all agents in the theatrical situation and also the memories active in it. They all contribute essentially to the adding of something new by the performance.

The second point is that another essay by Diderot is never read in connection with the essay on the theatrical paradox. It is the essay on people born blind, *Lettre sur les aveugles* (1749). Does it sound strange to you that I refer to an essay on blindness while discussing a predominantly visual art like theatre? But rather than trying to describe a deficient body missing a vital sense, Diderot is describing a bodily universe in its own right. He reminds us that also the most well-equipped body shows deficiencies: the seeing cannot see their own face (Diderot 1964, 85) or their own back, let alone their insides. The body is not available to us but through mediation by others, their looks and interpretations, or by sensory-enhancing instruments and so forth. And not everything received by the senses is registered by the bodily subject; we simply ignore some perceptions we get (Diderot 1964, 135). Therefore, those born blind may also have a complete picture of their world based on other details and filtering mechanisms than ours, including objects seen and told about by others (Diderot 1964, 85).

In other words: any body, with or without its complete sensory potential, is always organising a total universe through its senses. This is the new element the theatre adds to author, reality and spectator: a bodily universe of its own. What is added is not a new detail, but a new totality. This leads us to a particular interpretation of what senses are. They are first of all used to orient our world — or life-world, as it is called — only secondarily to inform us about and register the things contained in it. The senses do not separate us from things, marking the boundary between our bodies and other material phenomena. They make us partake in the world of objects so that my body is shaped not as a body but exactly as *my* body during this process of sensory and interpretational partaking.

When bodies are used on stage they represent this process of orientation; we are reminded what it means to be present as a body. In *Itsi Bitsi* the primary bodily action that takes place is how the bodies play with the importance of direction and distance; the things they see, hear and so on, or let us see and hear, are of secondary importance.

[Memory is presence]

This is the point of departure for Henri Bergson's theory of memory in *Matière et mémoire* (1896), to which I referred above. The pivotal point of Bergson's theory is the *present*, which to him is one and indivisible and basically determined by the fact that we as subjects are moving bodies. A present is always *my* present. The past is accessible as memory only through the present, released by the ambulating body in its presence and always reshaping the relation between past and presence; the mind is integrated into the bodily movements, reflecting on it, forecasting it, imagining it.

Pure memory, in his view, is processes of embodiment that organise the way in which the body is actually present. Memory for Bergson is not a way of reinstalling the present into the past or of filling it with the past; quite the contrary, it is way of orienting the present toward the future, for memory is a way of carrying something on beyond the point when it first happened. Memory is future oriented. Therefore, pure memory is only a transitional state; once inserted in the present it shapes the relation between present and future by way of past experience. There is always a tension between the memory of a certain message we have tried to learn by heart and to retain, and the memory of how and when we did it. The order of the first we cannot regulate without our memory being wrong; our situative memory, on the other hand, is subject to our selection, reorganisation and so forth without being wrong. An actor cannot change the lines of the first and the last part of a play; but he or she is free to reorganise how he or she memorises and tells about last night's performance as an event. Memory is always situated and thus related to an experience of a presence. What is added by the actor (cf. Diderot) is this sense of presence that embraces actor, author, spectator and reality. Memory does not remind us of the past, but of the experience of a present that made up our past and is repeated — hence Kierkegaard — as a new present when repeated. This is also what happens on stage: the repeated repertoire of a company is a reenactment of this repertoire as a present. Any new performance adds presence to the repertoire through the memorising of it.

If this view of how theatre and memory are linked together holds, memory is something enacted in the present making way for a dialogue between actor, author, spectator and reality. *Itsi Bitsi,* which occasioned my general reflection, gives special emphasis to memory in having as its topic a highly personal memory. We do not see it as transformed to a shared universe of meaning or potential meaning due to the general performative logic of theatre, but we encounter the very process of transformation. The play hereby shows what the spectator also has to do: confront intimate memory with the universe of others, confront my memories with what is foreign to them, confront individual memories with collective symbols that represent them.

[The body and cultural memory]

To wind up my argument I would like to add another dimension to theatre and memory. If I am right that the moving, mindful body more than the sealed off, disembodied mind is the driving force of memorising processes in general and not just on stage, then the use of the body on stage also refers to the way in which we in our culture deal with the problem of what bodies can contain, what they can express and how bodies can memorise. Theatre on the whole, Odin as well as any traditional theatre or amateur theatre, represents and reenacts our cultural memory of the body.

Diderot is placed at an important juncture in our cultural history of the body. On the one hand, he ushers in the idea that the body as a physiological unity and as a sign cannot be separated. The body is materialised meaning and thereby subject to a cultural change on an equal footing with biological change. On the other hand, he only focuses on specific bodies — that of the actor when acting, that of the person born blind when perceiving and organising the world. To him, the body of the spectator is still a passive receptacle for the unfolded talents of the actor.

The first aspect anticipates late 19th-century and 20th-century conceptions of bodies in anthropology, phenomenology, psychoanalysis, gender studies, discourse analysis, and in all the different theories and practices of performance connected with them. The second aspect is rooted in the conception of the body as a machine, widespread since Descartes, or as de-mentalised flesh, related to but hardly controlled by our consciousness; victim of passions and sin.

What is relevant in our context is how these two traditions have different views on how the body can express or represent memories, and how these differences influenced the theatre. The body as mere flesh has been known since antiquity as *soma*. Such a body does not contain or show other memories than traces of the bodily processes themselves: scars, signs of aging, gender characteristics and so on. Therefore, as a sign the body is or ought to be transparent and a carrier of natural signs that can be read immediately. This also holds when we come to passions or emotions realised through the body: love, lust, pain, envy and so forth. Signs for such states of the mind could and should be cleansed from their cultural disguises and brought back to their immediate natural state, and then be shown as an unequivocal sign. This is what is supposed to happen in science. In Diderot's days the physiognomics or phrenology of Johann Lavater or Franz Gall or the dramaturgic theories in Johann Jakob Engel's *Mimik* (1785-86) gave an example of how to detect the unambiguous sign of fixed character features — that is, permanent states of the soul that were otherwise hidden in the body. Such character types are still well known in popular fiction.

But already for the ancient Greeks the body is not only *soma*, but also *organon* (cf. Koselleck (ed.) 1978). It is part of something and consists of parts (limbs or senses). In its capacity as *organon* the body is integrated into a part-whole relationship and mediates between part and whole. This conception of the body implicitly directs Diderot's reflexions on theatre and on the universe of those born blind: by the body the senses are integrated into a situation of movement, by the body the mind is integrated into a social universe, by the body past memory is integrated into actual presence, and so forth. The body is materialised meaning and therefore also loaded with memories, not of the body as such, nor of the signs used to express the mind in the body, but of how the body has been and is actively involved in meaning creation. The signs used here are not immediately readable because they are not signs of something in the body or of the body itself. They are signs of how we take part in the world in being bodily subjects.

Using the body in a performance is also, I think, a staging of this history, of this age-old division in the European history of the body. Any performance reenacts the boundary between the body as *soma* without meaning and as *organon* with meaning. We cannot simply choose one instead of the other, just as we cannot choose what we want to remember and communicate. Because memory is bound to our bodies, it partly works randomly along the lines of the three reduplications I labelled above as communication, consciousness and representation. A common denominator for the performances of Odin Teatret is that it more clearly than most companies foregrounds this European history of the body. It makes this history a cultural memory in and by the presence of each performance.

I have not referred to *Itsi Bitsi* very frequently. But when I remind you of and you recall the opening lines, you will see that I have been talking about nothing else. Repeated now, at the end of my paper, they become part of a new context. They happen, again, here and now: 'My name is Jan. Now I am an actor. Before I was a musician. I was five years old when I started to play ...'

References

On Itsi Bitsi
The English manuscript, the Danish program, a videorecording, all from Odin Teatret. Also Iben Nagel Rasmussen (ed.) 1993. *Eik Skaløe. Breve til en veninde*. Copenhagen: Lindhardt og Ringhof, and Steppeulvene 1997 (1975). *Hip*. CD/Exlibris.

Other works cited
Bergson, Henri 1903 (1896). *Matière et mémoire*. Paris: Alcan.
Diderot, Denis 1964 (1749). Lettre sur les aveugles à l'usage de ceux qui voient. *Œuvres philosophiques*. Paris: Garnier. 73-164.

Diderot, Denis 1994 (ca. 1769/1830). Paradoxe sur le comédien. *Œuvres esthétiques*. Paris: Garnier. 289-381.

Engel, Johann Jakob 1971 (1785-1786). *Mimik* I-II. Frankfurt a. M.: Athenäum.

Gibson, James 1969. *The Theory of Ecological Perception*. Boston: Houghton Mifflin.

Kierkegaard, Søren 1983 (1843). *Fear and Trembling. Repetition*. Princeton: Princeton University Press.

Koselleck, Reinhard et al. 1978. Organ. *Geschichtliche Grundbegriffe* V. Stuttgart: Klett-Cotta. 519-622.

Larsen, Svend Erik 1994a. Body, Space and Sign. *Gramma* 2, Thessaloniki. 77-91.

Larsen, Svend Erik 1994b. Et in Arcadia ego. A Spatial and Visual Analysis of the Urban Middle Space. Thomas A. Sebeok and Jean Umiker-Sebeok (eds.). *Advances in Visual Semiotics* (= *The Semiotic Web 1992-1993*). Berlin/New York: Mouton de Gruyter. 537-57.

Larsen, Svend Erik 1997. La nature des sens dans un contexte urbain. Svend Erik Larsen, Morten Nøjgaard and Annelise Ballegaard Petersen (eds.). *Nature: Literature and its Otherness /Nature: la littérature et son autre*. Odense: Odense University Press. 205-20.

Merleau-Ponty, Maurice 1946. *Phénoménologie de la perception*. Paris: Gallimard.

Plato 1956. *Phaedrus* & *Theaetetus*. Irwin Edman (ed.). *The Works of Plato*. New York: The Modern Library. 109-89, 481-577.

Sennett, Richard 1994. *Flesh and Stone. The Body and the City in Western Civilization*. New York: Norton.

John Andreasen

[The Social Space of Theatre]
— *including Odin Teatret*

[This is the Player's Right]

If a player (*lekare*) is hit, one should pay no fine. If a player is wounded, one carrying a fiddle or passing with a drum, then someone shall take an untamed heifer and lead it to the Thing Hill. He shall shave all hair from its tail and grease it. He shall dress him with newly shined shoes. The player shall then grab the heifer's tail, and a man shall strike it with the keen cut of a whip. If he can hold it, he shall have the good animal and enjoy it like a dog enjoys grass. If he cannot hold it, he shall feel and bear what he has got, shame and hurt. He can never ask for more rights than a flogged bonds-woman.

'This is the Player's Right' (Dätta är Lekarens Rättighet) is a small part of the Swedish 'Västgöta Lag', which was probably written down before 1250 AD (Holmbäck & Wessén, 1946). I have chosen 'player' to connote both 'actor' and 'musician' — a wandering performer at fairs. This rule is even harder in the Swedish Östgöta Lag, where it is told that a 'player' can even be killed without penalty to the killer. A 'player' held the lowest status together with beggars and newly freed slaves in Sweden in the Middle Ages. My retired colleague Chr. Ludvigsen, who translated the 'Västgöta Lag' piece into Danish many years ago, considers it to be the first theatre law in Scandinavia — in reality a law against vagrancy.

This little law concentrates all the fear of and anger against different, 'useless' people who did not want, or were unable, to follow good customs and high principles and become decent, hard-working, happy citizens like everyone else. People who wished to differ from the majority — or were forced to it — considered sponging on the majority's labouriously gathered fruits and continuing to wander around as living scorn against these 'normal' people, perhaps inspiring more people to undermine society and authorities by their example!

750 years later laws are still passed all over the world against nomads of different kinds because of their special 'languages', interests and 'capabilities'. Not only 'players', storytellers and so on, but also various aborigines or minorities from all corners of the world. Fascinating and dangerous people; inspiring, tempting and seductive.

The status of theatre people has fluctuated in different cultures and periods, ranging from the most exalted to the most inferior rank. Around the year 2000, those actors who appear on film and television often have a minor god-like status. Still, even today most stage actors do not get rich and famous.

Some of the last remains of the public defence against vagrancy, artistic 'self-help' or the camouflaged regulation of commercial competition on the Danish theatre market was removed from the theatre law as late as 1990. Since then it has not been necessary to apply for permission from the local chief constable to perform in public indoors, but it is still necessary to do so if one wishes to publicly perform outdoors out of regard for traffic, public order, commercial interests and private property.

Perhaps Odin Teatret has been considered odd and 'dangerous' over the years on several of their tours in Scandinavia as well as under more distant skies?

[What are 'social' and 'space'?]

The word 'social' stems from Latin. According to *The Oxford Advanced Learner's Dictionary* (1995), 'social' has to do with the organization of and relations between people and communities. The negative contrast to 'social' is *a*-social or *un*-social: Unable to act according to the general interests of society.

Apart from a number of professional uses of the term 'social', it also inspires a lot of everyday associations. *Positively*, 'social' may mean 'caring for each other' or 'creating a good atmosphere'; *negatively*, it may signify 'empty social rituals', 'sickening, suffocating or false harmony', an 'easy solution' or ways of not taking oneself or others seriously enough to discover greater depths in the shifting 'communities' to which we belong.

'Space' is something very concrete and physical *and* a mental category. The social space of theatre does *not* depend on a certain style and form, a certain content or 'message', a certain place to perform, technical equipment, a certain dramatic text; nor is it limited, for instance, to certain kinds of audiences. Different types of theatre have at different times and in different situations and contexts performed different social functions for different participants and receivers. The social space of theatre can be viewed from different angles and studied in different types of research material. Most of my topical examples are taken from Danish and other Nordic materials.

[Legislation and 'social space']

A society's basic consensus is apparent in its legislation. The main purpose of the Danish *Theatre Law* (Teaterlov) from 1999 is to encourage and improve the art of theatre and theatre culture in Denmark. The law contains basic national rules concerning the following:

The Royal Theatre and Orchestra (the totally state-subsidised national theatre)
The Jutlandish Opera and *The Danish Theatre* (the two largest touring companies)
Touring and Visiting Theatre (smaller touring companies for children and adolescents)
The Province Stages (three large regional stages funded by the government and local counties)
The Theatre Supportive System of Copenhagen (an association of stages in Copenhagen subsidised by public funds)
Local theatres (smaller local stages subsidised partly by the State and the local municipality)
Small theatres in larger cities (similar to the *local theatres* but in the four largest towns in Denmark)
Theatre Council (funds of different theatre projects, children's theatre and others)
Ticket Subscription (provides subsidies for many local organisations of theatre distribution)
Special rules concerning children's theatre (lower ticket prices for children and youth)
Amateur theatre (a possibility for 'Artistic Amateur Theatre' to receive government funding)
(*Theatre education* has been removed and now falls under a general law about 'artistic educations' in Denmark)

The law is not entirely structured as a hierarchy, but almost: first the Royal (national) Theatre, then larger touring companies and regional theatres, followed by smaller local theatres, project theatre, children's and youth theatres, local theatre distributors, and finally amateur theatre and its national organisation. One can imagine another view of how to create a coherent mental 'system' of national theatre culture — an upside-down system: it would start by encouraging ordinary people to participate in amateur theatre, then encourage some to get more education and try to work as professionals on different levels, up to an excellent 'national' level; in short, a 'theatre ecology' with a multiplicity of intermingling layers and milieus.

[The economy and 'social space' of theatre]

Different official *statistics* show wishful public distributions of the 'social space' of theatre through the public economic support of theatre production and promotion.

According to *Kulturpengene 1999* (Cultural Money 1999), published by the Danish Ministry of Culture, the Danish State, the 14 counties and some of the 275 municipalities in Denmark officially supported theatre in the following way in 1999:

Receivers of public funding	Millions of Danish Kroner	
	(: numbers of theatres per category)	
The Royal Theatre	305.0	(1)
The Province Scenes	128.5	(3)
The Theatre System of Copenhagen	69.5	(6 + 2)
Jutlandish Opera + Danish Theatre	38.3	(2)
Local theatres	27.1*	(20)
Small theatres in larger cities	— *	(24)
Touring & visiting theatre	13.1	(7-10)
Touring & visiting ticket reimbursement	13.3	
Theatre Council	64.0	
Ticket subscriptions	64.6	
Cultural adjustable grants	40.2	
(= Regional Cultural Experiments)		
Miscellaneous	8.1	
Lotto & pool	15.9	
Undifferentiated municipal funding	138.5	
Total amount 1999:	926.1 million Danish kroner	
	(7.50 Danish kroner = 1 US Dollar)	

Besides these subsidies there are other possibilities for public funding. Large-scale private sponsorship of theatre in Denmark has only slowly become 'common' since the late 1980s.

[The economy of Odin Teatret in 1999]

Odin Teatret also receives public economic support, in part because it is a 'local theatre' (egnsteater) in Holstebro. In 1999 they had a turnover of approximately 11 million Danish kroner (1.46 million USD): 32% of this income stems from the municipality of Holstebro, 2% from Ringkøbing County, 18% from the Theatre Council, 14% from 'activity-based support' and 34% from self-earnings. If 'activity-based support' is counted as a part of the theatre's 'self-earnings', this constitutes 48% of the turnover in 1999. And that is a lot of money for a Danish theatre.

It takes around 1.46 million USD to run such a small 'concern' as Odin Teatret/Nordic Theatre Lab per year with its minimum of 18 employees, rent, insurance, production and promotion costs and so forth. It also requires great diligence, a lot of different activities, and beyond performances a good deal of networking, touring in different countries, strength, resourcefulness, endurance and perseverance, solidarity and thrift. A few of its members have worked together for 35 years and some for at least 25!

But the sources of Odin Teatret's income have also changed over the years. When the Danish theatre law was changed in 1970, a new subsection was added on alternative educations in acting (§30.2), mostly because of Odin Teatret even though at the time they had only been working in Denmark for four years, but with remarkable results. Of course experiments of different kinds were also being made in different group theatres at that time — as part of the *Zeitgeist*. But only Odin Teatret directly called their work 'education' and 'research'. Twenty years later, in 1990, the 'alternative' subsection (§29.2) was reformulated and the word 'research' was cut out, but basically the possibility for the state to support 'alternative' educational programmes was maintained — still mostly due to Odin Teatret. But in the late 1990s the subsection has slowly been emptied of government funding. This means, for instance, that Odin Teatret must apply for money from the Theatre Council, and until now they have managed to get their annual 267.000 USD, but no longer as a guaranteed government grant. On the road again![1]

[Organisation and 'social space']

In 1991 a Bachelor of commerce and a theatre researcher in Oslo published a working paper on theatre organisation (Gran and De Paoli, 1991). They define 'theatre' as *'an organised, artistic process'* (p. 2), underlining its character of live, human involvement, collective creative creation and communication among the people putting on the production and directly between these people and the audience (pp. 9-11). And they sketch some of the different physical and mental interests that can be involved in creating or blocking theatre communication: e.g. authorities, suppliers, competitors, substitutes, opinions, geographical contexts, producers, audiences and the 'art climate', elements that can develop different patterns to which the concrete theatres have to relate more or less consciously to survive on the market.

Gran and De Paoli construct 3 ideal-typical theatre cultures: 1) 'romantic', 2) 'modern', and 3) 'political' theatre culture. Some of their central characteristics are the following:

Romantic theatre culture has its starting point in the theatre view of the 18th and 19th centuries and focussed on the genius's ability to create art with a capital A around 'eternal ideas'.

Modernistic theatre has its starting point in the beginning of the 20th century and involved new creations, formal experiments and avant-garde theatre.

Political theatre has its starting point broadly speaking in the radical milieus of the 1920s and the 1960s, and concentrated especially on giving art a 'changing' role in society.
These basic views on theatre culture are then transferred to 4 ideal-typical models of theatre organisation: 'Factory Theatre', 'Director's Theatre', 'Group Theatre' and 'Project Theatre'. Below is a brief summary of what each model implies:

Factory Theatre is based on a *romantic* view of theatre, but it can also involve some 'modernistic' and 'political' ideology. First of all it includes the large institutional theatres that effectively produce performances based mainly on dramatic texts in a hierarchic organisation (pp. 26-30).

Director's Theatre operates with a less hierarchical organisation yet is clearly run by a charismatic director situated its centre like a romantic genius, creating concepts for performances that may or may not be based on dramatic texts. This type of theatre most often regards itself as experimental and 'modernistic' and may possess certain 'political' traits (pp. 30-32).

Group Theatre is a consensual theatre community with a non-hierarchical organisation and ad hoc traits. This type can have either a low or high degree of specialisation and may or may not base their performances on dramatic texts. Its work is based on common 'modernistic' and 'political' goals in a broad sense (pp. 32-35).

Project Theatre — in principle — has to rebuild its often rather non-hierarchical organisation for each new project. Many of its traits are shared by 'group theatre' (pp. 35-36).

But what about Odin Teatret? It is not an ordinary theatre, inasmuch as it also produces books, videos, artistic research and conferences and so forth. But often it is presented as 'the oldest group theatre in Scandinavia' even though it has replaced a lot of its members during its 35 years of existence.[2] Even more often, however, Eugenio Barba is referred to as the leader of the theatre, so is Odin Teatret really a 'Director's

Theatre'? According to different publications, the members of Odin think they create something new each time — often something in sharp contrast to the immediately preceding performance — so really one might say that Odin Teatret is a 'Project Theatre'? And, after all, are there not traits of 'Factory Theatre' in the theatre's working roles and planning routines, its mixture of protecting and challenging every single actor? It is not very easy to categorise such a theatre. Looking at Odin Teatret's self-image, it seems to contain 'romantic' creative traits, 'modernistic' form experiments and 'political' intentions in its choice of topics and collaborators. So the basic organisational question about any theatre is: What specific combination of elements from the different categories characterises *this* particular theatre as compared to another concrete theatre — at specific moments in history?

[Odin Teatret — an 'artistic theatre'?]

In 1981 the Finnish-Swedish director Ralf Långbacka published an anthology of articles in which appeared 'Eight Theses about Artistic Theatre' (Långbacka, 1981). Unfortunately, he does not say how many theses must pertain to a theatre, and to which degree, for it to be worthy of the name 'artistic'. It nevertheless seems as though most of them apply to Odin Teatret, which brings them into company with the leaders and ensembles from the 20th century that Långbacka has analysed as 'artistic': Stanislavsky & Moscow Artistic Theatre MXAT, Brecht & Berliner Ensemble, Strehler & Piccolo Teatro, Krejča & Divadlo za Branou, Ljubimov & Teatr na Taganke and Stein & Schaubühne. Långbacka's central characteristics — in my translation and abbreviation — read as follows (Andreasen 1998): 'Artistic Theatre'

1) implies a group or community with a common starting point and common goals that can gather around one or a few central persons;
2) opposes an old fashion, fossilised theatre, breaking with its ideology and production methods, ideals of style and fixed positions;
3) has to turn to a new audience and actively change the structure of the audience and its experience of theatre;
4) has a clearly selective repertoire;
5) looks for artistic ways of working implying a holistic view of theatre;
6) has an internal and external organisation to attain an optimal artistic result;
7) demands a lot of every single member of the ensemble as well as of the total community, and
8) has a motivation beyond the motivation to survive, to continue to exist.

Odin Teatret is clearly an 'artistic theatre'. But we who work outside Odin Teatret do not know very much about what kinds of consequences the 'artistic' way of living has had on the 'social' spirit *inside* the theatre. However, this situation may soon be remedied, since in the spring of 2000 a young PhD student from Aalborg University Centre, Jørn Bjerre, started an investigation of whether organisational theory can learn something from theatre. Bjerre is interviewing members of Odin Teatret to find out about 'good labour' and how to create results from that. His results will be ready three years from now.

[The 'social space' of 'theatre space' — an underestimated phenomenon]

My own experiences from my 'street theatre period' in the 1970s and 80s tell me to reflect on the physical, psychological/mental and symbolic arrangement, status and mood of a particular venue. Such a space can — maybe without total awareness of it on the part of the sender or the receiver — signal anything from extreme friendliness to extreme hostility towards those invited to participate or those who, in defiance of common sense, wish to play or experience playing in a precise venue, indoors or outdoors.

What physical and psychological elements promote or hamper the possible 'social' function of a venue for different target groups? What can be done to alter their expectations and experiences if necessary? Is it a place where people are used to coming and like coming? How can their interest be stirred with the personal, material and temporal resources we have? For instance, who will voluntarily come to a university studio to see a performance? Is Odin Teatret sufficient to make people interested — no matter what they play and where? (For a more detailed model of 'theatre space' for empirical analysis, see Bablet 1972).

[Audience statistics — who actually goes to the theatre?]

According to *Statistisk årbog* (Statistical Yearbook) in 1999 Denmark had a population of 5,313,577. But far less than half of the population is interested in theatre. According to *Statistiske Efterretninger* (Statistical Information), state-subsidised theatres in the theatre season 1998-99 consisted of: 117 theatres and single theatre projects with 448 productions and 11,629 performances for a total audience of 2,329,000 spectators. An average of 200 spectators per performance. There are no really good detailed statistics about who actually goes to the theatre — partly because certain types of information are difficult to obtain, partly because it would then be obvious that a minority buys or gets most of the tickets; it would be clear that nearly forty years' of political attempts to 'democratise' art and culture in Denmark have not succeeded well enough yet.

In the accounting year 1999 Odin Teatret showed 14 different productions at 190 performances in 14 countries: 75 performances in 24 Danish towns and 115 performances in more than 70 towns abroad (from *Beretning*). In addition, they put on 9 cultural 'barters' and other performance-like activities.

In a comparative Danish study of people's 'cultural habits' from the 1960s to the beginning of the 1990s, Torben Fridberg concludes that the level of education, mass communication, transportation, personal earnings and health in the Danish population in general has risen during this 30-year period. In his opinion, these factors must have affected the interest in theatre (Fridberg, 1997). He concludes that a minor adjustment between different layers of social status and between women and men has taken place such that more people from lower layers of society and more men are interested in theatre than previously. The best-educated and best-paid people living in the larger cities with the most varied offers are nevertheless the most frequent theatregoers. Social strata I-III are still over-represented and IV-V under-represented in the 1990s; so much for progress ...

Most theatre still only interests different 'elites'— including Odin Teatret. But the difference is that Odin know they are mostly for *connoisseurs*. As Eugenio Barba said to on Danish television (DR2) the night before receiving the Sonning Prize in April 2000 (my translation):

> Theatre is elitist because it applies to a minority that has certain needs. But is it elitist today? Theatre is an archaic way of communicating that demands great human, temporal and material resources to reach a result that will be seen by how many — a thousand? Thinking of all the other sorts of performative media, tv and film that can be seen by hundreds of thousands, the theatre is in a way elitist, and it does not matter if there are a thousand spectators or a hundred like at a Odin Teatret performance. Most important is the impact. How deeply can such a theatre hurt the conscience, history, fantasy — the way theatre is conceived and made?

[The spectator as recipient]

A lot of research on theatre spectators and reception situations has been done in different countries, most of which is research based on models of social strata. At the moment my young colleague Anne Marit Waade operates with 5 general types of recipients to search for contemporary competencies in relation to performances: *zapping, shopping, sightseeing, fucking* and *playing* (Waade 2000).

What do they have in common? They know much about the medium in which they are interested and they are very selective. They can be combined in different ways, but one by one they can briefly be characterised as follows:

The *zapping* spectator masters the ability to change frequently and rapidly between identification and distance and is fascinated by this.

The *shopping* spectator estimates the different offers on the 'market' and focusses on desire and primarily on the consumption of bodies.

The *sightseeing* spectator 'travels' between experiences and adventures looking for site-specific performance on the global wide screen.

The *fucking* spectator is characterised by some of the former elements yet focusses especially on erotic attraction in dance and movement.

The *playing* spectator is full of desire, self-activation, interaction, perceiving plays and performances with a view to some personal gain.

Waade seems to concentrate mostly on well-educated Western young or younger middle-class types of audiences, but the types may potentially be developed to something more detailed and specific in the future.

Odin Teatret should be able to address and please a lot of these spectators with its rapidly shifting and complex montages of pictures, movements and sounds. It may demand a highly developed ability to *hold on* to as well as *shift* between several different sensory impressions at brief intervals or at the same time.

[Theatre — activities and content]

Regardless of a particular theatre's theatrical activities, the core of its existence for a lot of artistic and other reasons is the performances. Odin Teatret/Nordic Theatre Lab is a 'local theatre' (egnsteater) in Holstebro in western Jutland, Denmark, with stationary as well as touring activities nationally and internationally: performances, demonstrations of the actors' techniques, workshops, artistic research, conferences, master classes, guest performances, a hiring-service, a library and archives, film, video and music production, publishing, a magazine, festival coordination and so on. And besides acting every actor has other tasks. In this way the company gets into contact with different social strata and subgroups, depending on the concrete activity and the concrete space it takes place.

One of Odin Teatret's special activities is called cultural 'barters', in which for a short period of time theatre representatives — more or less symmetrically — exchange different kinds of cultural goods for mutual inspiration, to celebrate universal human values or to show solidarity with certain groups. No money is involved but rather artistic activity is exchanged as mutual payment. Inspired by anthropological studies, Odin

Teatret started 'barters' in southern Italy in 1974, where they exchanged training excerpts and small scenes with, for instance, local people's songs. In 1999 they arranged 9 'barters' in different countries.

In the spring of 2000 in Aarhus — the second largest town in Denmark with its 250,000 inhabitants — an Odin actor arranged four barters in the shape of either the accordion-playing polar bear Otto or the clown van Gakk. The first barter was a short exchange with Danish folk dancers and Palestinian musicians as part of local Palestinians' celebration of 'Earth Day'. The second was a collaboration with normal and handicapped school children and a physically handicapped adult theatre group at a school, each group performing for the others. The same model was used in a local youth centre. And in the fourth barter 'van Gakk' exchanged scenes, things and personal poems with mentally ill adults in a local open institution. Each barter lasted between one and two hours for specially invited spectators.

Fortunately — to my mind — attempts to invite a wider audience to the barters failed. A barter is a prepared interaction between more or less equal parts and not a (peep)show for people without concrete and in-depth knowledge about the aims and resources of the participating parts. And even though the central organiser and actor is a very committed, inspiring and competent barterer, he is still only a *representative* of Odin Teatret, and it is *not* the famous Odin Teatret *as a whole* that does the bartering — as opposed to what some local collaborators might have hoped based on the image created by the publicity from some of the local organisers as well as from Odin Teatret itself.

[Three wishes for the theatre]

One of the exiting but also problematic views on the present time is the theory of *the* modern individual in contrast to *the* traditional individual — a daydream from the Age of Enlightenment at the end of the 18th century. It is the ideal of definitive liberation and emancipation from the trammels of religion, history, class, family, sex and other 'traditional' brotherhoods and communities. Being 'modern' is a certain, simple act of will according to a simple version of this theory. 'Modern' is pure progress, 'traditional' is pure retrogression.

Although this is also a reduction of reality, it seems more fruitful to regard a period in history in a somewhat more complex way. Experience tells me that a lot of different mental 'times' exist simultaneously: Different traditions and courses of action gathering and splitting individuals and groups across boundaries, frontiers and borders. Terrifying and terrific! Several changing and developing 'modern' *and* 'traditional' individuals created in many kinds of interaction. Passé, up to date, ahead of time.

Inspired by Ernst Bloch, the German philosopher from the 1930s, one might characterise any period as 'un-synchronous' (*Ungleichzeitigkeit*), or maybe even more fruitfully use the term 'social character' invented by David Riesman in *The Lonely Crowd* from 1950. He talks about three different dominating *groups* of 'social characters': *tradition-directed types* (dominant into the Middle Ages in Europe), *inner-directed types* (dominant until the beginning of the 20th century) and *other-directed types* (dominant from the beginning of the 20th century). The last one may even be more radicalised at the beginning of the 21st century, but all of them can still be found in the same societies and communities today — as germs, mature plants, residues — and are regarded as pro-active, active or re-active depending on personal values and the demands of changing realities.

And even a small — strong and vulnerable — unity like Odin Teatret probably consists of 'un-synchronous' individuals and subgroups doing 'un-synchronous' performances together such as for instance *Mythos* and *Ode to Progress*, where a mixture of all the values of Western times fight — and eliminate — each other misanthropically?

In general — and not only from Odin Teatret — I wish for three kinds of adult theatre in the near future: 1) Dilemma Theatre, 2) Positive Theatre and 3) Realistic Theatre.

1st wish: Dilemma Theatre

Theatre should use *all* its strength, *all* its amazing storytelling and other illuminating forms and techniques — all its 'gravity' in the best sense — to give us important messages to consider about the present times and times to come. It is hard to find solutions to dilemmas. You are forced to use all your will, brain and bone power to do it, like Antigone and Creon in the classical duel.'Dilemma Theatre' has to examine our complicated present times and future visions more directly, closely and deeply, creating a larger geographic, historical and cultural wing span to put us in larger, less narcissistic perspectives. 'Un-synchronicity' contains an endless amount of improving dilemmas!

2nd wish: Positive Theatre

And I would simply like more 'positive news' for adults in theatre! Good examples of human magnanimity, unwarier-like braveness, endurance and perseverance, generosity and so on. Variations on themes that strengthen human self-confidence, showing that human beings are not only stupidity, greed, violence and humiliation, but also positive will, courtesy, self-sacrifice; theatre to be proud of and happy about, theatre that shows possibilities of development, victory over difficulty, hope and not just cheap solutions. More 'deep happy ends'!

A lot of minor and major daily situations make a person happy, make families function, make teachers and students choose to stay together after all instead of splitting up and so on. Films like *Riff-Raff, Forrest Gump, Life is Beautiful* and *My Life as a Dog,* among others, celebrate man as a kind and surprising creature. Let these ideals invade adult theatre in the nearest possible future!

'Art shall provoke, challenge, disturb and make uneasy' is a mantra that we repeat unconsciously nowadays. But shall art only intimidate and scare people out of their wits and leave them hanging? Of course art may provoke, but those who provoke should risk something themselves, otherwise it constitutes a fake provocation, as the Danish 'situationist' Jens Jørgen Thorsen says. Yes, art must demand something from us, but it may also make us happy, calm, wonder, seek for understanding and desire for visions.

Considering Odin Teatret's performances and other activities, one might call them 'pessimists in theory, optimists in action'.

3rd wish: Realistic Theatre

I am far from only wishing for 'realism'; I *also* wish for full-hearted 'realism' in theatre! One bad theatre comparison in particular irritates me — in both versions: *Realism = social realism = bad theatre!* Or *Realistic theatre = livingroom drama = boring theatre!* This kind of automatism is silly. Can 'expressionism' replace 'absurdism'? Can 'surrealism' replace 'expressionism'? Can 'montage' replace 'linear drama'? Can 'performance style' replace 'melodrama'? And so forth. Of course not, but it seems as if 'realism' can be replaced by any other style. 'Realism' is a large branch on the tree of theatre history. Every period has had some realism or realistic traits in its theatre. And any style must be acted out with talent and commitment in order not to be considered dull and dusty!

'Realism' could also be defined as 'Life's incredible multiplicity of laughing and crying, believing and doubting — fights, defeats and victories!' And not only melancholy, nostalgia, sadness, prediction and boredom. 'Realism' can dig deeply into 'reality', the material and the mental sphere, to show fractal variations of real human desires, wishes, beliefs, self-illusions and deceits, attempts, cutbacks, comebacks and successes. Demonstrated with all the power of theatre!

And what about Odin Teatret? They are well known for their 'extra-daily movements' and special use of the voice. Still, in various performances they have also used *some* everyday movements, such as the cooking of soup in *Brecht's Ashes,* some of the preparatory movements of Judith in *Judith,* Oedipus moving through pebbles in *Mythos* and various other examples. Should Odin Teatret now turn altogether 'everyday' in their movements? No, but their work demonstration based on the last scene of Henrik Ibsen's *A Doll's House* in Aarhus, Denmark, in April 2000 indicates that we should perhaps expect something very different in the future. Concentrated, committed, attentive — 'realistic'?

[Spectator's Right 2000]

Starting with the socially negative *Player's Right* from approximately 1250, a more positive transition to the second millennium could be a wish for the most outstanding from all the history of performance in new, future combinations — surprisingly new 'social spaces':

> *Spectator's Right 2000:*
> *Shaman's Drum*
> *Storyteller's Circle*
> *Dancer's Space*
> *Mask's Darkness*
> *Puppet's Skin*
> *Actor's Pulse*

Notes

1. Odin Teatret was established in Oslo, Norway 1964 and moved to Holstebro in Western Denmark in 1966 under the organisational umbrella Nordic Theatre Lab for Actors' Art. Over the years they have taken in still more of the world. According to Odin Teatret's website the list of 'new' countries each year looks like this (and the brackets contain the number of countries visited that year): 1964: Norway (1), 1965: Denmark, Sweden (3), 1966: Finland (3), 1967: Iceland, Italy (4), 1968: France (3), 1969: Belgium, Germany, Holland, Yugoslavia (8), 1970: Switzerland (7), 1971: No tour caused to re-organisation of Odin Teatret in 1970?, 1972 (3), 1973: Poland (10), 1974 (2), 1975 (4), 1976: Venezuela (5), 1977: Spain (5), 1978: Peru (2?), 1979 (3), 1980: Japan, Wales (9), 1981: Mexico, Israel (5), 1982: Colombia (7), 1983 (6), 1984: Canada, French Antilles, USA (11), 1985: Hungary, India (6), 1986: Argentina, Austria, Uruguay (11), 1987: Brazil, Faroe Islands (10), 1988: Chile (7), 1989: Costa Rica, Cuba, Ireland, Estonia, Northern Ireland (12), 1990: Portugal (10), 1991 (12), 1992: Czechoslovakia, Greece (10), 1993: England (13), 1994: Scotland (15), 1995: Macedonia, Turkey (13), 1996 (12), 1997: Korea (8), 1998 (10), 1999: New Zealand (13), 2000 (10). The earnings have slowly increased over the years - with some waves - from 1.060 Danish Kroner in 1964, 18.280 in 1965, 113.286

in 66, 550.986 in 68 and slowly from 1 to 3 million through the 70s., between 5 and 6 in the 80s and between 7 and 11 million in the 90s. (7.5 Danish Kroner = 1 US Dollar April 2000).

During the 36 years Odin Teatret/Nordic Theatre Lab (NTL) has created more than 50 different performances in- and outdoor. Tony Cots' 'Basho' was a NTL-member 1984-86, Richard Fowler's 'The Canada Project' was a part of NTL 1984-91, and Iben Nagel Rasmussen's 'Farfa' has participated since 1983. According to the Odin 1999-poster that is revised every 5th year the original titles are: *Ornitofilene* (1965-1966), *Kaspariana* (1967-1968), *Ferai* (1969-1970), *Min fars hus* (1972-1974), *Dansenes bog* (1974-1979), *Johan Sebastian Bach* (1975-1979), *Gøglere og spaghetti* (1975-1977), *Callot parade* (1976), *Come! And the Day will be Ours* (1976-1980), *Anabasis* (1977-1984), *Millionen* (1978-1984), *Brechts Aske* (1980-1981), *Brechts Aske 2* (1981-1984), *Moon and Darkness* (1980-1990), *Puputan* (1980-1985, Basho), *Puthanas befrielse* (1980), *Bryllup med Gud* (1983-1990), *Oedipus* (1983-1985, Basho), *Wait for the Dawn* (1984-1988, Canada Project), *Oxyrhincus Evangeliet* (1985-1987), *Gnomernes indtog* (1985-1986, Farfa), *Såret af vinden* (1985-1986, Farfa), *Før Paris brænder* (1987-1988, Farfa), *Landet Nod* (1987-1989, Farfa), *Judith* (1987 -), *Ulven Dennis* (1987-1991), *Talabot* (1988-1991), *Rum i kejserpaladset* (1989), *Tristan og Isolde* (1989-1990), *Spor i sneen* (1989 -), *Itsi Bitsi* (1990- (Farfa/Odin Teatret), *The Castle of Holstebro* (1990-1999?), *Memoria* (1990-1992), *Klabauterfolket* (1991), *Den døde bror* (1992-), *Stilhedens ekko* (1992-), *Fædre og sønner* (1992-1996), *Junglebogen* (1993), *Kaosmos* (1993-1996), *Tankens veje* (1993-), *Shakuntala* (1993), *Mødre og døtre* (1994), *Den grimme, den grumme og den virkelig dumme* (1994-1996), *Hvid som jasmin* (1995-), *Doña Musica's sommerfugle* (1996-), *Whispering Winds* (1996-), *Ode til fremskridtet* (1997-), *I Hvalens skelet* (1997-), *Vincent van Gakk* (1997-), *Mythos* (1998-), *The Castle of Holstebro II* (1999-).

Odin Teatret's logos may also show some kind of artistic development. The first one from around 1966 shows Odin, the supreme Nordic god before Christianity on his 8-legged horse Slejpner followed by his messenger ravens Hugin and Munin. According to Christian Ludvigsen and Silvia Hagberg the motive is a reconstruction from a Swedish warrior helmet from the famous Vendel Era around the year 700, maybe from a drawing in a Scandinavian encyclopaedia. The present logo for Nordic Theatre Lab including Odin Teatret became official in 1984.

 Odin-logo 1965   Odin-logo 1984

It is taken from the Danish nuclear scientist, Niels Bohr. In 1947 he was conferred the highest Danish order, Knight of the Elephant, and for his oval coat-of-arms at Fredericksburg Castle he chose the taxitic symbol of yin and yang and the Latin words 'contraria sunt complementa', contrasts are complementary. Using this symbol suggests, that Eugenio Barba/NTL corresponds with the entire world through all ages combining in their lives and performances a lot of contrasting elements as a picture of life itself. PS In April 2000 Eugenio Barba was conferred 'Knight of the Order of Dannebrog' (the name of the Danish flag) by Queen Margrethe II.

2. Odin Teatret's staff 2000: Eugenio Barba (leader, director), Kai Bredholt (actor, barter), Roberta Carreri (actress, Odin-weeks), Jan Ferslev (actor, composer), Tage Larsen (actor, workshops), *Else Marie Laukvik* (actress, IT assistant), Iben Nagel Rasmussen (actress, actor students), Julia Varley (actress, theatre magazine editor), *Torgeir Wethal* (actor, film & video), Frans Winther (actor, composer), Patricia Braga Alves (tour manager, producer), Tine Bødker Christensen (technician), Anna Maria Hede (assistant accounter), Marie Holt (assistent producer), Hans Kobberø (technician), Sigrid Post (accounter, video publishing house), Pushparajah Sinnathamby (assistant), Rina Skeel (leader's secretary, producer, publishing house), Ulrik Skeel (producer, press manager), Ferdinando Taviani (dramaturge). The board: Søren Grundtvig Kjems (chairman, OT-administrator), Kirsten Justesen (visual artist), Per Kofod (publisher), Peter Laugesen (author), Bjørn Lense-Møller (former leader of Theatre Council in Denmark). Eugenio Barba (director), Julia Varley and Torgeir Wethal (actors) participate without vote.

According to Tony D'Urso/Eugenio Barba's *Viaggi con/Voyages with Odin Teatret* 2000 previous actors and central collaborators since 1964 have been: Ulla Alasjärvi, Louise A. Andersen, Judy Barba, Leif Bech, Hans Martin Berg, Jan Erik Bergström, Torben Bjelke, Lena Bjerregaard, Marianne Blichfeldt, Cécar Brie, Jens Christensen, Mona V. Christensen, Ragnar Louis Christiansen, Bernard Colin, Toni Cots, Berit S. Duusgaard, Christoph Falke, Tom Fjordefalk, Richard Fowler, Marisa Gilberti, Naira Gonzales, Cecilie Grieg, *Anne Trine Grimnes*, Juha Häkkänen, Falk Heinrich, Malou Illmoni, Fernando Jacon, Hanne Birgitte Jensen, Lis Jensen, Martin Kim Jensen, Lars Göran Kjellstedt, Bente Knudsen, Knud Erik Knudsen, Elsa Kvamme, Dorthe Kærgaard, Sören Larson, Anna Lica, Yves Liébert, Christian Ludvigsen, Giancarlo Marchesini, Dag A. Moe, Heidi Mogensen, Per Moth, Dan Nielsen, Tina Nielsen, Reidar Nilsson, Karl Olsen, Lars Oppegaard, Simon Panduro, Francis Pardeilhan, Grethe Pedersen, Silvia Ricciardelli, Carita Rindell, Gustavo Riondet, Stanley Rosenberg, Lucca Ruzza, Pia Sanderhoff, *Tor Sannum*, Jens Silverstersen, Agnete Ström, Odd Ström, Jan Torp, Isabel Ubeda, Kathrine Winkelhorn, Walter Ybema, Poul Østergaard, *Toril Øyen*. (*Italics*: founders together with Eugenio Barba). In spring 2000 Barba talked about difficulties in integrating new actors in Odin Teatret nowadays. It takes a long time to make them familiar enough with the 'old' actors' way of creating together. So Odin Teatret might not take in new actors in the ensemble from now on?

References

Andreasen, John 1998. Janus Teatret 9 - 10 - 8. Elin Andersen and Niels Lehmann (eds.). Teaterlegeringer. Aarhus: Aarhus Universitetsforlag.

Bablet, Denis 1972. Pour une methode d'analyse du lieu théâtral. *Travail théâtral* no. 6, mars 1972, pp. 107-25. (Translated to Swedish as: För en metod att analysera teaterplatsen. Kurt Aspelin (ed.) 1977. *Teaterarbete.* Stockholm: PAN/Nordstedts, pp. 93-118).

Beretning 1. januar 1999 - 31. december 1999. Holstebro: Odin Teatret (unpublished).

D'Urso, Tony and Eugenio Barba 2000. *Viaggi con/Voyages with Odin Teatret.* Milano: Ubu-libri.

Fridgaard, Torben 1997. *Fra eliteforbrug til masseforbrug. Interessen for kultur 1964-1993.* København: SFI.

Gran, Anne-Britt and Donnatella De Paoli 1991. *Teaterorganisering. En tverrfaglig tillnærming.* Oslo: Handelshøjskolens Bedriftsøkonomiske Institut.

Holmbäck, Åke och Elias Wessén 1946. *Svenska landskapslagar tolkade och förklarade för nutidens svenskar.* Stockholm: Gebers Förlag.

Kulturpengene 1999. København: Kulturministeriet.

Langsted, Jørn 1980. *Teaterlovgivning 2.* Graasten: Drama.

Långbacka, Ralf 1981. Åtta teser om konstnärligt teater. *Bland annat om Brecht.* Stockholm: Norstedt.

Oxford Advanced Learner's Dictionary 1995, Oxford UP.

Riesman, David 1971 (1950). *The Lonely Crowd.* Yale UP.

Statistiske Efterretninger. Uddannelse og kultur 2000. 1. København: Danmarks Statistik.

Statistisk Årbog 1999, København: Danmarks Statistik.

Waade, Anne Marit. *Zapping, shopping, sightseeing. Nye resepsjonskulturelle mønstre; teateropplevelsen som forskningsobjekt.* Æstetisk Seminar 16.02.2000, Århus (unpublished).

Niels Lehmann and Steen Sidenius

[**Postromantic Romanticism**]

A Note on the Poetics
of the Third Theatre

[**A theatre of the actor**]

Dealing with the theoretical work of Eugenio Barba presents certain difficulties. Barba does not think highly of the purely theoretical concept. Like so many other artists, he believes that by its very nature it tends to violate the richness of life. To artists like Barba, conceptualising something means imposing on it a particular vocabulary that only allows us to acknowledge a small fragment of the described piece of reality. According to this view (which, it should be noted in passing, is defended by theoreticians as well as artists), language will always lag behind reality. Consequently, Barba often cautions us not to take his words at face value. For instance, in a discussion of his central notion of the pre-expressive level of the actor's work, he suggests that we think of this notion as 'an epistemological illusion [en erkendelsesmæssig fiktion]' (Barba 1994, 124, our translation). Furthermore, he insists that his theory concerns what he calls the logic of the process and that, consequently, it should only be seen as an attempt to come up with solutions to the concrete problems with which the actors in Odin Teatret are faced.

Now, the difficulty with interpreting a corpus of theoretical writing based on such a self-conscious devaluation of the conceptual work to an illusion suited for solving practical problems is, of course, only that one may always be accused of being beside the point if one tries to analyse the inner logic of the theory. Though we realise that we may distance ourselves unduly from Barba's intentions, we would nevertheless lie to run the risk and undertake such an analysis. We find the approach legitimated by the fact that, if taken literally, Barba's texts seem to be founded on a rather consistent theoretical framework. If by poetics of the theatre we mean a set of presumptions about what theatre is and should be, i.e. a set of guiding principles that determines the practical work, we contend that Barba's writing does indeed display a poetics.

Not only is it evident that Barba opts for a form of theatre in which the actor is the undisputed heart of the matter; for Barba, theatre only exists because of the actor:

> In the moment of truth, in front of the spectators, but only if the presence of the actors catches us and throws us into a whirl of reflections and experiences that are different from everyday life, only then *does the theatre exist because the actor exists*. (Barba 1989, 89, our translation)

This definition is less innocent than it may seem. A definition of theatre in general based on the belief that theatre only exists because of the actor excludes from the notion of theatre a whole range of theatre forms that do not make the actor the centre of everything. For the sake of it, let us mention the theatre experiments in the tradition of Edward Gordon Craig and Oscar Schlemmer based on an attempt to rid the theatre of the human, all too human actor. We also find it appropriate to mention so-called per-formance theatre, in which the actor is but one element in the overall stage image that is considered to be no more important than, say, a video projection or a particular soundscape.

We point out Barba's initial exclusion of theatre forms which are not based on the presence of the actor not so much in order to highlight the fact that he, like many other theoreticians, displays a general normativity when he founds his poetics on an ontolog-ical definition of theatre; by arguing that Barba's reasoning only applies to a certain form of theatre, we simply wish to suggest that his theoretical endeavour is based on a particular poetological will (*ein Kunstwollen*, as it were), i.e. the attempt to discover the secrets of 'the actor alive'. This is underscored by the fact that, in the eyes of Barba, it is only a particular type of performer who is in fact entitled to be called an actor: 'An actor who is not effectful on the pre-expressive level, is not an actor. [...] An actor's effectiveness on the pre-expressive level is the prerequisite for his integrity as an indi-vidual and as an artist' (Barba 1994, 125, our translation). Barba demands, it seems, not only a certain form of theatre, the theatre of the actor should also be carried by a very definite kind of actor.

The longing for a type of actor whose work can guarantee the quality of the par-ticular theatre of the actor has indubitably been the heart of Barba's poetological will throughout his career. From the attempt to create an anthropological theatre to the for-mation of a theatre anthropology aimed at a transcultural investigation of the work of the actor, the presence of the actor has been on the agenda. Consequently, Barba's po-etics first and foremost unfolds as a representation of the strategies by which he hopes to increase the probability that the audience will experience a hightened presence on stage. As far as we can see, this representation relies on a certain poetological logic. In the following we shall try to unfold this logic as we believe it to be staged in Barba's texts. It should be mentioned, however, that due to the space available we are only able to draw a very rough sketch.[1]

[The problem with rationality]

The logic governing Barba's poetological will might best be characterised as 'post-romantic formulas romantically interpreted'. This is, at any rate, the general point of view carrying the following argument. We acknowledge the fact that, strictly speaking, it is probably highly problematic to talk about romanticism and post-romanticism as such; thus we suggest both that there are no differences between philosophers and aesthetes like Schelling, the Schlegel-brothers, Hölderlin, Novalis and Hegel and, furthermore, that the philosophies of every thinker since Nietzsche — for instance, Heidegger, Derrida and Deleuze — are all the same. Of course, neither of these views would be correct. However, we hope to be excused for this gross simplification as we only evoke the distinction between romanticism and post-romanticism for strategical purposes. It simply helps to shed some light on the logic of Barba's poetological thinking.

To begin with, it is the critical attitude towards our rational and secular Western civilisation that is only rarely explicitly stated in Barba's texts but seemingly all the more *implicitly active* that brings the romanticist-post-romanticist tradition to mind. This postulate is probably in demand of some justification. However, we must restrain ourselves to one example. In his text on the Euro-Asian actor, Barba suggests that we do not concern ourselves with the superficial differences between the European and the Asian traditions. In spite of their obvious differences, both traditions come from the same source; they both originate from the same transcultural dimension, 'the tradition of the traditions' as Barba calls it. However, if Barba thus attempts to surmount the differences by probing into the common ground of the two types of actors, i.e. into what precedes difference, in order to get at the very foundation of acting, he still tends to favour Asian culture at the expense of Western culture. In conclusion, Barba opts for the Euro-Asian theatre built upon the tradition of the traditions, which he finds necessary at the threshold of the twenty-first century. Barba seems to think that whereas the Asian audience is already equipped for this theatre, the Western audience is not:

> It is only the Western spectators who are not used to jumping from one role to another in the company of the same actor; who are not used to relating to somebody whose language they cannot easily understand; who are not used to a physical expression that is not immediately mimetic or that does not belong to the conventions of dance. (Barba 1989, 202, our translation)

How should this be read, if not as a criticism of Western culture, a culture so superficial because excessively dependent on rationality that, due to its insensitive ideology of understandability, it deprives its inhabitants of the more subtle aesthetic experiences of a theatre based on bios, not logos?

Later, when Barba returns to the issue of the Euro-Asian actor, he substitutes the opposition between an Asian and an European actor with a juxtaposition of the actor from the North Pole and his counterpart at the South Pole. However, this manoeuvre does not really alter the image of a wise culture on the one hand and a somewhat superficial and rationalistic culture on the other. The drift is still the same. What is needed according to Barba, is a transgression of the immediate differences of the two poles in order to find the 'recurring elements' proper to both traditions. Barba suggests this change of vocabulary explicitly in order to avoid the differences to be related to specific cultures. So far so good, but the implicit hierarchy is still maintained. In spite of Barba's explicit intentions it soon becomes clear that the actor from the North Pole is valorised and the actor from the Southpole depreciated. Why? Firstly, because only the North Pole actor understands the necessity of working from *basic principles*. As opposed to the actor from the South Pole, who is defined as the actor without a set of rules and who is therefore bound to construct his own rules along the way, the actor from the North Pole 'forms his scenic behaviour according to a thoroughly tested set of rules' (Barba 1994, 21, our translation). Secondly, because the lack of guiding principles so typical for the Southpole actor evokes the image of 'the culture of dissolution' from which Barba distances himself when describing his experiences of a secular culture without a common faith (Barba 1994, 11). In Barba's view, like the actor with no set of rules, the secular human being experiences among other things a lack of orientation, a split between thought and action and a static and deadly specialisation.

We take pains to unravel this implicit depreciation of Western culture because it seems to agree with the negative feelings towards our culture shared by romanticists and post-romanticists alike. In romanticism the analytical reason of the Enlightenment in general and of Kant in particular is considered highly problematical. At best, it is seen as superficial because it is incapable of bringing us in contact with the essential dimensions of life. At worst, it is seen as a destructive force because in its attempt to break everything up into small components no cohesion can withstand it.

This feeling of uneasiness towards rationality is shared by post-romanticists, but for thinkers following in the footsteps of Nietzsche it seems necessary to extend the criticism to the entire history of metaphysics, i.e. 2500 years of Western philosophy. From this radicalisation of the scope of the criticism not only follows that the sting is now turned against reason, logos, *as such*; it also implies that the metaphysics of romanticism is included in that which is being criticised. This feature is, in fact, what makes the use of the term post-romanticism feasible. If we are not completely mistaken, post-romanticism should be understood as a philosophical position that inherits the romanticist criticism of analytical reason but which is also marked by an attempt to transgress the limits of romanticism.[2]

[The work of art and the art of living]

When it comes to the question of what they have to offer in replacement of the rationalistic culture of the West, post-romantic philosophers also seem to reveal themselves as critical heirs of romanticism.

The aforementioned suspicion towards the capability of language to represent reality in a straightforward manner has its origin in romanticism. This kind of scepticism is, thus, a central element of the romanticist criticism of rationality. As opposed to modern scientists who generally hold a belief in the possibility of immediate representation, romanticists pin their faith on the work of art. In doing so, they reverse the long tradition in the wake of Plato, according to whom art should be condemned. To the romanticists the reverse is in fact true. Because art does not attempt a straightforward representation, but takes a detour around an indirect and metaphoric kind of expression, they find it much better suited to getting in contact with reality than the ordinary use of propositional statements. As a work of art is believed to be enigmatic by nature and therefore, in principle, inexhaustible as far as meaning is concerned, according to the romanticists it is capable of doing what ordinary language cannot, namely, letting the ineffable be expressed. With his famous dictum, 'je poetischer, je wahrer', Novalis puts into words the general feeling on which, it seems, romanticism is built (cf. Frank 1989, 123ff). The hope that romanticists pin on art is fundamentally based on *the creative dimension* of art. Artistic creativity is regarded as the prerequisite, the condition of possibility, as it were, for propositional truth, which, consequently, must be seen as a mere derivation of a more original form of truth, a truth of a second order. With Frank, the romanticist insistence on art's birth right to truth may, perhaps, be summed up by a phrase borrowed from Klee, who once said: 'Art does not reflect the visible, it makes visible' (cf. Frank 1989, 18).

The most important trait in this profile of the romanticist attitude is, it seems, that it is not representation, *mimesis,* as such that is being attacked. Insofar as art is seen as a kind of mirror that can do what ordinary representational statements cannot, i.e. bring us in contact with a deeper kind of truth, what is at stake, if anything, is the search for *an improved form of representation*. At least, this trait is the most important one if one wishes to compare romanticism with post-romanticism. In the latter we also find the critical attitude towards direct representation and a positive attitude towards art. But in philosophies that are critical towards romanticism, art does not represent a

175

LIVERPOOL JOHN MOORES UNIVERSITY
LEARNING SERVICES

privileged access to truth. As a matter of fact, post-romanticists have given up on the quest for truth. This act of active forgetting is a consequence of the attempt to formulate a philosophy of pure immanence, i.e. a philosophy based on an acceptance of the impossibility of transgressing time and chance. This acceptance not only implies turning Platonic philosophy upside down, as it is founded upon an insistence on the materiality of life, it also means giving up the belief in a fixed identity of, or a timeless essence of, things. As things are seen as being in a constant flux, or in duration, to quote Bergson, they are always already differing from themselves. As opposed to a philosophy based on the notion of *being*, a philosophy that takes its point of departure in *becoming* focusses on the inevitable transformation of identity into difference.

It goes without saying that this displacement is ripe with consequences, the most important of which may be illustrated by a reference to one of Nietzsche's famous remarks. When criticising his own early work on the birth of tragedy, he considers the main advantage of the work its tendency 'to evaluate science from the perspective of art and art from the perspective of life'. Had he only found the first part of the formula feasible, he would probably have discredited the book altogether, as it would have contained nothing but the artist's metaphysics of romanticism that Nietzsche came to find despicable at the end of his career.

The second part represents, however, the beginning of Nietzsche's break with romanticism. Seeing art from the perspective of life means considering whether a particular piece of art is beneficial to life or not. When setting out to evaluate the work of art along these lines, one is only a short step away from giving up the production of art in favour of an attempt to live artistically, if by this we mean living according to values one has created oneself. This attempt to generalise the creativity of the artist to the practice of everyday life is one of the central trademarks of the philosophy of immanence in the wake of Nietzsche. In this philosophy there is no need for works of art as a means of true representation, as there is nothing to be represented, not even something ineffable to be stated indirectly; there is, however, the need to experiment with the practice of living, since a life conceived as contingency has to be created over and over again.[3]

With this movement from valorising art to generalising creativity to an art of living, Nietzsche prepares the project of sublating art, i.e. transforming art into reality, performed by the historical avant-garde at the beginning of the twentieth century (cf. Bürger 1973), as well as the attempt to live creatively by way of an individuation without subjectivity suggested by Deleuze at the end of this century (cf. Deleuze 1980).

[Individual development through theatre]

Now, how does Barba appear in this light? On the face of it, much of what Barba says seems to rhyme with post-romanticist thinking. In Barba's view, working with theatre first and foremost seems to involve a project of development for the actors, a constant creation and recreation of the self. This seems to be the main implication in the demand for an acculturation that will allow the actor to rid himself of the automatisms of the practices of everyday life. The ideal of constant personal development also seems to be the rationale for using individual exercises rather than general ones as well as for the need 'to efface 'the actor' in my friends, to wash off their roles, destroy the theatre in our relationship, so that we could meet like humans' (Barba 1998, 61, our translation).

Furthermore, the implications of the name that Barba invents for the actors who are willing to take part in the developmental work and embark on a floating island, 'the travellers of speed', also point in the direction of post-romanticism. In part, because Barba underlines the corporeity of the traveller, the body being understood as the very space in which the travel of speed takes place: 'My body is my country. The only place where I always *am*' (Barba 1989, 90, our translation). This accent placed on the bodily dimension, on the bios of the actor, definitely brings the philosophy of immanence to mind; in part because of the insistence on speed, which appears to be akin to the philosophy of becoming.

Reflecting on the necessity of acculturation, Barba explains that 'the search for our *bios*, our own 'country', our body-alive [...] is an attempt at continuous development' (Barba 1989, 96, our translation). Barba even finds it necessary to warn the actors against the dangers of being caught in a new fixed bodily culture when trying to escape the inculturation. A new set of ekstra-daily movements may easily turn into a prison house no less suppressive than ordinary inculturation. Apparently, the aim of travelling is to constantly become other.

It should not be overlooked, however, that the developmental process that Barba has in mind is occurring *through art*. Faced with the difficulties of becoming liberated from the automatisms of inculturation in the predominant rationalistic culture, Barba turns to the art of theatre. To him, art represents a sort of refuge (cf. for instance Barba 1980, 13). Moreover, it is not any art that can bring forth the desired result. Authentic liberation can only be obtained by *true art*, it seems. At any rate, it only seems to be true art that can bring us in contact with profound truth:

> Our anatomical theatre does not just concern the human body. It concerns human actions and its relationships, in the light of the events of society, in the light of historical conflicts: the tensions and contradictions which are the profound (dybereliggende)

rules for the different realities. This means: establishling the vision of what is hiding underneath the skin. (Barba 1980, 68, our translation)

To us, two things are particularly striking in this quote. Firstly, it is obvious that Barba applies a hermeneutics of depth. Barba leaves no doubt that the indirectly stated ineffable is more profound, truthful and authentic than any straightforward meaning. Secondly, Barba's theatre is about visualising something that is not immediately visible. This fits in nicely with the enhanced mimesis of romanticism.

No wonder, then, that the program of 'effing' the ineffable is restated by Barba. Discussing the difficulties with language, Barba poses the question of whether it is possible to communicate one's own experience in order to point out the essential. To this question he answers:

It presupposes that the word, when it is no longer communicated directly, renounces its will to say, withdraws and lies in wait [...] The word will array, therefore, in artistic knowledge and experience, point at rules and discoveries. But its truest value — if it succeeds in conquering it — will be *to say without saying*. (Barba 1980, 19, our translation)

As we have already seen, Barba believes that in order to get at the essential elements of experience, in the wake of the Romanticist poetics as it were, that one needs to use indirect, artistic language. The point we would like to make here, however, is that the actor's development is not just about personal growth. It is first and foremost about obtaining the skills for producing the enhanced mimesis, for making the invisible visible, for letting the skeleton appear beneath the flesh, for giving speech back to life itself, and so forth.

Barba even claims to know what we will find when we obtain the necessary skills: the dialectics that governs life' (Barba 1991, 70). The decision that life is ontologically ruled by dialectical laws places his poetics at odds with post-romanticism. Barba often talks about the play of oppositions, and occasionally he even uses phrases that could have been lifted out of the philosophy of difference of, say, Derrida or Deleuze.

Dialectics is not a fact that rests in itself. It emerges from the intention to control forces that, if left alone, would be at war with, or destructive for, each other (Barba 1994, 109, our translation).

Here, dialectics is not conceived as an ontological condition of life, but rather as something which must be actively intended in order to surmount the real ontological condition which is represented here as a battlefield of forces ever at war. This corresponds with the view of the tragedian, the philosopher of 'original' difference, who neither believes in the capability of dialectical reasoning to bring the various forces of life in agreement, nor finds it likely that we will ever obtain a true understanding of the becoming of being. Such a statement is, however, a very rare occasion in Barba's theoretical writing. Normally, he talks like a dialectician who sees dialectical movements at the heart of life, and insofar as he claims to have knowledge of the dialectical rules governing life, he reinstates being in the becoming.[4]

In this light the only difference between Barba and the Romanticist seems to be that Barba prefers to substitute the aural metaphor of the ineffable with the visual metaphor of the invisible or, perhaps, that his entire poetics has been built upon an ongoing clash between two mutually exclusive philosophies. However, neither of these images would be a correct representation of Barba's theatre poetics, we believe. What we are dealing with seems rather to be a post-romantic version of the attempt to arrive at the ineffable:

> This is a fundamental principle in [Odin Teatret's] theatre work: On stage the action must be real, but not necessarily realistic. The actor does not revive the action but *recreates life* in the action. (Barba 1994, 41-2, our translation, italics added)

Thus, in Barba's theatre the enhanced mimesis takes the form of *a recreation* of life. If the true dialectics of life shall become visible, the actor must be 'for real', so to speak. There is no doubt in our minds that this is the reason why Barba is doing theatre with real actors of flesh and blood instead of writing, say, poems or novels. The call for *a scenic bios* seems to state the two dimensions of the poetics *in nuce*. On the one hand, Barba goes for the actor's *bios,* the body in becoming. On the other hand, it is the *scenic* bios — i.e. a body transformed into art, or to be slightly more precise: into *true* art, thus leading us towards true life — that has his interest. Like so many of Barba's theoretical constructions, this seems to be a post-romantic formula romantically interpreted, if there ever was one.

Notes

1. For a more thorough investigation of the logic at work in Barba's poetics from a slightly different perspective, see the unpublished thesis by Sidenius on this subject.
2. For the romanticist position cf. Frank 1982 and Frank 1989. For an exposé of the critical inheritance of the romanticist project by philosophers and artists in the wake of Wagner and Nietzsche, cf. Frank 1988. Cf. Frank 1984 for a thorough investigation of the reactualisation of the critical project in so-called poststructuralism.

3. The self-criticism is found in Nietzsche 1988.

4. For a closer look at the difference between 'the becoming in being' og poststructuralism and 'the being in becoming' of Barba, see Sidenius 1998.

References

Barba, Eugenio 1980. *Modsætningernes spil*. København: Berg.

Barba, Eugenio 1989. *De flydende øer*. København: Borgen.

Barba, Eugenio 1994. *En kano af papir*. Gråsten: Drama.

Barba, Eugenio & Nicola Savarese 1991. *The Secret Art of the Performer. A Dictionary of Theatre Anthropology*. London: Routledge.

Bürger, Peter 1973. *Theorie der Avantgarde*. Frankfurt a/M: Suhrkamp.

Frank, Manfred 1982. *Der kommende Gott. Vorlesungen über die Neue Mythologie*. Frankfurt a/M: Suhrkamp

Frank, Manfred 1984. *Was ist Neostrukturalismus?* Frankfurt a/M: Suhrkamp.

Frank, Manfred 1988. *Gott im Exil*. Frankfurt a/M: Suhrkamp.

Frank, Manfred 1989. *Einführung in die frühromantische Ästhetik*. Frankfurt a/M: Suhrkamp.

Nietzsche, Friedrich 1988. *Die Geburt der Tragödie*. In Colli, Georgio & Mazzino Montinari (eds.). *Kritische Studienausgabe*. München: Verlag de Gruyter.

Sidenius, Steen (unpublished). *Det tredje teater. Eksistens, kunst og videnskab i Barbas poetik*.

Sidenius, Steen 1998. Barba and Poststructuralism. The Metaphysics og the Third Theatre. In *Nordic Theatre Studies*, vol. 11. Helsingfors: Föreningen Nordiska Teaterforskare.

Torunn Kjølner

[**Searching for Differences**]

Odin Teatret did represent something different from the very start. The group of people who started to work together in Oslo in 1964 called themselves a theatre. Odin Teatret was different because it was a theatre laboratory, a place to investigate acting through experimental exercises. It was different from the theatre school run by the Norwegian government, Statens Teaterskole, in that the 'school' of Odin Teatret did not have a fixed idea of what kind of actor it would turn out at the other end. In fact, they did not even think in terms of an end to their training. Training soon became the essence of Odin Teatret and was not something one could leave behind

> Training is an encounter with the reality which one has chosen: whatever you do, do it with your whole self. For this reason we talk about training and not learning or apprenticeship. Although all our actors are formed here in our theatre, we are not a theatre school in the usual sense since there are no teachers or study programme. The actors themselves elaborate and are responsible for their training. But in order to achieve this degree of freedom, there must be self-discipline. And this is why training is a necessity for everyone, irrespective of how long one has been working in the theatre. (Barba 1979, 68)

This statement was made more than thirty years ago. However, it is still impossible to understand Odin Teatret without understanding how training and, based on this, a constant search for a different kind of theatre has been the very foundation of Odin Teatret.

In Norway the only door leading to a professional acting career was (and still is) a theatre school run by the state. It was a brave and provident move of Barba to recruit group members from a list of people who had failed to gain entry through the only sanctioned door. Brave because it seemed an impossible task to challenge the monopoly of the school, and farsighted because such a group of people obviously had a love of theatre to invest in their work. Everybody was in a position to look for something else. Barba wanted to do the following:

LIVERPOOL JOHN MOORES UNIVERSITY
idne arts L.R.C.
. ∩
3701/3634

[...] create a new language, which will lead us towards a new form of contact, increasing our possibilities of approaching other individuals. A language that can strike us with the same immediate force as the sight of a mother protecting her child, or a man who, in cold blood, kills another in the street. Even if we have not had the similar experience, or are not prepared in any way to interpret it, nevertheless we will still be touched in a direct, physical way. (Barba 1979, 29)

This statement still seems like a striking metaphor for what Odin Teatret has been searching for — theatre that touches us in a direct, physical way, theatre that does not lend itself to immediate interpretation. To look for the difference that Odin Teatret makes today is perhaps a different task than in the sixties when Taviani wrote these lines:

Isolated and autodidact, the people of the Odin are forced to draw inspiration from books by great masters of the past, in particular Stanislavskis and Meyerhold. But what they do is not *recognizable*. They haven't the possibility of referring to other experiences possessing a certain measure of prestige in order to back up their practical choices. [...]. An actor who trains daily and doesn't limit himself to rehearsals and performances is totally unknown, or known only in the context of the distant oriental civilization rooted in traditional values. (Barba 1979, introduction)

Today many different actors-to-be have studied the great masters and many are exploring the art of acting in many different kinds of laboratories. Odin Teatret has moved out of its isolation and many theatre schools have moved in the direction of actors' laboratories.

Barba created the Third Theatre to search for something different than what the First and Second theatres had in his view. He seemingly still regards the First Theatre as the commercial theatre and the Second Theatre as the avant-garde. During his visit to Aarhus in the spring of 2000, Barba maintained that the Second Theatre seemed to have 'evaporated' or been swallowed up by commercial interests, like so many other new forms of art. This also opens up for questioning, one should think. What has made it possible for the Third theatre to avoid commercialisation? Is it still interesting to ask what difference the Odin approach makes? Yes, I believe so, and it seems impossible to avoid focussing on acting if one does look for the difference. Is there a real difference between a 'first' and a 'third' concept of acting?

[The laboratory revisited]

The whole idea of the actors' laboratory is based on the presumption that there is more potential in human material as art than what is exhibited at first sight, and that these potentials can only be displayed and investigated in real action. Stanislavsky saw the art of acting in terms of natural laws. Being an artist, Stanislavsky admits that he can only talk about these laws in everyday terms — or use metaphors to explain what he means. A lot of Stanislavsky's metaphors are related to the idea of birth and organic growth. As such the idea of the organic is a vital backdrop for his theories of acting. Likewise, Barba turns to the organic when he investigates and explains the art of acting. To Barba it is life itself, *bios*, that is the base in acting. The human being is, of course, the sine qua non of this bios — and therefore of theatre as such. Life is not just to be represented by the actor. The actor must be *present in life* on stage for theatre to happen. So, basically Barba treats acting as a quality, not as a profession or a craft. There is a kind of hierarchy in his terminology which makes him draw a dividing line between bios and form. Bios ranges far above form because form to Barba is a result and as such something fixed, inorganic and overt: '[...] the fixity of the Form seemed irreconcilable with the changeable, living, continuously metamorphosing nature of the performance and of its artists.' he writes in 1995 (p. 103). The actress of the Third Theatre cannot rely on mere craftsmanship. To learn a craft is to learn something that is already known in an already known form. One would perhaps suspect that talent, then, must be a big issue for Barba, but actually it is not: 'We do not choose our actors because of their talent, but because of their strength of character, their generosity, their perseverance' (Barba 1979,26). Contrary to Stanislavsky, who deals with talent as an almost ontological issue in many of his books, Barba starts from other sources. Like Stanislavsky, Barba is concerned with the rules that govern acting, but whereas Stanislavsky studied, and even copied, what the great actors of his time did on stage — and backstage — Barba studies the great traditions or cultures of acting. Stanislavsky also studied himself and very consciously took notes. His notes include successes as well as failures. Stanislavsky did not consider himself to be a natural talent. He had to work hard to achieve his successes. He also worked hard to accept his failures. Stanislavsky's theses of acting and his discovery of laws for good theatrical conduct drew from both experiences. Among other things he found that a lot of bad acting stemmed from copying exterior forms of acting, from copying stale conventions or actions that had lost their reference to modern society. Stanislavsky reacted against theatre that mimed theatre and not real life, in this case nature or social reality. His obvious solution was to make the actor look to nature, including the nature of social forms, to understand what could take place in a human being behind — or even beyond — exterior forms of social conduct, because in real life one experiences a difference between an 'inner' and an 'outer' life. To make the exterior forms truthful and convincing on stage, the actor must find a way to deal with the forces that lead to the particular form of conduct of a character in a particular situation. He should learn to think in terms of what happens, or in the well-known 'chains of actions'. What the character says must, of course, be considered in terms of the same logic. Words are actions. The words grow from actions, which themselves grow from an inner source in an organic way. Stanislavsky seems to treat talent like an ability to work on such connections so that they flow freely and create a real relationship between the actor and his role that has a similar flow. To Stanislavsky acting relies on craftsmanship, but craft alone does not make a great actor or actress. To play a character who convincingly interacts with others implies that one has reached a particular control over one's body, one's voice, one's psyche and one's environment. In short, we owe to Stanilavsky the idea that acting requires an ability to master oneself as artistic material in a fictitious role — and to be present as a living person at the same time.

Barba's organic approach and his focus on physical personal presence is a heritage from his master Stanislavsky. Nature, however, seems to play a more central role in Barba's conception of acting. It is not enough to consider nature as involved in acting. Nature — or in Barba's version — the organic, *is* acting. Barba does not believe that representative actions in terms of social behaviour can really cultivate the organic, so he wants to do the following:

> Cut through the stereotypes of social reactions which is the usual theatrical model. We are trying to go beyond our socially determined reflexes, to reach our living and basic nucleus, disciplining this process through signs and situations. (Barba 1979, 27)

To Barba, the actor's psycho-physical possibilities are his or her voice and body. In other words, the nature of social life is not really natural because it is culturally determined. Realistic acting can be acting in some cases, but there is no real bios in representation as such. To find this bios, the actor has to look for something that makes the actions stand out as something different from our commercialised and culturally meagre everyday life conventions — something 'extra-daily' in Barba's terminology.

I have tried to understand how Stanislavsky's laboratory experiences can be a main reference to understand how Barba links his organic concept of acting with the conscious and detailed montage he undertakes when he directs Odin Teatret's performances.

[A new language?]

Barba has been more interested in finding a 'new language' than in actively breaking the laws of an old. He has been looking for something beyond theatrical forms. 'What matters is what lies behind the results', he argues in *Modsætningernes spil* in 1980. The actor must not look for an effect on the audience, but for what works for himself as an individual actor. To explain this personal approach to acting, he uses a whole range of metaphors, that are taken from the natural sciences, particularly the fields of physics and electricity. Thus the concept of *energy* is central. Behind these metaphors we find a deep respect for principles for how the body acts and reacts in extra-ordinary moments of life. These principles or laws are linked with a basic belief in dialectics as a main driving force in human life. I shall not discuss these concepts here, just remind the reader that Barba's prescriptions for a new language are thought of in terms of coherent principles of acting, not in terms of individual praxis. The individual actor discovers the principles through conscious training. Barba does not talk about acting as a craft one can learn, but about the principles of acting inherent in different theatre cultures. He studies how these principles manifest themselves as 'pre-expressivity', which he defines as a level of organisation that can be virtually separated from the expressive level. Thus, pre-expressivity is a metaphor, or 'an experiential fiction', as Barba calls it.

Certainly, there have been some changes in respect to the way Odin Teatret worked in the sixties and seventies, perhaps in particular when it comes to the use of voice and the use of texts. Most of the original principles are nevertheless more or less intact. It is the work of the individual actor that matters. The 'process itself, the development of personal research' is essential. Discipline, precision and the desire to transgress social conventions are still prerequisites for Odin Teatret. Today we see some interesting consequences of Barba's poetics. Each individual actor or actress in Odin Teatret has developed not only an individual stage personality, (some would call it 'style') but their approaches to training and working with a text also differ considerably. To talk about one way of using the voice and one way of approaching the text in Odin Teatret today would lead us astray. Some work with musical scores, some have started to adjust connections between the voice, the text and the physical scores they produce in their training or rehearsal situations, some even say that training is no longer their main point of departure for finding stage actions. Music has taken on a greater importance and different kinds of dance have been applied and explored. However, Odin Teatret's performances, like *Mythos,* have one director, namely Barba, and it is he who in the end creates the performance as a *montage* of the different stage personalities.

LIVERPOOL JOHN MOORES UNIVERSITY
Aldham Robarts L.R.C.
TEL 0151 231 3701/3634

[Organic montage?]

For a start Odin Teatret does not practise to 'suit the action to the word — and the word to the action' as Shakespeare let Hamlet command his actors. At least not in the traditional way. When Barba digs for sources of acting, he does not look to the great actors of his time. Barba looks for rules behind the rules. In an almost Darwinist way he has spotted principles that seem to have survived time and cultural changes, principles still fit for life — extraordinary life. Like Stanislavsky, Barba does not want the ordinary on stage. Barba's opposition to state-supported and commercial theatre practise has the lifelessness of conventional acting as its main target. Barba's insistence on finding the essentials of on-stage life can be seen as a driving force against the commercialisation of theatre. It can also be seen as the conviction that the secrets of acting are to be found in the *principles* of acting, not in the actor. This may seem inconsistent thinking. It makes sense, however, in light of Barba's notion of a new language or a Third Theatre. Insisting that there is only one real difference, the difference between live acting and not acting at all, Barba avoids dealing with the issue of good and bad acting or of talented or untalented actors. Seeing acting as an organic quality that transgresses theatrical forms changes the orientation of the discussion to a field that is principally without aesthetic judgement: that of presence. Barba's notion that there is acting, which is organic and essentially filled with life, and 'something else', which may look like acting but which is really something deadly and commercial, might, however, make it difficult to explain if and when acting can take place in the commercial theatre. More intriguing still is the question of whether 'something deadly' can happen if and when the actor knows and applies the right principles. The Third Theatre does not expect its audiences to interpret something recognisable. So the audience should principally suspend aesthetical judgements from their reception of what they see. Avoiding any discussion of acting in terms of bad and good dissolves the issue of talent. Talent can not be explained in terms of principles. Insisting that acting is a quality then explains why discipline must be the core of acting.

What at first sight seems impossible is the combination of organic acting and a conscious montage of elements to form performances like those of Odin Teatret. One explanation could be that in montaging the organic bios of the individual contributions of his actors, Barba acts like the gardener who weeds to leave space for the most able plants to grow. The director thus actively selects and links up his selections. The theatre is the actor, Barba maintains. Is directing then a version of acting based on the same principles? Or are there other secret principles that lead the director in his dramaturgical choices? What to me seems different is the notion that form or aesthetic ideals does not really belong to the art of acting. An actor who wants to become a good actor by means of mastering the conventions, the ideals of vocal and corporal beauty, artistic originality and the aesthetic ideals of a contemporary theatre culture, will have difficulty seeing Barba's universal secrets of acting, because they are hidden neither in the form nor in the recognisable movements and sounds of the actor. Acting is not talent. Acting can not be judged in terms of bad and good. Barba and his researchers of theatrical anthropology maintain that the principles can be explained and studied. *The Secret Art of the Performer* from 1991 is an attempt to do so. The searching actor (and director?) can start from this lavishly illustrated dictionary of theatre antropology and take the path through training. There is no end result. *There are no secrets* is the reply Peter Brook sends through his book a few years later. But who really knows? Answers differ — as does taste ...

References

Barba, Eugenio 1979. *The Floating Islands*. Graasten: Drama.

Barba, Eugenio 1980. *Modsætningernes spil*. København: Berg.

Barba, Eugenio 1991. *The Secret Art of The Performer*. London: Routledge.

Barba, Eugenio 1995. *The Paper Canoe*. London and New York: Routledge.

Brook, Peter 1993. *There are no secrets*. London: Methuen.

The Sonning Prize
University of Copenhagen

[Eugenio Barba awarded the Sonning Prize 2000]

The winner of the Sonning Prize for the year 2000 is Italian born Eugenio Barba, the founder and director of Odin Teatret. The official ceremony will take place on Wednesday 19 April 2000 at Copenhagen University.

The Sonning Prize, comprising 500,000 Danish Kroner, is awarded every other year to a person who has made a significant contribution to European culture, the winner being elected by a committee established by the Senate of the University of Copenhagen. In 1991 it went to the Czech playwright Václav Havel, in 1994 to the Polish film director Krzysztof Kieslowski, in 1996 to the German author Günter Grass and in 1998 to the Danish architect Jørn Utzon.

There are few who have kept theatre alive and at the forefront of European culture as has Eugenio Barba. In his capacity of theatre pedagogue, researcher and creator over a period of 35 years, he has succeeded in implementing his ideas in accordance with the changing artistic, political and social circumstances in such a way that theatre stands out as a vital source of artistic and cultural renewal.

In giving the Sonning Prize to Eugenio Barba we are honouring a man who is not merely a researcher into the fundamentals of the art of theatre, but is at the same time an outstanding creative artist. Through his art and his theatre research he has managed to carry his craft forward as well as connect his wide European background — reaching from Italy to Norway and from Poland to Denmark — with a worldwide network spanning the Far East, over Eastern and Western Europe as far as Latin America, and consisting of theatre people he has influenced and collaborated with. Eugenio Barba is an original artist and a true European in an age of globalisation, rooted in ancient culture yet with apprentices and collaborators around the world.

University of Copenhagen, 19 November 1999
Kjeld Møllgård, Rector

Prizewinners

Albert Schweitzer (1959), Bertrand Russell (1960), Niels Bohr (1961), Alvar Aalto (1962), Karl Barth (1963), Dominique Pire (1964), Richard von Coudenhove-Kalergi (1965), Sir Laurence Olivier (1966), W. A. Visser't Hooft (1967), Arthur Koestler (1968), Haldór Laxness (1969), Max Tau (1970), Danilo Dolci (1971), Karl Popper (1973), Hannah Arendt (1975), Arne Næss (1977), Herman Gmeiner (1979), Dario Fo (1981), Simone de Beauvoir (1983), William Heinesen (1985), Jürgen Habermas (1987), Ingmar Bergman (1989), Václav Havel (1991), Krzysztof Kieslowski (1994), Günter Grass (1996), Jørn Utzon (1998). In 1950 an extraordinary award was given to Sir Winston Churchill.

Kirsten Hastrup

[For Odin!]

Dear Odin, Dear Eugenio Barba

It is a great honour and no less a pleasure to have been asked to give this talk as part of the motivation for awarding you the Sonning Prize for this year. It appears so patently right that Eugenio Barba and his colleagues at Odin Teatret should be distinguished for their contribution to European culture, even if the theatre and the theatre anthropology thereby honoured are not at all limited by the ever more fluid boundaries of Europe.

The more than twenty performances that Odin has put on during 35 years of activity, and the equal number of books produced by Eugenio Barba, on his own or in collaboration with colleagues, have made a lasting impact on our understanding of theatre as a peculiar space, a floating island, that may, in principle, anchor everywhere. If nothing else, this, by itself, makes 'Europe' just one possibility among others.

The work of Eugenio Barba is, to a rare extent, marked by a fusion of traditions. Theatre historians will be able to identify elements from East and West, inspirations from near and far, and repercussions all over the world. It may be seen like a quite unwarranted honour for this country that a world theatre like Odin Teatret has chosen Holstebro as its anchor place, when the floating island sometimes needs to rest. It speaks loudly and clearly of Barba's loyalty to the town that first invited Odin to settle.

It is worth noting, however, that for Eugenio Barba and his colleagues, the 'homeland' of theatre is as much a time as it is a place, as he says in *The Paper Canoe* (1995). There are no geographical boundaries, only contemporariness or the opposite, ancestors and successors, within and outside the traditions of theatre, and each with its claim to respect. As recurrently stressed in a number of works, the homeland of theatre lies in those hidden experiences that all actors must seek to tame and transform, in order to catch the spectator by the heart. In a transcultural theatre, the experiences are shared human experiences.

It is difficult to speak to, and about, a theatre group which has perfected a mode of expression that says more than words can contain. Odin Teatret has developed its own theatrical culture, which, more than anything, is a poetics of space. It has replaced the grand dramatic narratives by 'poems of action' that, like other poems, are so condensed that their meaning may explode in all directions. In this spatial poetry, the actors combine their movements and their voices in a way that permits the individual to seek his or her own truth, while also contributing to a totality of condensed meaning.

Even if it may thus be difficult to do Eugenio Barba and his theatrical work verbal justice, something must be said on this occasion. And we may take comfort in what Barba himself has said about the zone of silence: 'It is one's duty to speak. Precisely because the essential is mute' (Barba 1999, 50). What seems to be absolutely essential is expressed in the title of Barba's latest book: *Theatre: Solitude, Craft, Revolt* (1999). And I shall borrow those three words as key words in this partial motivation for awarding Odin the Sonning Prize.

[Solitude]

It may seem paradoxical that a theatre which has won international fame on the basis of performances that are, by definition, public and dependent on dialogue, and which, furthermore, is renown for all kinds of spectacles, should still see itself as based in a profound sense of solitude. The point is that to go one's own way and follow one's own paths, of necessity leads to solitude. We also know that as scholars; the most profound insight occurs as a result of a profoundly solitary process, not independent of tradition, but certainly in temporary exile from well-known theoretical landscapes.

In Odin Teatret, one speaks of a theatre of exile: a travelling theatre that must cut its roots to follow new paths over and over again. It started almost by accident, or so it seems, because the group was not accepted by the ordinary public and the critics. The first group of actors that Eugenio Barba got together in Oslo in 1964 had all failed to gain admission to the theatre school. They decided to go their own way, against the current, and across the boundaries, whether linguistic, political or geographical. The exile thus started as a conscious break with conventions, but was soon established as a principle of work within the Third Theatre.

The word 'ghetto' has also been used about Odin and its philosophy. Normally, the ghetto is loaded with negative connotations, but for Barba, it is not so simple. He says that the ghetto is a 'place that implied the limitation of certain elementary liberties, but which allowed for the preservation of others: the freedom to follow one's own cult, to speak one's own language, to live according to one's own norms. The ghetto was a place where one could preserve one's own identity, where one could defend and hand down the essential values of a culture of which one felt a part' (Barba 1979, 152). It is necessary to stress, too, that even in the most fearful of times, the people and the economy of the ghetto were vital parts of the surrounding society.

So also for Odin Teatret; it must be a ghetto, in the sense that it has to remain separate to stay alive, and to avoid levelling to conventional theatre. Odin has also shown how it is possible to remain apart and stay different without being isolated, by constantly engaging in barters with any temporarily surrounding community. In that way, they have retained a vision of a theatre which has gradually expanded the notion of the ghetto, and transformed solitude to a shared experience.

Solitude, exile, ghetto: these are words pointing to a certain kind of silence, which also allows the spectator to understand what cannot be said, including that which has not been said about the unknown spectator him/herself. In the theatre of silence, there is neither past nor future, only a suspended present. Any narrative or interpretation is a 'presentation' or a choice of a particular present, but the unknown historical potentiality remains on the edge of silence. In this insight lies one of Odin's great contributions to our culture, however defined.

[Craft]

It has always been important for Odin to stress the importance of the theatrical craft. Theatre is not only art, but like all true art, it is also a craft, a controlling of energy. The technical mastery of Odin's actors is legendary, and evidently it is obtained only through years and years of training and investigations into the expressive faculties of the body and the voice. Thanks to work demonstrations and an extensive pedagogical programme, the legend has become accessible for all (if not easily duplicated). In itself it is highly laudable to be willing to unveil the secret art of the performer: the techniques that make the actors leap from ordinary to extra-ordinary behaviour, and that make it possible for them to invite the spectators into another reality.

Eugenio Barba and his colleagues have created a theatre laboratory, which can be likened to a scientific laboratory, where the material at hand is researched in a systematic and empirical manner. Where one starts all over again when the experiments are not successful, but also where one uses previous results in new analytical contexts, new experiments. In the case of Odin, it is well known how many of the characters that have come to life in particular plays are recycled or reborn in new performances. The characters take on their own life and become archetypes that we may meet in unprecedented situations and connections, which they help to explore and lend new meaning.

From this theatre laboratory a particular kind of research has emerged, called theatre anthropology, about which Barba says:

Performance study nearly always tends to prioritize theories and utopian ideas, neglecting the empirical approach. Theatre Anthropology directs its attention to empirical territory in order to trace a path among various specialized disciplines, techniques and aesthetics that deal with performing. It does not attempt to blend, accumulate or catalogue the performer's techniques. It seeks the elementary: *the technique of techniques*. On one hand, this is Utopia. On the other, it is another way of saying, with different words, *learning to learn*. (Barba 1995, 10)

If Odin has carved out a peculiar place for theatre, Eugenio Barba and his colleagues have also created a particular space for theatre anthropology. This space is called ISTA, or The International School of Theatre Anthropology, and it is recreated every two years, somewhere in the world. Theatre professionals of all kinds are drawn to it, and for a couple of weeks they form a peculiar village with its own structure and its own ambition of searching for the technique of techniques together (see Hastrup 1996). Actors from East and West, North and South, all of them masters of their own traditions, bring their experience and their tacit knowledge out into the open. In the process, it becomes open to general inspection and to further investigation in the laboratory, where others seek the scenic *bios*, the biological level of performance, that which does not change, and which transcends personal, stylistic and cultural differences.

This bios is used creatively in Odin's own plays, which are both exemplars of knowledge achieved in the laboratory, and experiments that potentially threaten that very knowledge. Both the example and the experiment confirm that the craft is, and remains, the cornerstone of Odin's house.

[Revolt]

One can always ask how important theatre is, and how much it has influenced culture and society over the centuries. It is also possible to question the effect of Odin's own revolt on the world at large. But this essentially quantitative perspective should be replaced by a more qualitative one, if we are to take Odin seriously.

When Eugenio Barba speaks of revolt, he does not mean that theatre must overthrow society, as in ordinary revolutionary rhetoric. That it may do so is a distinct possibility, but above all, theatre must contribute to change by 'shouting against the wind', by insisting on its own course of action, and refusing to bend to external demands of content and form, whether deriving from society at large, or from a narrow theatrical convention. Theatre must remain distinct, and follow only its own ways. The course must be determined by personal and performative necessities, not particular ideological programmes or hopes of economic gain. This is the demand of the exile, and the condition for the actors' sacrifice of themselves.

The sacrifice does not lead to a self-centredness that excludes interest in other people. In the world of theatre, 'others' are always implicitly present, in the shape of spectators, whose attention must be caught for the play to work. The actors' technique is, to a large extent, a means of catching and keeping the attention of the spectator, who is always the 'third part', even when physically absent (as during rehearsals), and who therefore functions as a kind of guarantee of objectivity, as Barba says.

However, in relation to the spectator, there is also a kind of revolt going on, of which it has been said: 'the demand for a new ethic for the actor has always been the moving force of all theatre revolutions: to liberate the actor from servitude to the public, from the conventions and the conveniences of fashions and the theatre market' (Taviani 1986, 256). Liberating the actor from servitude means that even though a relationship between the actor and the spectator must be created, it should not be on the latter's terms. When it comes to Odin's plays, it usually holds true that the audience does not understand everything. But then, possibly they understand something of a different kind. To ask for total comprehension is to ask for total recognition, and this would run counter to the ethics of the exile. The most comprehensive revolt in the theatrical work of Odin, and one I would also like to see in scholarship, is the revolt against a utilitarian logic. Barba offers the following comment on that:

> Occasionally they ask: 'What use are you? What use is your theatre?'
>
> To answer would be to accept the reasoning that only he who produces has the right to exist, and he who does not produce has no function, must be isolated, eliminated, because he is socially de-funct, literally: dead.
>
> He who asks, 'What use are you?' should beware of himself, of his attitude, which makes him deny the value of trees that bear no fruit. The tree that bears no fruit — one proverbially useless — becomes essential in cities without oxygen. (Barba 1979, 149)

If one were a pedantic, one could claim that in this argument one utilitarian consideration is simply replaced by another. But I still believe that the image is clear: in theatre it is not a question of usefulness, but of renewal. The value is not instrumental, but expressive; by giving its own condensed expressions, Odin has fulfilled the ambition of renewal or recreation in the most impressive fashion.

Barba has characterized theatre as an empty and useless ritual that each of us may fill out with our own personal longings and beliefs. If the actors or directors are not possessed by their own drives and beliefs, the spectator will not experience renewal, only recognition or a lack of involvement. The poem of action must proceed according to a feeling of an inner necessity to express what cannot be said, but which must be sensed. As condensed potentiality, theatre gives the spectator an experience of the yet inexperienced, and a sense of the unprecedented. This is where the source of change is located.

[Closing remarks]

As a final observation, I want to stress that Odin Teatret's remarkable position in the international world of theatre is owed to the group's unique power to condense expressions in poems of action of unprecedented meaning and beauty. At the same time, Eugenio Barba has shown that art and science are not opposites, but mutual preconditions. In this sense, too, Odin has contributed to a new renaissance in Europe.

Most important, perhaps, Eugenio Barba has contributed to a diminishing of the distance between action and words, about which he has said, in a letter to Jerzy Grotowski: 'We know that only the action is alive, but only the word remains, in the spectacular desert of dirty cities and outsized museums' (Barba 1995, 138). In this desert, Odin represents an oasis of life.

Congratulations and Thanks

References

Barba, Eugenio 1979. *The Floating Islands*. Graasten: Drama.

Barba, Eugenio 1986. *Beyond the Floating Islands*. New York: PAJ Publications.

Barba, Eugenio 1995. *The Paper Canoe. A Guide to Theatre Anthropology*. Translated by Richard Fowler. London: Routledge.

Barba, Eugenio 1999. *Theatre. Solitude, Craft, Revolt*. Aberystwyth: Black Mountain Press.

Hastrup, Kirsten (ed.) 1996. *The Performers' Village. Times, Techniques and Theories at ISTA*. Graasten: Drama.

Taviani, Ferdinando 1986. The Odin Story. In Barba 1986.

*The Sonning Prize
2000:
Judy Barba and
Eugenio Barba.
Photo: Bo Amstrup*

196

Eugenio Barba

[Sonning Prize]

Acceptance Speech

Copenhagen University, 19 April 2000

Dear friends

I would like to begin with a dream. A man, bound to a stake on the terrace of a temple, tries to free himself. In vain. He persists. Spheres of glass fall from his eyes and shatter into a thousand splinters as they touch the ground. Two jaguars approach, upright, on their hind legs, dancing on the crystal splinters, and their feet — not jaguar paws but human feet — leave streaks of blood on the earth. Suddenly one of the jaguars thrusts a flintstone into the heart of the prisoner. From the gaping wound spurts, not blood but a burning book, and then a second, and a third, one after another: dozens, hundreds of books in flames which pile up in a gigantic pyre at the feet of the man at the stake.

The dreamer, whose name is Kien, is a scholar, a man who loves books. In his troubled sleep he shouts: 'Close your chest, close your chest'. The prisoner hears him and in a superhuman effort unlooses his bonds, puts his hands to the wound and tears it still wider open so that a stream of burning books tumbles out.

The sleeping man, unable to bear this sight, leaps into his own dream and into the fire to save the books that are turning into ashes. The flames blind him. Hundreds of desperate people scream at him, trying to grab him and stop him from saving the books. He tears himself free from their grasping hands and runs away, shouting insults at them. Once at a safe distance, he watches as men, women and children slowly turn into books and are silently consumed by the flames like heroes or martyrs.

Kien, the dreamer, is the protagonist of a novel by Elias Canetti, a Jew who was born in Bulgaria, studied in Germany and later, in England, wrote the books which won him the Nobel Prize. The same Canetti, towards the end of his life, used to say that one does not inhabit a country, but a language. What then is left of a human being who has lost both country and language? Perhaps the essential. And what is the essential for us from Odin Teatret who cannot be identified by a language or a country?

For the sake of convenience or custom, prizes are often awarded to one person and thereby connected to a name. But that name conceals a microcosm that palpitates, lives and acts. The person and the name are the top of an iceberg whose solid hidden bulk consists of an intricate network of relationships, collaborations, affinities, exchanges and tensions — a living organism that navigates on the currents of time, sometimes following them, sometimes opposing them, but always taking a stand.

It is to this iceberg that the Sonning Prize has been given. It is to the entire Odin Teatret — to this group of men and women belonging to different nations, cultures, religions and languages — that the University of Copenhagen has conferred this honour and a monetary reward in recognition of its life's work.

But this iceberg has slopes that far outnumber those that have formed and still form Odin Teatret. It also includes those Holstebro politicians who welcomed us when we were so small that we could pass through the eye of a needle, when we were anonymous and young at a time when to be young was not a sign of vitality and creative potential, but merely of inexperience. It is to the whole of Odin Teatret as well as to the Holstebro Town Council which has stood by it for over 35 years that this prestigious prize is awarded today.

The essential always emerges through privation. In the beginning there is a lack, a loss or an exclusion. For Odin Teatret the exclusion was double. We wanted to do theatre, to enter into the milieu and the history of the craft, but were denied the possibility. We were considered incompetent. At that time, in 1964, there were no theatre groups. No alternative performance culture existed to inspire us and in which we could be integrated. We were excluded. Theatre was our personal need. Nobody had knocked at our door begging us to become actors because the world needed us. We assumed the consequences of this situation: theatre was necessary only to us, and therefore we would pay for it out of our own pockets.

That is the origin of Odin Teatret in Norway: a tiny amateur theatre, dreaming of becoming professional, only five people who had to learn by themselves the essentials of the craft in solitude, outside the realms of the then recognised and recognisable theatre.

Barely two years later this little group of people moved to Denmark, accepting the extraordinary offer of the municipality of Holstebro. It was the first time that 'adults' — what is more, politicians — looked us in the eyes, bestowing a value on what we were doing. For the first time we were aware that we had a meaning for others, too.

By moving to Holstebro we suffered a mutilation: we spoke a foreign language. We lost *the word* which at the time was the essential channel of communication in theatre. In Norway we had been a Norwegian group consisting of Norwegian actors, with a Norwegian author, Jens Bjørneboe, performing for Norwegian spectators. In Holstebro we became a Scandinavian group with actors from Norway, Finland, Sweden and Denmark with irremediable difficulties of verbal communication with our spectators.

It is impossible to understand the history of Odin Teatret if we ignore these two exclusions: rejection by the theatre milieu and the amputation of language. We transformed that situation of inferiority and mutilation into a sense of honour and a source of strength. But where could we learn the essential? The living were neither willing nor able to teach us. To whom could we turn?

Theatre became the place where the living met the non-living. The non-living are not just the dead, but also those yet unborn. It is to them that you have to turn when the present does not take you into consideration. Then you can speak with assurance, through shouts and silences, to the older brothers who preceded you and the younger ones who will follow, to those who have already undergone the experience and to those who will face the same situations in which you find yourself; derided by the spirit of the time, alone against the indifference of society and the coldness of the craft.

The biographies, the words and the work of the theatre reformers of the 20th century were the burning books that illuminated our path. Their flames guided us towards that technical knowledge which is an individual way of breathing, something that only belongs to us. Thus we built our performances, with a layer of light and one of darkness, safeguarding the essential: the humblest details, often invisible, which conceal the embrace of opposites, the interweaving of tensions which allow life to flow. Perhaps the living, the spectators, will not be able to distinguish these details, but the non-living will accept your work and judge it by the care taken over these details, by the personal temperature with which you alternate the layers of light with those of darkness.

In order to reach the non-living, those still unborn, your performances must become burning books. You must scorch the sensibility of your spectators, haunt their imagination, illuminate their most personal wounds, coax them on into the mute landscape of their most intimate self, in that part which lives in exile within them. Only in this way can Odin Teatret become a legend which its spectators will pass on to those not yet born.

It was the theatre reformers, those heretics, nihilists, revolutionaries or mystics — from Stanislavski to Grotowski, from Meyerhold to Julian Beck, from Artaud to Judith Malina, from Brecht to Copeau, not to mention our Latin American colleagues Atahualpa del Cioppo, Vicente Revuelta, Augusto Boal, Santiago Garcia, Osvaldo Dragún —who showed us how to give the most of our most to the spectators who, for their part, come with an extraordinary gift. They offer you two or three hours of their life and place themselves, trustingly, in your hands. You must repay their generosity with excellence, but also with an obligation: you must put them to work. The spectators must be put to the test. With all their senses and all their experience they must scale an impervious wall of impulses and reactions, allusions and meanings, they must themselves resolve the enigma of a performance-sphinx that is about to devour them.

The spectators must be cradled by a thousand entertaining subterfuges, sensual pleasure, artistic quality, aesthetic sophistication. But the essential resides in the trans-figuration of the transient character of the performance into a splinter of life thrust into the ribs of the spectators and which will stay with them for years to come. Like an insect, the performance makes its home deep within the spectators, gnawing at their psychic, mental and emotional metabolism, and is converted into memory. The actions of the actor must leave an anonymous yet indelible mark on the spectator. This mark is the anonymous and unplanned message that you deliver to those who are not yet born. You must open the spectator's eyes with the same delicacy with which you close the eyes of someone who has just died.

The burning books of our elder brothers whispered all this to us. It is essential to get rid of illusions but not to lose your ideals, especially when recognition threatens to bury you alive beneath a monument. Do not forget that a good performance does not improve the world, but a bad one makes it uglier.

You must be a stone which does not roll with the currents of time but resists them. You must strike roots with which to cling. The currents will change. Sometimes they will submerge you, appear to obliterate you. But you are still alive, visible even to those who may not see you in your lifetime. In order to achieve this, you must grow roots, find the right ground.

El hombre es tierra que anda, according to an Inca saying: man is earth that walks. This wandering earth is our homeland. It is made up of the actions of particular men and women. They are our Polar star, the example to emulate, the frontier to reach. The mute essence to be passed on is contained in this earth made up of the actions of single individuals. This human earth is scattered all over the planet, in many continents, throughout the ages.

A few clods of this earth are in Denmark. They have nourished our roots, helped Odin Teatret to find its destiny. First of all, Ole Sarvig and Peter Seeberg, those extra-ordinary poets and novelists who gave us encouragement by writing plays for an unknown theatre group. And then Christian Ludvigsen and Hans Martin Berg who guided us in our ingenuousness, helping us to uncover what was fermenting inside us. Finally Kai K. Nielsen and Jens Johansen, Holstebro's mayor and municipal director, who won over the entire town council and received Odin Teatret without obliging us to become integrated in the little Danish garden. They did not ask to see results straight away. They left a strange bush to grow according to its own rhythm, following other seasons, with its wild branches. And thus they allowed the Odin to become a fertile part of the multiplicity, diversity and extraneousness which characterises our contem-porary culture.

We began in the shadows and in the shadows we prefer to live. It is in the anonymity of the daily work that we encounter the ceaseless challenge that tests the intensity and the credibility of our motivations. We came from the darkness and you must wish for us that when we vanish into the darkness again, our last dream will resemble the first one of our youth: to be like the San nomads of the Kalahari desert who move towards the lightning, because where there is storm, there is water, vegetation, life.

Together with the whole of Odin Teatret I am proud of this prestigious Sonning Prize. However we cannot accept the money. The money will journey on, divided into three portions. The first is destined for Holstebro Folkegave, a collection of associations and individual citizens from Holstebro who are building a youth club in Tirana, Albania. The second portion will cross the sea to Cuba for the theatre magazine *Conjunto* which, for 35 years, has witnessed the struggle by the theatre of the Latin American continent against violence and oppression. The third portion goes to Antigone's grandson, the Danish priest Leif Borch Hansen who followed the impulse of his conscience and hid refugees who the Danish police had orders to deport. By doing so he didn't respect the law of the State, following the example of the few Danes who opposed the Danish government in April 1940 when it asked its citizens to collaborate with the occupying German forces.

There was once a group of wandering players who lived in West Jutland. They journeyed to villages and towns, climbed up the tallest building, tied a rope to the roof and threw the other end into the air. Then they walked on it, one after the other, concentrating so as not to make the slightest false move which could jeopardise the balance and progression of the individual and the whole group. Their performance was acclaimed as a great artistic feat. Applause and acknowledgement: this was truly avant-garde at its most extreme, experimentation at its most daring. The years went by and the strolling players were still doing the same thing. They did not renew themselves, they didn't adapt to the times. They used a rope to get closer to the sky, ignoring the latest technological finds: helicopters, jet planes, missiles. Deaf to any comment or advice, they persisted in visiting the same places, meeting again their old spectators whose number was diminishing as time went by, and smiling at the young people who had never before seen such a performance: fixing a rope to a rooftop, casting it to the sky and dancing on it. One day they vanished into the void. Their rope dangled in a stormy sky that was heavy with black clouds and pierced by lightning. The ashes of a burning book fell to the ground. Only a page was left whole. On it was written: AThat which you must do, you must do. And don't question, don't question'.

Editors' note on Odin Teatret and awards

Odin Teatret and individual members of the theatre has got a number of international awards over the years. When Barba received the Pirandello Award in 1996 he had the relief remelted into more than 60 earrings, that were separately given not only to members of the Odin staff, but also — unofficially — as an encouragement to a lot of artistic fiery souls around the world. And apropos encouragement: Odin Teatret has had its own foundation since May 1982: The Stanislavsky Foundation. The purpose of the foundation is to give support to: 1) Theatre research, 2) Individuals connected to the field of theatre, 3) Theatre groups, 4) Social and cultural purposes other than above mentioned. The foundation's funds are raised by private donations, contributions from public authorities, etc. Members of Odin Teatret can voluntarily donate a percentage of their income to the foundation. The Stanislavsky Foundation has supported several persons and projects over the years. The Board of Directors are: Søren Kjems, Torgeir Wethal and Julia Varley. One cannot apply for support.

Chr. Ludvigsen

[Open Letter 36 years later]
— a Framework of Moles

> ... suit the action to the word, the word to the action.
> (*Hamlet* act III, scene II)

> Well said, old mole; canst work i' th'earth so fast?
> A worthy pioneer; — Once more remove, good friends.
> (*Hamlet* act I, scene V)

Dear Eugenio & Company

We are both very grateful, Silvia and I, to have had the opportunity to follow you and Odin Teatret so closely over so many years. Culminating so far with the stimulating seminar in March-April of this year, with your entire repertoire of newer performances, and yourself as guest-professor at the Department of Dramaturgy, again so near our own residence, where an important meeting took place 34 years ago.

According to our recent research, including Silvia's letters to her parents, I had invited you and Tiemroth, the new director of Aarhus Teater, to meet here from early morning on Palm Sunday, April 3, 1966, till late in the evening (10 pm). The next evening, we had a good talk with professor Albeck at an improvised *souper* at his home. He had also mobilized his old friend, Jens Kruuse, as expert-adviser, together with his wife. All because I had promoted you as a future teacher of modern theatre at the University of Aarhus, maybe including a theatre-laboratorium. A promising meeting!

But this would take time! So I understood your very good reasons for choosing the better and quicker offer from Holstebro, forwarded by Inger Landsted, who might have learned about your visit to Aarhus in early April '66 from the newspapers. Kruuse was culture-editor of the newspaper *Jyllands-Posten* and, as Silvia said in her letter of April 7th, 1966:

On Tuesday there were photographers, and interviews with Eugenio Barba, who may now move to Aarhus with what he calls his laboratory and his British wife.

You and Odin Teatret have, of course, visited Aarhus regularly since then, both as teachers at the university and with your performances, and we have joined you in Holstebro with our little family, beginning in July 1966 for the first Grotowski & Odin Teater seminar. And now a kind of family-reunion!

On this background, your latest visit to Aarhus was a very great experience! For me, it clarified some (important) problems concerning the relationship between (spoken) text and stage movement, which has puzzled and interested me for more than 45 years, ever since I began to translate Beckett... and had the texts performed by both amateur and professional actors, dating from 1956.

Dear Eugenio, in later years you have asked me to look back in time, to the beginning of Odin Teatret, before it was even born as such, to our very first meeting in the tiny flat in Vangede (later occupied by Dan Turell, also a Beckett-fan and close friend of Peter Laugesen) on Wednesday, July 22, 1964 — the date being confirmed by a letter from Silvia to her parents, dated July 23, 1964.

Recently, you published your memoirs, *Land of Ashes and Diamonds*,1999, including a kind of 'subterranean (theatre) history' about the more or less important 'moles' you met in your search for a new theatre in the early 1960s, but based on ex-periences from older 'master moles' such as Stanislavsky, Meyerhold, Copeau, etc. I became one of your new moles after July 22, 1964.

'But why?' you asked me a few weeks ago, in March, 2000. 'I still don't under-stand why you should be interested in me, with only vague ideas of a theatre magazine. And later offering a performance acted by very young amateurs, some years before youth itself became a qualification???'

It is impossible to find an easy answer, but your new book provided some clues to trigger my memory and revive my own interests of that time. I was also helped by old papers, letters, etc., more or less forgotten until now.

In my own way, I too, was *In Search of Lost Theatre* — as your first book on Grotowski was titled (in Italian, 1963). You could say that, in some respects, we made a 'barter' long before Odin Teatret used this expression, about 2 months before its offi-cial birth. I learned from your book that it was Jess Ørnsbo who recommended me as someone who, in his opinion, 'might be interested in this type of theatre' (op. cit. 85).

Though I then had a certain reputation for more alternative theatre initiatives, such as introducing Beckett and Ionesco, and partaking in the leadership of the first avant-garde theatre in Denmark after the Second World War, Fiol Teatret in Copen-hagen, Ørnsbo must have been more than clairvoyant in this case!

My earlier vague memory of this first meeting has been corrected by various sources, incl. my own, now activated, memory: I'm quite sure you didn't try to promote Grotowski on that summer evening, as you were previously used to do. You were now 'persona non grata' in Poland (op.cit. p.84).

You were promoting yourself and your vision of a new theatre, based on experiences from older masters, and including an ambitious project for a theatre magazine, to introduce these masters' written texts in Scandinavian languages.

For me (and Silvia) it became an evening to remember, though we were informally interrupted by the Swedish poet, Stig Carlson (a friend of the coming Odin Teatretmole, Ole Sarvig), who on this special occasion may have acted as a catalyst?

I'm sure I didn't promise too much that first evening, but in some ways I was convinced of the future possibilities in your visions, also for my own task at that time. We made an agreement something like this: 'If you present me with some concrete results, such as the first issue of the theatre magazine in print, or maybe a performance? I will, in turn, offer to help you in Denmark, to recommend you to my personal network of 'moles': persons who 'might be interested in this type of theatre.' (Or who trusted my judgement!)

And so I did in the following years, beginning with the relatively new Ministry of Culture. On October 31st, 1965, I applied for a travel grant for Odin Teatret and *Ornitofilene*'s first tour to Aarhus, Viborg and Aalborg on November 13th-17th, 1965. I had the pleasure of reconstructing the situation with the first 'mole' of mine to subsidise you: J. Harder Rasmussen, who was present at your Sonning Prize reception at the University of Copenhagen in April, 2000.

In the following years, our good connections and eager molework with the Ministry of Culture resulted in a special paragraph in the revised Theatre-law of 1970, when Odin Teatret almost got its own paragraph, in §30,2. In my translation: 'Furthermore, subsidies may be granted to experimental activities related to theatre training and -research.'

As Kirsten Hastrup pointed out in her Sonning Prize lecture, you, together with your company, have really done your duty as regards theatre-research on an international level!

[**My own research**]

At our first meeting, I already had a vague idea that your vision of a 'new theatre' might clarify or demonstrate some of my research-interests concerning stage-directions in a text by a dramatist — as his own director!

In July 1964, I had received a scholarship from the University of Aarhus to do research on the first modern stage-director in Denmark, William Bloch (1845-1926), engaged by The Royal Theatre in Copenhagen from 1881. He directed modern dramatists such as Ibsen (and later even Holberg), in the naturalistic-psychological style, in many ways a Danish pendant to the early Stanislavsky's work with Chekhov in 1898. Bloch also founded the first official School for Actors (1886), and was himself, on a smaller scale, a dramatist and translator of drama.

Bloch's force as a director was his ability to conceive a complete so-called *mise-en-scène*, incl. all positions and movements for all actors for the entire performance, before the first rehearsal: the French model for a mise-en-scène at that time.

Both as dramatist and director, Bloch had an extraordinary gift of adding smaller scenic actions to the main dialogue, to demonstrate a person's character and feelings at that very moment, in the form of carefully elaborated stage-directions. In all his 'domestic' dramas, Ibsen, used, to a certain degree, to incorporate a hidden mise-en-scène of this kind into his written (and printed) drama texts, in an effort to, in some way, direct future performances of his plays without being present himself.

Ibsen's stage-directions are very well done. This was confirmed by the famous Danish actor, Poul Reumert, during two interviews I had with him later in the autumn of 1964. Reumert was one of Bloch's most outstanding pupils. According to Reumert, Ibsen was an exception, as he puts it in his impressive memoirs *Teatrets Kunst* (The Art of the Theatre 1963, 48):

> Is Henrik Ibsen not the only one whose stage directions you can fully trust?
> (Er der overhovedet andre end Henrik Ibsen, hvis Parantheser man trygt kan stole på?)

And Reumert was not the only professional of that opinion. Normally, you still delete nearly all stage directions by the dramatist in the text copies delivered to the actors: 'Either the 'scenic movement' is obvious from the dialogue itself, so the stage directions are superfluous, or they are wrong', as William Bloch himself puts it. By 'wrong' he meant contradicting the literal meaning of the text, as interpreted within the framework of his very fine, but limited artistic craftsmanship, which dominated Danish theatre for the next 2-3 generations.

My recent research to reconstruct aspects of our first meeting confirmed that I was well aware of this problem of disrespect for the stage directions of the poor dramatist, who normally was denied admission to rehearsals of his own plays, even at The Royal Theatre in Copenhagen. He was degraded to a 'persona non grata' and only invited to the opening night.

The dramatist was often more literary than theatre minded, as our mutual friend Gordon Craig puts it in his *First dialogue* of *The Art of the Theatre* (1905):

The first dramatists were children of the theatre. Modern dramatists are not. The first dramatists understood what the modern dramatist does not yet understand. He knew that when he and his fellows appeared in front of them, the audience would become more eager to s e e what he would do than to h e a r what he might s a y ... (my 1962-edition, 141)

(Did I ever tell you that Ole Sarvig visited the very old 'child of the theatre' — Craig was born in 1872 — in the early 1960's along with Peter Seeberg, whom Craig at their leave-taking advised: 'Take good care of your father'— yet another of the underground stories about Odin-Teater moles: Ole had a substantial red beard; Peter was only 3 years younger than Ole). On page 151-2 (op.cit.) Craig has a short dialogue about the playwrights' attempts to master 'the art of stage-directions':

PLAYGOER: Then is all the stage-direction of the world's plays worthless?
STAGE-DIRECTOR: Not to the reader, but to the stage-director, and to the actor — yes.

[Dramatists as directors in their own text?]

We must have discussed this problem earlier, maybe as early as July, 1964? I remember your comment very clearly, also because you used a Norwegian expression — new to me — about that kind of stage-direction in the dramatist's texts: 'It is buttered bacon' (Det er smør på flæsk) — like saying the same thing twice.

But I'm sure you agreed that Beckett, et al., have created other possibilities for stage directions in more concrete detail. It is quite impossible to cut all Beckett's stage directions, leaving only the naked dialogue. Beckett's stage-directions are part of the drama text, often in contradiction to the spoken words. And will remain part of a stage partiture! As at the end of both acts in *Waiting for Godot*:

ESTRAGON: Well, shall we go?
VLADIMIR: Yes, let's go.
              (They do not move)
CURTAIN

The only difference between the 2 acts is that the two persons exchange their text. You can't cut the stage directions without betraying Beckett.

One result of these first dialogues between us concerning the playwright's part in the performance was, of course, that I recommended to you authors (Sarvig and Seeberg) of a type unusual in Denmark at that time.

Another result already appeared in issue no. 5 of your theatre magazine project, *Teatrets Teori og Teknikk (TTT)* 1967: 'The Playwright as Director in his own Text' — a year after the establishing of Odin Teatret in Holstebro in Denmark.

Together with my own book, *Moderne Teaterproblemer* (1964), this issue of *TTT* also became documentation for the renewal of my scholarship at Aarhus University. Only in 1969 did I become more permanently employed — 4 years before Dramaturgy as a subject became a separate department in 1973, with a theatre room in the shape of an empty space with a flat wooden floor, also suited to guest performances by Odin Teatret. You accepted this 'new area' for *TTT*, as you put it in a brief preface to no. 5 when you said:

> Normally, *TTT* doesn't consider dramatists. But in this case it isn't their dialogue etc. that commands our interest, but their comments about the way of acting. Jean Genet, and especially Beckett, seem to deeply mistrust the ability of both the director and the actors to transform their texts to theatre performance.
>
> They present very precise stage-directions, nearly a firm partiture, both in movements, voice intonations and pauses, which they expect both the director and the actor to respect. In reading the texts by Genet and Beckett, we are very surprised at their amazing technical knowledge, their ability to think in the visual categories of the theatre, and that sense of scenic dialectics which excludes every tautology, every buttered bacon. Their stage directions often build on a contrast between the spoken words and the physical action, which — according to their suggestions — is to contradict the (verbal) meaning of the text. That was what Meyerhold, as early as 1906, called 'movements not corresponding to the words'.

[From Ornitofilene to Kaspariana]

I know you remember some aspects of the problems concerning possible texts for (originally Norwegian) Odin Teatret, after the June 1966 settling in Holstebro as a Nordic theatre laboratory, open to new actors with other languages: Danish, Swedish, Finnish, Italian etc. In your first performance, *Ornitofilene*, it was easier. Our mutual friend, Jens Bjørneboe, offered you a rather normal dramatic text, not yet quite finished, as I understand. He was very satisfied with your version, and told me he had actually used some of your inventions to complete the final version of his drama, *Fugleelskerne* (The Birdlovers) (1966). Ole Sarvig agreed to inspire the next performance, *Kaspariana*, based on the story of the different phases of the civilisation of the mythic Kaspar Hauser, from his appearance in Nürnberg 1828 — of unknown origin, quite uneducated; he couldn't even speak — to his sudden murder in 1833.

After we had elaborated a scenario for the progressive situations in Kaspar's education, Ole gave further stage-directions, more like inspirations for the individual actor, in the form of selected quotations from different poems, acting as a kind of stage-directions.

Your actors were relatively free to interpret. The words could be spoken in any language, the scenic actions told the story to the audience, transcending national boundaries of language.

[No text or hardly any?]

Odin Teatret had — by chance or necessity — already become more international by the opening night of *Kaspariana* in 1967.

As a theatre laboratory, Odin Teatret was not obliged to produce a certain number of performances each year, but still, as literate adviser, I thought we should think of the next performance in due time.

I remember we asked Peter Seeberg to try, as early as 1967. But meanwhile, I had tried another solution as the result of a very interesting correspondence I had with Beckett, concerning his practical experiences with his on-stage directions in performances, as research for *TTT* no. 5.

As in the French tradition since Molière, Beckett was always present during the rehearsals, as co-director, in fruitful dialogue with his first French director, Roger Blin (a 'pupil' of Artaud). In a letter I received from Beckett, dated December 8, 1966, he pointed out:

> ...The mental stage on which one moves when writing, and the mental auditorium from which one watches it, are very inadequate substitutes for the real thing... And yet, without them, it is impossible to write for the theatre. My experience is that the mental vision and consequent stage-directions are valid on the whole, but must often be corrected, and even altered in function, not only of the real theatre space, but also of the performers...
>
> On the whole Blin has followed my indications without demur. I know there is a certain rigidity in them which is alien to him...
>
> *(Two shorter examples of corrections during rehearsals to be maintained in all productions).*
>
> To sum up, if familiarity with the mental stage, auditorium, lighting, acoustics, actors, set etc. is indispensable to the writing of a play, the results are only valid in so far as they function satisfactorily under given real conditions.
>
> The ideal would be to work, knowing in advance these real conditions. I dream of

going into a theatre with no text, or hardly any, and getting along with all concerned before really setting out to write That is to say, a situation where the author would not have privileged status, as is the case when he arrives with a text already set, but would properly function as a specialist of neither more nor less importance than other specialists involved ...

I discussed the letter with you and — perhaps a little hesitantly — we agreed to ask him to join Odin Teatret, incognito if he so preferred. I wrote him an invitation, which is printed in my publication *Det begyndte med Beckett...* (Aarhus 1997, 73). But he didn't answer until July 1967. Meanwhile, he had had a bad accident, falling into an auto pit, a result of his failing vision, badly decimated by cataracts (which, however, were later operated with good result).

Now, he was on his way to direct *Endgame* at Schiller Theater in Berlin in the autumn of 1967, the first time Beckett was the only responsible director, 'under given real conditions'. He was quite familiar with the German language, and had a remarkably fine dialogue with his German translator, Elmar Tophoven, whom he sometimes quoted when I posed interpretative questions to Beckett's dramatic texts.

In a way, he may have thought that Danish was a kind of German dialect, but of course, he knew better, as he referred several times to his older master, James Joyce, and his attempt to pick up some Danish-Norwegian in Copenhagen, in order to be able to read/understand Ibsen as a preparation for the multi-languaged *Finnegan's Wake*.

My idea of inviting Beckett to be the next literary adviser for Odin Teatret might have been 'the real thing' — even though in retrospect it seems a bit too brave at that time!

Recently, you commented on that possibility with a question: 'What would have happened if Beckett had arrived in Holstebro in 1967 — as a specialist of neither more nor less importance than other specialists involved?'

With *Kaspariana*, you and your actors had proved an outstanding ability to create a performance based only on a scenario — in a way like a *Commedia dell'arte* production — but stimulated by selected poems, as, for instance, later, in *Mythos*, though the poet was now quite absent.

[Hardly any text?]

In December of '67 I presented you with a concept based on the Greek myth of Alkestis and her sacrifice/suicide — like a Buddhist-monk in Vietnam, and later, Jan Palach in Prag, 1968 — combined with the Nordic myth of King Frode's might, even after his death, with his embalmed body brought on tour around his kingdom as symbol of the old power. (Similar, in a way, to Lenin on the Red Square, though nowadays the people must bring themselves to the meeting place).

Maybe your actors didn't need more material than this, even in 1967? It's easy to see other possibilities now, especially after we have followed the later development of Odin Teatret — from as early as 1972 without the base of a written, elaborated text by a more traditional playwright, or rather without it as trampoline for the actors' more mimical and corporal expressions and performance.

[The mental stage? The playwright's or the actors'?]

Later I have had opportunities to learn more about *the mental stage* of Beckett at that time. Important material about his function as his own stage-director has been published, beginning with *Endspiele* in Berlin, 1967. He tried unceasingly to clarify his visions for a very *precise connection between scenic movements and the words*, if he used spoken words at all!

Endgame starts up with a *written* 'good morning'-pantomime and was originally conceived to be followed by another pantomime, *Act without Words*.

Of course you can protest against a *written pantomime*, as your actors were primarily trained to express their own, more personal, corporal expressions, without more academic mime education, like Decroux.

The statement by Hamlet mentioned, 'suit the action to word, the word to the action' has puzzled me since my first studies in theatre-history at the University of Copenhagen — which happened to be almost parallel to my first translations of dramatic texts such as Beckett, etc. from 1953, when I moved from literature to theatre at the university.

I thought that Hamlet's actors were probably trained in a kind of rhetoric 'mime-language' — as recommended by Melanchton in Wittenberg! English actors were able to tour on the continent in the 17th century, crossing the language-borders.

In this scene, especially, Hamlet — with Shakespeare's words — speaks as both stage director and playwright with personal experience as an actor. He continues:

And let those that play your clowns speak no more than is set down for them...

They should not improvise, as in the Commedia dell'arte-tradition, not create their own scenic movements or words, but stick to the text; in the case of *Hamlet* even including a text for a pantomime. Beckett was very familiar with Shakespeare as dramatist, and often quoted him.

Molière as dramatist wants to direct his fellow actors — contrary to the improvisations of the Commedia dell'arte tradition (cf. *L'Impromptu de Versailles*) — by writing the text down before the rehearsal, more or less fixed, for later performances of his texts, as Corneille had recommended in his *Trois discours sur le poëme dramatique!* (1660) about what he called 'un mot d'avis à la marge' (cit. from my 1964-edition of *Trois discours*, 136). Corneille argues further for his marginal advice, because 'the printed text could fall in the hands of provincial actors' ('... nos pièces entre les main des comédiens des provinces ...') where he couldn't be present as playwright/director, to protect 'the real vision' behind the performance.

[The supremacy of the written text
(which comes first: word or action?)]

At that time, 1953, I still believed in the text's supremacy; literature seemed to some extent a finer art than theatre, at least written theatre-texts had a longer life, incl. the latent possibilities of passing on time-honoured human experience through generations: 2500 years from the old Greek dramatists as classics to modern theatre interpretations.

I was both provoked and inspired by reading Artaud in 1958-9. *Le Théâtre et son Double* (Paris 1938) had a renaissance after World War II, promoted by the new generation of French theatre-people like Jean-Louis Barrault and Roger Blin. In his chapter VI: *En finir avec les chefs-d'œuvre* (*No more masterpieces*) Artaud is ready to drop (almost) the entire literary heritage: like this:

> ... Masterpieces of the past are good for the past: they are not good for us ...
>
> ... If the public does not frequent our literary masterpieces, it is because those masterpieces are literary, that is to say, fixed; and fixed in forms that no longer respond to the need of our time ...
>
> ... We must get rid of our superstitious valuation of texts and written poetry ... let the dead poets make way for others ...

I introduced Artaud in Denmark with an article in the newspaper *Information* on July 6th, 1959, reprinted in my book: *Det begyndte med Beckett ...* (Aarhus 1997). In 1967, Klaus Hoffmeyer translated *Le Théâtre et son Double* in extenso, with your commentary, Eugenio. And during the seminar, in your dialogue with Klaus Hoffmeyer on April 5, 2000, you declared that you wanted to reconsider your comments, based on your practical experience since 1967. As 'old mole' I immediately contacted Bent Jacobsen from the publishing company 'Drama' to reprint Artaud with both your old and your new comments. Bent Jacobsen immediately seized on the idea!

[Last experience with a written drama at Odin Teatret]

In 1967-68, I think we both believed in some kind of supremacy for an author's written text, complete with dialogue, etc.? At least we agreed to offer Peter Seeberg my material on Alkestis, now daughter of the late King Frode. Peter had dropped his own project, and agreed to our suggestion, which he fulfilled in the summer of 1968 with a nearly complete dramatic text, later called *Ferai* in the printed edition. (ARENA 1970, incl. some alterations from the rehearsals at Odin Teatret 1968-89 — dedicated to me).

I remember very clearly your first comments on Peter's text:

> In our case it is a mistake to let a messenger tell about important events such as the duel between the claimants to the crown seeking to marry the late king's daughter (Alkestis), and the peoples' effort to confirm the myth of Old King Frode carrying his embalmed body around. These events must be shown to the audience.

And so you and the actors did, after many rehearsals, even when Peter, present at rehearsals, was at first very disturbed by your ensemble's disrespect for written words; later he became more cooperative and impressed by your theatrical use of, for instance, a tiny stage-direction — *Alkestis dies* — transformed to a 4-5 min. long, very moving, wordless suicide scene performed by Else Marie Laukvik from the original Norwegian troupe. Even though the performance of *Ferai* at Théâtre des Nations in Paris in June 1969 became a first breakthrough to later international fame, you altered the course of your 'ship' and gave up the possibilities of more or less complete written author-texts as trampolines for the next production of Odin Teatret, *Min fars hus* in 1972 (*My Father's House*), based on Dostoevsky's prose works, from which you let the actors themselves choose characters and dramatic situations.

This was the new course for Odin Teatret, with you and the actors as combined actor-authors and you as stage director.

[Epilogue: To continue ...]

My latest research on the value of the dramatist's stage-direction in this special case still remains.

From a remarkable book: *Beckett in the Theatre* (ed. D. Macmillan and M. Fehsenfeld. London & New York 1989) I've learned a lot more about Beckett as stage director in his own plays, always combining the words with action. Or conversely! I quote from page 90-91:

... In 1962 he had told Jean Reavey that with *Godot* and in part with *Fin de partie* he had just written dialogue, without seeing the stage movement in strict detail. In the later plays, he had been aware of every movement of the actors, even before he wrote the dialogue ... (Unpublished journal in possession of Jean Reavey, the wife of Beckett's early publisher George R.)

'To be aware of every movement' and then somehow add the words, sounds in my ears like the opposite of normal practice for a playwright, but why not?

At the seminar in Aarhus (April 11, 2000) Iben Nagel Rasmussen demonstrated the creation of her extraordinary autobiographical performance *Itsi Bitsi* (1991). She was able to demonstrate the different phases of its creation from the very beginning, with 'improvised movements', for which her two accompanying musicians, Kai Bredholt and Jan Ferslev, later added music incidental to different parts of the now fixed improvisation.

At that stage, they presented their work to you. You were not present that day, but Iben told us that you had suggested her to be inspired by *Oedipus at Colonus* by Sophocles, where the old man memorizes his past, his very special biography.

Iben pointed out that she answered something like this: 'But I'm not Oedipus, the keywords here are rather a special biography ...' And you suggested that Iben write her own biography from the time, just before she joined Odin Teatret (1966), when she was a flower-power child, very close to the famous musician and poet, Eik Skaló, who committed suicide in 1968, only 25 years old, on the border to Nepal.

Iben followed your advice, and you selected some passages in her text suitable to add or 'suit to the action', bit by bit. What was first in Beckett's 'mental stage'? — The action or the word (logos)? 'In the beginning was the word (logos) ...' as stated by St. John in his gospel. Or ...?

I assume you will put forth objections here? — But 'even writing includes an element of improvisation', as Niels Bohr once pointed out in his lecture *Unity of Knowledge* (printed in 'Naturbeskrivelse og menneskelig erkendelse', Copenhagen 1985, p. 36) as a comment on his own struggle to find adequate words for his complementarian conception of our world. Ying and Yang at the same time?

Good old Aristotle suggested that a dramatic performance is a kind of *harmonizing* of *rhythm* (= controlled movements) and *logos* (= language).

You might continue our dialogue, quoting Gordon Craig's *First dialogue* (1905) where the wise stage-director asks:

... Do you know who was the father of the dramatist?
Playgoer: No, I do not know, but I suppose he was the dramatic poet.
Stage-director: You are wrong. The father of the dramatist was the dancer. (op.cit. p. 140)

As a still rather naive playgoer, I could add: I've still a lot to learn from you and the Odin Teatret-company. Let us keep up our tradition for long-lived dialogue.

The very best wishes for the future to you all — and thanks to the kind fate that let us meet in July 1964.

from your 'old mole'

Tony D'Urso

[**Pictures of Odin**]

When I think about my photographic work with *Odin Teatret*, I can't help going back to my first encounter with the group — when I first met Eugenio Barba outside the deconsecrated church where *Min Fars Hus* ('My Father's House') was being performed. We were at Belgrade's International Theatre Festival, in 1972. I arrived there with a letter from an Italian weekly review, with the task of making a reportage of this happening. I was very young at the time, and I was looking for a personal identity, after the two years' course of photography at the 'Umanitaria' in Milan, and a period of political engagement in the left-wing groups which were very active in those years. Apart from the risks you ran in following demonstrations and the clashes with the police, however, there was not much chance of making a living from that kind of photojournalism.

The first meeting with Eugenio comes back very clearly to my memory — his surprised smile when I asked if I might take photographs of the performance, his curiosity about my work, his surprise in finding out we were both from the same area of Southern Italy. He invited me to watch the performance first, and then to talk to the actors in order to decide whether I could take pictures or not. I was astonished by the performance, and afterwards I told Eugenio about the impressions I had, watching it. He translated them directly to the actors, and they were amused and surprised at them. I eventually managed to take some photos. I was away from the performing area, high up on a kind of balcony, hidden by a black cloth — a really odd situation: I felt like a legalized spy; also, I couldn't possibly fail this one chance which was being offered to me.

We wrote our 'contract' on a scrap of paper soon after the performance, and made an appointment in Milan, where Odin Teatret was going to be for the last tour with *Min Fars Hus*. I remember clearly my emotions at Iben's and Eugenio's reactions when they saw the scene with Tage and Ragnar in the black-and-white photograph.. The film had been stretched to the maximum of its potential, with the incredible result of capturing the highly energetic atmosphere of the performance — with the figures of the actors striving to emerge strongly from the foggy light, created with small light-bulbs hanging from a rope — which surrounded actors and spectators.

This situation — to which I always return when I think about my work with Odin Teatret — is strongly impressed on my memory, and has been like a compass by which I have later oriented my professional and existential choices. Some comments on the photos I have chosen:

LIVERPOOL JOHN MOORES UNIVERSITY
Aldham Robarts L.R.C.
TEL: 0151 231 3701/3634

Iben and Odd's picture in *The Book of Dances*, in a courtyard in Martano — a village near Carpignano, where I spent quite a long period with Odin Teatret. This long stay in Salento gave me the chance to re-establish a connection with the land of my birth — a bond which emigration had suddenly interrupted. I again found gestures, songs and dances — the cultural variety and richness which was part of my childhood, and which I could remember only in fragments after so many years away from it. During that period Odin Teatret had the idea of the barter, and each performance was the pretext for an exchange: the group offered its performance, and the hosting community 'repaid them' with its dances and its songs.

This photo portrays Iben in Sardegna, meeting 'Zi Gavina', and playing a melody on the flute for her. I made a reflection on that particular occasion, in which Iben and I went alone to meet the people of Saule — a village near Nuoro. In that very unusual situation, my presence as a photographer functioned as a bridge between the actress and the curiosity of the people at seeing this strange figure go around their village. For the first time, I didn't feel like an aggressive thief of images, I was at ease in my role, which almost justified this vision of an elf, which Iben was evoking with her white costume, her mask and her drum, going around barefoot, dancing, and making strange, mysterious sounds with her voice.

In this photo, Mr. Peanut (Julia Varley's character on stilts) is visiting the Palacio de la Moneda in Santiago de Chile.

On this occasion I felt again that cringing of the stomach which I often felt when I was photographing clashes with the police during political demonstrations in my first years as a photographer. I used that experience on this occasion to rescue the pictures of the scene. Soldiers had quickly and roughly managed to restore order in a few seconds. The cringing of the stomach which this situation provoked in me — the violence with which soldiers had immediately blocked the entrance to the square and loaded Julia and Eugenio into their prison vans — fortunately did not make me lose control. I managed to hide myself and my camera in the crowd, disguising the moment of panic I was going through. I had only one purpose: saving the photos, the cameras, and myself.

[Act IV] *Behind the Curtain*

The picture of Iben and her mother Ester laughing — taken during the 35th anniversary — made me think of the complex and tangled course of events which I experienced during almost 25 years of collaboration with Odin Teatret.

I was deeply moved when Iben talked about her memories in that very special situation. I realized that I had shared many very intense moments of life with these people — the Odin Teatret crew. Some of these moments are impressed on my film; some are entirely entrusted to my memory.

Janne Risum

[ISTA — What's in a Name?]

In 1979 Eugenio Barba founded the International School of Theatre Anthropology (ISTA). He designed this intercultural and interdisciplinary theatre laboratory to serve as an intermittent and mobile complement to his more constant pursuits in Odin Teatret since its start in 1964. ISTA is his cross-cultural master class, based on the Eurasian axis on which modern theatre is founded and designed as a meeting point for aesthetics and science. By its very design ISTA reflects his views and, by the very definition of a master class, it invites anything but passive indifference.

The core artistic and scholarly staff that he involves in the ISTA sessions would agree on the necessity of continuing this pursuit, but would do so for different reasons and with different priorities.

ISTA teaches and compares the basics of various performance traditions. The core artistic staff are masters of Indian Odissi dance, Balinese dance theatre, Japanese Kabuki and Nihon Buyo, Brazilian Candomblé, the corporeal mime of Etienne Decroux, and Barba's own actors from Odin Teatret. A wide range of other performance traditions have occasionally been presented as well: for example, Peking opera, clowning, flamenco, classical ballet, European opera, European acting based on texts, Stanislavsky etudes, modern dance, Meyerhold's biomechanics, Brechtian acting, Dario Fo and Franca Rame, Grotowski, contact improvisation, Japanese butoh ...

The core scholarly staff are European theatre professors and professors in related subjects. The ISTA sessions have an interdisciplinary scholarly approach, focussing on the rich potential of the human body-mind and on the mutual inspiration between old and new performance traditions and their spectators. A wide range of other scholars and scientists from different fields have also contributed to the sessions and presented their views. Their backgrounds encompass, for instance, anatomy, neurophysiology, psychology, theatre studies, studies of sport, musicology, anthropology, cultural studies, philosophy and philosophy of science.

As for the participants, ISTA is also a meeting point for performers (actors, mimes, dancers and singers), directors, pedagogues and scholars from all over the globe.

[The ISTA sessions]

An ISTA session presents work demonstrations, practical classes, lectures and research symposia. Directed by Barba, the Asian actors and the Odin actors also create the joint public performance *Theatrum Mundi*, where they interact while following their own various conventions. All scenes have a cross-cultural casting, and although they may be derived from one of the conventions involved, they develop into archetypal situations.

Each *Theatrum Mundi* is unique. From session to session over the years the performance has steadily grown and changed and its manifest themes have varied. Recurrent European themes are Faust, Hamlet, and Don Juan; however, its overall mythological theme is global Armageddon. The performance normally ends in this explosion, only to dissolve into some final first steps of resurrection. The Armageddon conflict activates all the mythologies involved and, for instance, borrows central turning points from Shakespeare's *The Tempest*.

The 11 ISTA sessions so far have been hosted by theatres, festivals and local communities and have been funded by cultural organizations from all over Europe and from Brazil.

An approximate estimate of the progression of ISTA over the years may be formed by studying the session titles.

Each session is unique and a fresh start. They all explore the same basics. However, as reflected by the different titles of the sessions, over the years special themes have grown or varied, each has a special focus and is never repeated in exactly the same way. Each one indicates a new aspect or point of view. A session title may follow the European university tradition of stating an exact scholarly definition of the topic that is to be explored; other session titles state the topic using the professional working language of European theatre. Some sessions seem to have more poetic titles. Some of those nevertheless refer to well-established notions in the working language of Asian theatre, while others state notions invented by Barba. In any case, once a theme is introduced at ISTA it is never abandoned, and each point of view serves as a frame for more general explorations.

[Intertwining perspectives]

The first methodological step joined the forces of esthetics, scholarship and science in a cross-cultural and interdisciplinary comparison of the basic elements of the Asian and European performance conventions represented. This implied discussing the possible epistemology of a scholarly paradigm, which allows for cultural difference and for the dynamics of coexisting points of view. The title of the Ist ISTA in Bonn, Germany, in1980, determined its field of research as *Theatre Anthropology*, defined as 'the study of human beings' socio-cultural and physiological behaviour in a performance situation', and special seminars posed the question of *The Performer's Art: Talent or Science?*. The key notion suggested by Barba, *pre-expressivity*, in relation to the dimension of improvisation, determined the approach of the IInd ISTA in Volterra, Italy, in 1981, entitled *Pre-Expressivity/Improvisation*. A concluding public symposium focussed on *Theatre and Anthropology*.

The second step addressed more specific cross-cultural performance studies. The IIIrd ISTA in Blois-Malakoff, France, in 1985, pursued *Dialogue Between Cultures*, and its concluding public symposium, *Le Maître du regard*, studied how performers mould their actions so as to create diverse points of view for their spectators. The IVth ISTA in Holstebro, Denmark, in 1986, investigated *The Female Role as Represented on the Stage in Various Cultures*, including cross-gender acting.

The third step explored possible methodological links to spectator studies and semiology, and the epistemology of a scholarly working language that more openly admits the inevitable component of subjectivity. The Vth ISTA took place in Salento, Italy, in1987, and was entitled *The Actor's Tradition and the Spectator's Identity*. It held a concluding internal symposium on *Theatre Anthropology* and a final public symposium on *Semiology of Performance and Theatre Anthropology*.

The fourth step addressed the epistemology and methodology of theatre historiography, in the sense of writing history from a point of view, or re-writing it from another. The VIth ISTA in Bologna, Italy, in 1990, explored the theme of *Performance Techniques and Historiography*, and two concluding public symposia addressed the questions of *Theatre Anthropology: Ethos and Expressivity* and *Performing Techniques and Historiography*.

Continuing the creative fusion of esthetics and scholarship, the VIIth ISTA in Brecon-Cardiff, Wales, in 1992, looked into *Working on Performance East and West*, especially scrutinizing the notion of *subscore* suggested by Barba (as opposed to Stanislavsky's notion of subtext). The final public symposium addressed the topics of *Fictive Bodies, Dilated Minds, Hidden Dances*, as suggested by Barba.

The fifth step reclaimed the crucial question of tradition (as opposed to avant-gardist rejection). The VIIIth ISTA in Londrina, Brazil, in 1994, was titled *Tradition and Founders of Traditions*. The concluding public symposium had the same title. So far ISTA had exclusively explored an Eurasian axis. The Londrina ISTA took the important step of adding Afro-Brazilian candomblé dance to the permanent core group of codified conventions studied.

The sixth step explored the intrinsic qualities in the formal patterns on which performance traditions are founded and which help them survive, or make it possible to change or to revive them. The IXth ISTA in Umeå, Sweden, in1995, focused on *Form and Information* and was part of the local World Culture Festival *Crossroads*. The case studies included Meyerhold's biomechanics. To present an impressive cornucopia of many such live traditions within theatre and dance became possible in the context of Copenhagen being nominated as the 1996 Cultural Capital of Europe. The title of the Xth ISTA in Copenhagen, Denmark, in 1996, *The Whispering Winds in Theatre and Dance. The Performer's Bios*, reflected the practice of some Asian traditions to refer to the performer's energy as a wind (*bayu*). The final symposium focused on *Theatre in a Multicultural Society*.

The seventh step looked at the organic quality of acting and dancing. The XIth ISTA in Montemor-o-Novo and Lisbon, Portugal, in1998, simply bore the corresponding title, *O-Effect*.

The eighth step will be to address the question of dramaturgy. The XIIth ISTA in Bielefeld, Germany, in 2000, focuses on *Action, Structure, Coherence. Dramaturgical Techniques in the Performing Arts*.

[Giving]

The basic artistic 'economy' of ISTA is one of extravagant giving, of co-operatively exploring some basic performance skills and some basic questions concerning value in performing for a number of intensive days.

During a session the meaning of the title may metaphorically extend well beyond its professional focus, and furthermore in quite unexpected ways. During special shared moments the meaning of the seminar may obtain profound personal significance to a large group of participants, and even years later it may still designate a unique common experience to them. At the same time, the session titles and key notions have invariably aroused heated arguments or been met with derision, hostility or open revolt. Some participants have left, others taken different stands overnight. A title or notion may of course also prove not to matter so much as what is going on. Whichever attitude is adopted, they all reflect the session as a group event and ISTA as an environment.

Most participants attend only one session. Some ISTA veterans keep turning up, including some inveterate scepticists. Quite a few keep relating in some way or other to the informal ISTA network of artistic or scholarly friendships.

One thing is certain: the personal artistic revelations or explosive idiosyncrasies — both may be highly productive — which the participants may bring home with them differ considerably. At the end of the day, how they may integrate them into their own artistic or scholarly work remains a personal matter. Why settle for anything less?

Many publications have been written about ISTA. Some idealize it, others demonize it or question Barba's intellectual property right to the notion of theatre anthropology. Still others relate to their ISTA experience and to ISTA notions only when they wish to do so, or enter dialogues with ISTA approaches from different angles. ISTA reflects the modern condition of living in a global village. Without the ensuing cross-cultural clash of ideas, counterpoised by moments of sharing, ISTA could not have survived as an environment; more precisely: it would have failed.

References

Barba, Eugenio 1981. Theatre Anthropology: First Hypothesis. In *Theatre International* 1981/1, Paris.

Christoffersen, Erik Exe, Kirsten Due Kjeldsen, Janne Risum og Eddy Thomsen (eds.) 1987. *At synliggøre det usynlige. En antologi.* Aktuelle teaterproblemer 18. Århus: Institut for Dramaturgi.

Hastrup, Kirsten (ed.) 1996. *The Performer's Village. Times, Techniques and Theories at ISTA.* Gråsten: Drama.

Kowalewicz, Kazimierz (ed.) 1999. *Living in the Performer's Village.* Łódź: University of Łódź, Chair of Sociology of Culture.

Skeel, Rina (ed.) 1994. *The Tradition of ISTA.* Londrina. Brazil: Filo.

The emblem of ISTA comes from the Hopewell culture (Ohio 300 A.D.).
The engraving shows two versions of the human hand, one realistic and the other arctistic, presenting the dialectic nature-culture.

Ulrik Skeel

[Dancing without Light]
A Note from the Administration

Since Odin Teatret was born in 1964, a considerable amount has been written about it. About the performances, its scenic language, its unusual placing in a small provincial town, outside the contemporary theatre environment; about its international composition, its constant nomadic life around the globe, its barters; its working discipline, and about its ability to survive without loss of identity. That so much has been written about Odin Teatret is, of course, connected with the fact that it, through its primary activities, has stimulated descriptions and reflections. But also the fact that Odin Teatret has manifested itself through so many different activities besides the performances has contributed to the high number of utterances about it. To mention but a few of these: theatre pedagogy, theatre anthropology, film, publishing house, festivals and festive weeks, seminars and conferences.

In everything — or almost everything — written about Odin Teatret, it is, naturally enough, the professional side that has animated the utterances: the impressions the performance made, the benefit gained from a seminar or course, the dynamics set off by the theatre during a barter in a distant or neighbouring country, the theatre theories seen as a starting point for the work of the theatre, etc. In other words — everything that Odin Teatret's actors and director stand for. It is they, the actors and director, around whom revolve the utterances about who they are and what they are doing. It is they who have been pioneers in a desert without oases. It is they who have travelled so far away that one didn't know if they were going to fall off the edge. It is easy to understand that their words and actions have given rise to interpretations, reports, articles, letters, dissertations, and even books, in a gentle flow.

Should one, on the other hand, have the mad idea of writing something about the group at Odin Teatret which is not seen on stage, does not appear in interviews or is depicted on press photos: the anonymous staff behind the lines, the administration; one would find it very difficult.

What should you write about? In the first place, administration is not about the central element in theatre: representation. No performance is taking place in the office (none which you would pay to see). No one is affected, as they are during a stage scene, by the tingling excitement of what will happen next, at the sight of an office team at work. When the paper is changed in the copy machine, the head of the observer hardly buzzes with a multitude of associations. The fascinating discharging of energy of an actor's well-trained body is totally missing in the tired administrative employee, sitting bent over the reply to the day's tenth letter asking when the next course at Odin Teatret will take place. Secondly, the administrative staff has neither formulated revolutionary new ways of applying to the minister, nor developed new and different types of contract formulas. Thus there seem to be nothing to write about when speaking of the administrative staff and its work.

The administration of Odin Teatret consists, here at the beginning of 2000, of a Danish, bank-educated bookkeeper; a former organiser of festivals, from Brazil — now a Danish citizen; a former microbiologist from Argentina; a refugee from Sri Lanka — now a Danish citizen; a Danish lawyer, who is also chairman of the board of the theatre, and who carries out his functions from his address in Aarhus and through regular visits in Holstebro; a Danish, office-educated assistant to the book-keeper; a Danish, former actor at Odin Teatret; a Danish former office head at Odin Teatret, employed part time; a Danish M. A. in French and History; a Norwegian actress and co-founder of Odin Teatret; and, of course, Eugenio Barba. Add to this that several of the centrally placed Odin Teatret actors carry out administrative tasks.

They are the administrative staff, which keeps the tracks clear. Both the ones which have been paved, and those which are to be trodden. This is the group of persons who, among other things, must keep up contact with the authorities and other financial sources on several levels, in order to ensure the operational — and other means for productions, projects, festivals, visits, trips, meetings, publications, film, various arrangements, courses and guest performances. They must keep the accounts, transfer salaries, collect accounts owing, answer telephones, e-mails, letters, faxes. Order flight tickets, send presents, thank-yous, telegrams, flowers and arrange insurance. Translate books, programmes, leaflets, articles, lists. Collect articles, produce magazines, write contracts, keep up the clipping-, film-, library-, article-, dissertation-, address-, and other archives and indexes. Send out invitations, information, advertisements, programmes. Procure contacts, organise tours, book hotel reservations, accommodate. Take care of the maintenance and cleaning of the theatre, cultivate contacts and carry out lobbying activities, phrase invitations, write reports, sell books, films and posters, as well as catalogue, systematise and pass on information.

Afterwards, they will have to inform about the theatre, order equipment, find texts, cultivate networks, write recommendations, file statistics, send photos, collect information, procure collaborators, be responsible for the sale of tickets and reservations, hold long planning meetings, look after logistics and copy all sorts of material.

All this must be carried out locally, nationally and internationally. Over several continents and in a good many languages. A member of the administrative staff must be kind, extrovert, helpful and obliging in character.

There is one thing which is important to understand about Odin Teatret: its activities consist of a mixture of routine, the challenge from insoluble problems, plus unpredictable surprises. The art of administration at Odin Teatret consists in avoiding drowning in the routine or being paralysed by the insoluble problems, and in learning to treat the surprises as if they were routine. In the good old days, when the wind alone propelled those sailing ships which were wont to go into waters filled with sharks, one could manage with the proper sailors. That won't work in our time, where the techno-industrial development has created completely different conditions for crossing the oceans.

Jørn Bjerre

Odin Teatret and the Art of perpetuating
[Creativity through Difference]

If everything is uncertain, then the future
is open to creativity.
Wallerstein

The purpose of this article is to show that Odin Teatret — a theatre laboratory — not only can be seen as a laboratory of art, but also as one of human organisation.[1] And that their experience with working as a team, with highly advanced creative work, can be used within the framework of organisation theory, to meet the task of understanding some of the central challenges of today. With the development of information technology, a new ethos of work has evolved around themes like constant change, life long learning, flexible organisation, and the strategic use of human resources. This means that the roles of the workplace are being defined anew, in ways that crave new types of analysis and theory.

[Man as a tool]

As part of the overall shift in perspective, learning has become one of the most central notions in contemporary business language: In what is called the 'knowledge society', where knowledge is the prime resource, learning becomes its motor, and man, therefore, the prime tool. This being precisely the case in *Human resource management*, where man is defined in strategic terms in a much more specific way than ever before. The managerial intention behind this development is widely acknowledged, and has been criticised in various ways (Kamoche 1995; Kamoche and Mueller 1998; Legge 1995). One intrinsic problem with the expansion of strategy within the individuality of the worker is that it might prove dysfunctional: strategic thinking is not always strategic when it comes to human organisation — aiming at excellent results — because such organisation does not revolve around rational strategy, but around creativity.

If we want to understand how to handle such creativity within the learning-oriented field of organisation, we must make room for a level of learning which is open to mastery in other ways than the strategic-technical. In order to do so, Bent Flyvbjerg (1990) departs from the learning theory of Hubert and Stuart Dreyfus (1988). They argue for a qualitative differentiation between learning as rule-based, technical learning, and learning as a virtuoso type of learning, that 'simply does not use rules' but works 'holistically, and intuitively on the basis of experience' (Flyvbjerg, forthcoming, 30f). This second level of learning paves the way for understanding how creativity comes into play in human organisations (Flyvbjerg 1990), whereas the first level only helps us explain how learning is strictly related to competence (mastering the rules of the game). Understanding the move from the first to the second level of learning and beyond, towards a level of creativity and innovation, is highly relevant to the field of organisation theory. This is especially the case in relation to organisation in the high-tech world, where creativity has proved the only way to survive. It is in the quest to understand the art of obtaining and perpetuating creativity that we here turn to Odin Teatret.

[Teams]

The spirit of this flexible work-ethos is, according to Richard Sennett (1999), teamwork, which he describes as 'an ethos of work which remains on the surface of experience.' It 'is the group practice of demanding superficiality', while this 'keeps people together by avoiding difficult, divisive, personal questions' (p.108). Odin Teatret can be seen as an experiment with teamwork that overcomes this superficiality by having virtuosity and creativity as a strategy, rather than formal competence and techniques.

Working creatively in a group means moving from a social setting around rules and definitions to another level of problem solving, which includes a much more integrated part of the people involved. This also makes it dangerous, as Iben Nagel Rasmussen explains in an interview on her experience with groups:

> A group is unable to survive, if you do not discover the real tensions, the powers that circulate, and that do not come to expression through discussions about ideas. It is these powers that make the group grow, if they meet and change to something else. But if they are not discovered and oriented precisely within a creative field, they become destructive. It is no longer earth, which lets each individual develop, but quicksand, which strangles.

Groups can mean growth or quicksand, depending on how we use their real tension. When speaking of the superficial level of teamwork, we speak of quicksand, which people don't stay in, because they are all too busy. The fact, however, that they only stand in it until their shoes are covered, and then leave for other places, does not dispute that they walk on quicksand. The strategy of skipping between groups, in order not to take root, is likely to mean that you won't grow. In order to grow, the character needs to be rooted in the real tensions of working in groups in order to work with itself and others. This takes time.

[Understanding process]

Superficiality, speed, and the acceptance of empty rhetorics are ways to pave the quicksand, which accelerate anxiety and lead to a spirit of compliance that is directly opposite to a spirit of creativity. Therefore, the word 'creativity' should not be understood in the narrow sense of the word, relating to invention and expression; it should be understood as the art of making processes of invention and expression possible within a given life form of an organisation. As such, the story of Odin Teatret can be analysed as a multitude of stories of processes: (1) on the personal level of the actors and the director, (2) on the level of the development of plays, and (3) the overall evolution of the theatre from the will of a bunch of newcomers to the status of a professional, widely recognised, team of innovators.

What characterises the process on all these levels is that it is at the same time open and focussed. Which is exactly what constitutes the difficult art of creativity, where it is easy to be open, if you don't have to focus, or to be focussed if you don't have to be open. Being both at once is very difficult.

[Laboratory: building organisation]

From the beginning, Odin Teatret has been motivated by a will to produce quality theatre (focus), while at the same time learning what theatre is, or ought to be (open). Being autodidact in this context means being rounded of something other than what is normally expected within the field where one works. Motivated by something other than carrying on the tradition. It means being forced to question basic assumptions, definitions and ways of the theatre, in the search for mastery of what one, through working experience, comes to see as theatre. You are, in other words, forced to assume, define and create yourself, and thereby build the power of judgement and selectivity on the solid ground of your self in the world. That means constructing the way you walk, while you are walking. This defines 'the focussed open process' of creativity, based on the capacity to select and judge objectively from a very personal point of view.

Barba explains how, when they moved to Holstebro in 1966, and founded a theatre laboratory, nobody — including himself — knew what a theatre laboratory was. His definition to the Mayor of Holstebro was 'a theatre that does not play every evening'. This very open definition meant that they took the responsibility of finding out what such a laboratory is — which is inventing it. In this sense, learning and teaching have taken place at the same time. This way of organising as an open process is a way of rooting creativity in everyday work.

[Phoenix: building character]

On a personal level, creativity has more to do with what someone does not have than with what he has, because it is in the process of achieving and becoming that creative energy lies. In his work, the individual must be allowed to go into the unknown, which is the only place from where he can expand. The great task of organisations is making room for such walking off; just as it is the task of the leader to see in the person what he is not yet, but is able to become.

When Iben Nagel Rasmussen began at Odin Teatret in 1966, she was shocked by the lack of explanations. Thirty five years later, she explains:

> To me it was a shock that nothing was explained. I had expected some philosophical explanation of what it was all about, and how it should be done. That was not the case! One was thrown into these very demanding physical tasks without any explanation. It was an extreme experience that it was the body that had to learn, because through the whole school system we unlearn our bodies; the head is separated from the body.

Later, Nagel Rasmussen created her own training as an answer to the basic question: 'what is a dramatic action to me?' She relates this development to the metaphor of Phoenix. She was forced to rise from the ashes (of not having), and develop her own way. This meant that she not only developed a language (competence), but her own language (vernacular), i.e., a place of your own from where you can experiment in any direction.

[The inner need: building praxis]

Building organisations and building characters takes place in a praxis based on what can be seen as inner competencies. A letter from 1967, where Barba corrects the inner conviction or motive of an actor, can illustrate the importance of this:

> First of all, it seems as if your actions are not driven by any inner conviction or irresistible need which leaves its mark on your exercises, improvisations and performance. [...] The second attitude I see in you is your embarrassment in considering the seriousness of your work. [...] It is as if you want to flee from the responsibility that you feel is inherent in your craft, which consists in establishing communication with human beings [...]. (Barba 1979, 37-38)

Working out of a need, the quest for communication with fellow humans, is what it is all built on. There can be no other fixed positions than this: finding an inner need in each particular individual that can drive it towards the other. This is also valid today: 'All the activities that I engage in are activities that interest me', Barba explains. Torgeir Wethal, who can look back on 35 years of working with Barba, has observed this as a matter of having a vision: Barba 'has always had a vision that was great enough to encompass all the other visions in it. Or, as he puts it, he had a vision that needed the visions of others [the actors], in order to become more than just the thoughts of a single person'.

[Difference]

Organisations that seek to adapt difference to specific sets of values or defined cultural goals tend to take possession of the others' otherness, thereby killing creativity. Drawing on Todorov (1993), Levine (1999) explains:

> Where culture incorporates a set of roles and positions with predetermined modes of life, creativity is inconsistent with social meaning. You cannot both be in society, because the structure of society is organised around compliance with externally given norms. But where culture affords the individual a 'vernacular' rather than a set of rules, it enables the individual to be creative and establish a unique way of being. (Todorov 1993, 241)

The challenge to the organisation lies in limiting itself to providing a vernacular to be used by someone else in his or her way, not dictating specific contents by imposing one's own words, values and culture on them. Leaving be, letting go, making space for the other, is the way to organise creativity. Having open processes where each and everyone seeks their own way is the only way to reach unity:

> If you will reach a unity, you must strive towards difference and a differentiation process based on mutual trust without illusions. Down under the differences, a common and sustainable ground arises. The shallow unity, also with regard to ideas and intentions, will, on the contrary, be swept away at the first puff of wind. (Barba 1989, 16)

The creativity pivots, not on the group process as such, but from the letting go of the other, so that the process unfolds as an open-ended exploration, trusting to the process to release, through the making of space for otherness. The synergy of the group has to come from this. As explained by Torgeir Wethal:

> When you are in a group, it is important to make room for some rather individual developments, which, after a while, can turn out for the best for the group. But that is not the starting point. The starting point is what you really want to do ... This means that you disappear, move onto a sidetrack, and it looks as though you disappear from the group. But you do so in order to bring back new things to the group.

Perpetuating creativity in human organisation demands that we focus on 'the difference of the individual as a character' rather than starting with a conception of the 'identity of the group', as an inclusion system through which personal differences must be cultivated. We must give up the organic metaphors of organisations, conceiving them as units of parts. Group creativity thrives on growth on an individual level, by transcendence from this. Groups that organise from this perspective of difference, and not, as normally anticipated in organisation theory, from the perspective of identity, can prove to be best fittet to the challenges of the new economy.

[The unpronounced culture beyond theatre]

The creativity base of organisations cannot be enunciable in praxis, where they are at work. Enunciation will always become identity formations, hardening processes of difference into culture building. Letting difference be — making space for growth, is the challenge. That is, building an unenunciated culture of difference, differing from the managerial strategies, which seeks to overcome difference with identity creation. Silence about the central values — and making room for this silence — is crucial. The creative aspects only thrive in the dark mystique of the person. A theory of the un-enunciated culture of difference lets the organisation theory of post-modernity converge with what has been called the ethic of post-modernity (Bauman): namely that of Levinas and others, focussing on the irreducbility of otherness, inherent in the concept of *exteriority*. This means that the other can never be reduced to definitions made by the self, but always escapes any such definition. The other is transcendent in a way that originates from human organising in itself, namely from the resistance of social plurality towards any logic which seeks to totalise it; i.e., the resistance of difference towards the superficiality of any notion of sameness.

Creativity thrives on this exteriority of the individual in the work context. It revolts against the totalising tendencies of group processes, and promotes an understanding of the individual as infinite. Perpetuating creativity within the organisation depends on the ability to handle this well, springing from personal difference. To put it bluntly, the ability of each member to be him/herself, while providing others with the same freedom.

Winnicott speaks of living creatively, as living with a connection to one's true self. '*The true self* is the body when it is creative', the Norwegian psychiatrist Skårderud says, paraphrasing this thought (Skårderud 1999, 87) in a way that echoes the central notion of Odin Teatret: *bios*, the body-alive. Which is exactly the process where one strives 'to be in constant development, and thereby avoid living in what one has accumulated, to reject the capitalisation of skills and theories or to settle in one specialised field.' (Barba 1989, 96). This process is what being alive means. *Human resource management* strategies must — if they mean *human* resources — start here.

Note

1. This article is part of a larger investigation of creativity, difference and the new work-ethos. It is based on interviews with Eugenio Barba, Kai Bredholt. Roberta Carreri, Jan Ferslev, Tage Larsen. Iben Nagel Rasmussen, Julia Varley and Torgeir Wethal in the period from March 21 to April 4. The idea of working with Odin Teatret in this connection with the investigation came from H. Shapiro (Danish Institute of Technology) and C. Steyaert (Copenhagen Business School).

References

Bacon, Nicolas 1999. The Realities of Human Resource Management? *Human Relations*, vol. 52, no. 9.

Barba, Eugenio 1979. *The Floating Islands*. Holstebro: Drama.

Barba, Eugenio 1989. *De flydende øer (The Floating Islands)*. Copenhagen: Borgen.

Bauman, Zygmunt 1993. *Postmodern Ethics*. Oxford: Blackwell Publishers Ltd.

Dreyfus, Hubert and Stuart 1988. *Mind Over Machine: The Power of Human Intuition and Expertise in the Era of the Computer*. New York: The Free Press.

Flyvbjerg, Bent (forthcoming). *Making Social Science Matter. Why Social Inquiry Fails and How It Can Count Again*. Cambridge University Press.

Flyvbjerg, Bent 1990. *Rationalitet, intuition og krop i menneskets læreproces: Fortolkning og evaluering af Hubert og Stuart Dreyfus's model for indlæring af færdigheder. (*Rationality, Intuition and Body in Human Learning: An Interpretation and Evaluation of Hubert and Stuart Dreyfus's Skill Acquisition Model). Aalborg University.

Kamoche, Ken 1995: Rhetoric, Ritualism, and Totemism in Human Resource Management. *Human Relations*, vol. 48, no. 4.

Kamoche, Ken and Frank Mueller 1998. *Human Relations*, vol. 51, no. 8.

Legge, Karen 1995: *Human Resource Management. Rhetoric and Realities*. London: Macmillan Press.

Levine, David P. 1999. Creativity and Change. On the Psychodynamics of Modernity. *American Behavioral Scientist*, vol. 43. no. 2.

Nagel Rasmussen, Iben. *De stumme fra fortiden — svar til en kvindelig tilskuer* (The Mute From the Past). From the program to *Itsi Bitsi*.

Sennett, Richard 1998. *The Corrosion of Character. The Personal Consequences of Work in the New Capitalism*. New York: Norton paperback.

Skårderud, Finn 1999. *Uro. En rejse i det moderne selv* (Unrest. A Journey into the Modern Self). Copenhagen: Tiderne Skifter.

Starkey, Ken 1998. What Can We Learn from the Learning Organisation? *Human Relations*, vol. 51, no. 4.

Todorov, Tzvetan 1993. *On Human Diversity. Nationalism, Racism, and Exoticism in French Thought*. London: Havard University Press.

John Andreasen

[Ode to Odin 2000]

You, who travelled far,
found fabulous creatures
& legendary figures,
strange sights you brought
from territories under other suns,
twilight times' twined talking
rushed against us:

Grotowski & Panigrahi
Brecht & Stanislavsky
& faint figures like
Baargeld, Bach, Bakunin,
Baj & Bartók
blaze behind Barba, you Baal,
blustering fertilizer
of the tribe of Odin,
B&O

Anna Maria, Else Marie, Eugenio,
Frans, Hans, Iben, Jan & Judy,
Julia, Kai, Marie, Patricia & Pushparajah,
Rina, Roberta, Sigrid, Søren & Ulrik,
Tage, Tine & Torgeir
& other floating islands

Inhabitants of Babel,
heretics', liars'
& sinners' healthy lye,
balm, embalming,
balsams, bedouins

You fairly succeeded
calling yourself hubristic
Odin, First name of the North
from the season of your dawn

Call you grinning and giddy
deeply encumbered by heartfelt delight
you misanthropic aspirating,
(ana)chronic avant-garde:

Night-white jasmins,
whirling, whispering winds,
the sounding echo of silence,
trackless traces in the snow
— tacit knowledge

Broken masks inside the skeleton of the whale,
the suckling, dead old man in the castle of Holstebrow,
Doña Musica's soaring skirts painfully shrinking
to the (dead) brother's lounge suit cocoon,
Judith's joyful, bloody marriage
to the silvery head of Holophernes,
Kattrin's scissoring S.O.S.,
the indomitable clubfoot of courage
— a race with wild, blind horses

The ode to progress dying away
in uncertainty's shrilling, scraping laughter,
Sisyphus the First,
tired & tireless collecting
his numerous, dying troops
— the hero of Mythos in red,
the deaf-blind Samaritan,
a fool off to Nowhere Hill
a dim hot club rush night,
when snow was seeping subacidly
into wide open veins, Itsi Bitsi,
to Dylan's rhetoric blues
& a bittersweet polar bear teddy

vigorously & sonorously
grabbed all existing accordions
in yet another barter
some whirling place in the world
— theatrum mundi

Still, Odin will perish
& sink in the sands of time,
still solidly deposited
in the streams of
many minds & memories

Strange visitors vanish,
sights & saying slowly cease,
globes reluctantly return to previous orbits
— kindred spirits take insensible shortcuts!

Odin Teatret in Aros AD 2000

Odin Teatret:
Ode to Progress.
Photo: Jan Rüsz

Editors' Epilogue

[On the Authors]

of Odin Teatret 2000

ELIN ANDERSEN (1938), associate professor at the Department of Dramaturgy, Aarhus University, Denmark. Her recent publications on the issue text and theatricality include: 'Reading the Image' in *Nordic Theatre Studies*, vol. 10, Gideå, SW. 1997 and 'Øjeblikke af skønhed og grusomhed' in *Teaterlegeringer*, eds. Elin Andersen and Niels Lehmann (Aarhus Universitetsforlag, 1998). She has treated *A Doll's House* in her book *Den bristende uskyld* (Copenhagen, Reitzel, 1986).

JOHN ANDREASEN (1947), associate professor at the Department of Dramaturgy, Aarhus University, teaching theatre production and cultural politics. Published 'Flodens aske' ('Ashes of the River') on Odin Teatret in *Børneteateravisen* nr. 32, 1981. Recent publication in English: *Drama Teaching & Mnemonics*. Dept. of Dramaturgy (Aarhus 1995). Editor, with Annelis Kuhlmann, of *Odin Teatret 2000*.

EUGENIO BARBA (1936), director, writer, founder and leader of Odin Teatret since 1964 and ISTA, International School of Theatre Anthropology, since 1979. Has directed more than 22 performances at Odin Teatret. Recent publications: *Theatre: Solitude, Craft, Revolt* and *Land of Ashes and Diamonds. My Apprenticeship in Poland* (Black Mountain Press, 1999). Honorary Doctorate in Canada (Montreal), Denmark (Aarhus), Italy (Bologna) and Peru (Ayacucho).

JØRN BJERRE (1969), MA in Religious Studies and Social Theory from Aarhus University (1998). Is currently a PhD-student at the Center for the Interdisciplinary Study of Learning at Aalborg University on a project on the relation between organization, creativity and learning.

ROBERTA CARRERI (1953), joined Odin Teatret in 1974, during their stay in Carpignano, Italy. Her experiences as an actress are presented in *The Actor's Way*, edited by Erik Exe Christoffersen. Roberta gives workshops for actors all over the world, along with her work demonstration, a professional autobiography called *Traces in the Snow*. She also leads the semiannual *Odin Weeks* in Holstebro.

ERIK EXE CHRISTOFFERSEN (1951), associate professor at the Department of Dramaturgy. Has written books and articles on Odin Teatret: *Skuespillerens vandring* (Klim, 1989), *The Actor's Way* (Routledge, 1993), *Teaterpoetik* (Klim, 1997), and made a video for Italian RAI 2 (1991) on Odin Teatret 1964-1990: *On a Way Through Theatre*.

TONY D'URSO (1947), photographer, Milano. Has collaborated with Odin Teatret since 1972, and published *Viaggi con/Voyages with Odin Teatret* with Eugenio Barba in 1990 (reprinted in 2000). Tony D'Urso was cameraman on Torgeir Wethal's films *Dressed in White* (Vestita di bianco) from 1974, and *The Gospel according to Oxyrhyncus*.

KIRSTEN HASTRUP (1948), professor of Anthropology at the University of Copenhagen. She has done research in theatre anthropology, and has participated in a number of ISTA sessions. In 1988 Odin created a play, *Talabot*, partly based on her life story, including her experiences from anthropological fieldwork in Iceland. Editor of *The Performers' Village. Times, Techniques and Theories at ISTA* (Graasten 1996).

KLAUS HOFFMEYER (1938), director, artistic leader of Drama at The Royal Theatre in Copenhagen, former dramaturge with the Danish TV-Theatre and Aarhus Theatre. Has, among other things, directed Wagner's *The Ring of Nibelungen* with the Jutland Opera, and translated Alfred Jarry's *Ubu Roi* (1965) and Antonin Artaud's *Le théâtre et son double* (1967) into Danish.

TORUNN KJØLNER (1952), associate professor at the Department of Dramaturgy, Aarhus University. MA in Drama from the University of Bergen, Norway. Diploma in Speech and Drama, Royal Scottish Academy of Music and Drama, Scotland. Has written articles on drama and theatre in education, actors' training, improvisation, the actor as readymade, and on devised theatre.

ANNELIS KUHLMANN, (1960), assistant professor at the Department of Dramaturgy. PhD in 1997 with a dissertation on *Stanislavsky's theatre concepts*. Takes regularly part in ISTAs. Has written 'This is not a meeting. About the theatricality of the meeting in the case of Odin Teatret' in Kowalewicz, Kazimierz (ed.). Meetings with Odin Teatret. Łódź: University of Łódź 2000. Editor, with John Andreasen, of *Odin Teatret 2000*.

MORTEN KYNDRUP (1952), professor of Aesthetics and Culture at Aarhus University. He has treated art theory and enunciational analysis in connection with literature, film, theatre, and pictures. His books include *Det Postmoderne* (Gyldendal 1986), *Framing and Fiction*, (Aarhus University Press 1992), and *Riften og sløret. Essays over kunstens betingelser* (Aarhus University Press 1998). He is the editor of *Æstetikstudier* (1995 ff.).

SVEND ERIK LARSEN (1946), professor at the Department of Comparative Literature, Aarhus University. Books and articles on literature and urban culture, literature and semiotics. On the subject of the theatre, he has written about Büchner's *Woyzeck* (1982, 1985), Dumas' *La dame aux Camélias* (1984) and the intrigue (1986). He has contributed to *Théâtre. Modes d'approche* (1987), *Approaching Theatre* (1991) and co-produced the video *Theater Codes* (1991).

PETER LAUGESEN (1942), writer, dramatist, translator, member of the board of Odin Teatret since 1999. Has published many books since 1967, the newest being *Trashpilot* (March 2000). Danish translator of Antonin Artaud. Awarded a number of prizes, notably the Danish Academy Prize in 1992. Has since become a member of said academy.

NIELS LEHMANN (1962), associate professor at the Department of Dramaturgy, Aarhus University, PhD in 1994 with a dissertation on deconstruction and dramaturgy. Since then articles on the aesthetics of performance art, including the theatre of Grotowski, Foreman and the Wooster Group.

CHR. LUDVIGSEN (1930), MA in Literature, specializing in the Danish stage director William Bloch, 1958. Translator introducing the 'Theatre of the Absurd' in Denmark, especially Beckett. Appointed to the University of Aarhus 1963-97. Odin Teatret-collaborator since 1965, chairman of the board 1969-83.

IBEN NAGEL RASMUSSEN (1945), was the first actress to join Odin Teatret after its arrival in Holstebro in 1966. Her experiences as actress are published in *The Actors Way*, edited by Erik Exe Christoffersen. She established the group *Farfa* in 1983, and since 1990 she has had a yearly gathering of actors from different countries called *Vindenes Bro* (The Bridge of Winds). Among other things she has published *Breve til en veninde* (1993) and *Den blinde hest — Barbas forestillinger* (1998).

JANNE RISUM (1947), associate professor at the Department of Dramaturgy, Aarhus University. She has been widely published in the fields of acting and the history of theatre, and on the subject of women in theatre. She is a participant in the International School of Theatre Anthropology.

STEEN SIDENIUS (1964), MA 1997, PhD-student with a project entitled *Forms of Tragedy* at the Department of Dramaturgy, Aarhus University. He is the author of the thesis, *Det Tredje Teater — eksistens, kunst og videnskab i Barbas poetik* (unpublished) and the article *Barba and Poststructuralism. The Metaphysics of the Third Theatre* (1998).

ULRIK SKEEL (1949), actor at Odin Teatret 1969-1974 and 1978-1987. On the administrative staff from 1987.

ALEXANDER THIEME (1953), educated at The Academy of Arts in Leningrad (1971-77). Instructor at Højskolen på Helnæs (the Folk-High School for adults at Helnæs) since 1995. Has had a number of exhibitions, including an exhibition of more than 60 watercolour paintings of Danish manor houses and castles together with his wife, Tatiana Thieme, in June, 2000, at the Clausholm Castle. Among his paintings are modern, religious icons as well as two miniature portraits of Queen Margrethe II (1996).

JULIA VARLEY (1954), actress, joined Odin Teatret in 1976. Julia's writing has been published in publications such as *Conjunto, Lapis and Mascara, Mime Journal, New Theatre Quarterly* and *Teatro e Storia*. She has directed two performances for the Theater in Pumpenhaus (Germany) and is a member of the Magdalena Project. She is also editor of *The Open Page*, a journal devoted to women's work in theatre.

FRANS WINTHER (1947), composer, studied at the Aalborg Music Conservatory and composed for various theatre groups. He joined Odin Teatret in 1987, and has worked in, and composed for, various performances, among others *Memoria, Kaosmos, Mythos* and *Ode to Progress*.